The Hypothesis of Undesigned Coincidences

A SELECTION OF PUBLICATIONS
BY MICHAEL J. ALTER

What Is the Purpose of Creation: A Jewish Anthology (Jason Aronson, 1991)

Why the Torah Begins with the Letter Beit (Jason Aronson, 1998)

The Resurrection: A Critical Inquiry (Xlibris, 2015)

A Thematic Access-Oriented Bibliography of Jesus's Resurrection (Resource Publications, 2020)

The Name Israel (Resource Publications, 2023)

The Resurrection and Apologetics: Jesus' Death and Burial Volume 1 (Resource Publications, 2024)

The Hypothesis of Undesigned Coincidences: A Critical Review (Resource Publications, 2024)

The Hypothesis of Undesigned Coincidences

A Critical Review

MICHAEL J. ALTER

Foreword by Evan Fales

RESOURCE *Publications* • Eugene, Oregon

THE HYPOTHESIS OF UNDESIGNED COINCIDENCES
A Critical Review

Copyright © 2024 Michael J. Alter. All rights reserved. Except for brief quotations in critical publications or reviews, no part of this book may be reproduced in any manner without prior written permission from the publisher. Write: Permissions, Wipf and Stock Publishers, 199 W. 8th Ave., Suite 3, Eugene, OR 97401.

Resource Publications
An Imprint of Wipf and Stock Publishers
199 W. 8th Ave., Suite 3
Eugene, OR 97401

www.wipfandstock.com

PAPERBACK ISBN: 979-8-3852-3472-1
HARDCOVER ISBN: 979-8-3852-3473-8
EBOOK ISBN: 979-8-3852-3474-5
VERSION NUMBER 11/14/24

Unless otherwise noted, Scripture quotations are from The Holy Bible, English Standard Version (ESV)®, copyright © 2001 by Crossway Bibles, a publishing ministry of Good News Publishers. Used by permission. All rights reserved worldwide.

The July 4, 2023 Independence 5K Run & Firecracker Dash in Redondo Beach, CA. Credit: Scott Christopher Stolarz Photography, SCS Photoworks, LLC

Map: Jesus Ministry in Galilee
Map used with permission by David Barrett from the Bible Mapper Atlas (biblemapper.com/blog).

To Sophie for her graduation

Contents

List of Images and Tables | ix
Foreword by Evan Fales | xi
Preface | xv
Acknowledgments | xix
Abbreviations | xxi

1 The Hypothesis of Undesigned Coincidences: Introduction, Key Terms and Definitions, Methodological Problems, and a General Critique of the Hypothesis | 1
2 The Hypothesis of Undesigned Coincidences: How Well Does It Explain the Gospel Accounts of the Feeding of the Five Thousand? | 61
3 The Philip Controversy and Summary of Problems with the Hypothesis of Undesigned Coincidences | 129
4 Summary of Problems with the Hypothesis of Undesigned Coincidences | 149
5 Conclusion: The Cumulative Argument against the Hypothesis of Undesigned Coincidences | 157

Bibliography | 163
Name Index | 173
Subject Index | 177

List of Images and Tables

IMAGES

1. Map: Jesus Ministry in Galilee | 78
2. The July 4, 2023 Independence 5K Run & Firecracker Dash in Redondo Beach, CA. | 135

TABLES

Table 1. John's Use of the Hebrew Bible: Biblical Quotations and Allusions in the Fourth Gospel | 25

Table 2. Parallel Gospel Accounts of the Feeding of the 5,000 (ESV) | 62

Table 3. A Comparison of 2 Kings 4: 38–44 and Mark 6: 30-44. | 66

Table 4. Mark 6 and Psalm 23: A Comparison | 67

Table 5. Was Mark 6 Adapted from an Exodus Motif? | 69

Table 6. Looking for Food | 84

Table 7. Parallel Texts: Mark 6 and Luke 9 | 114

Table 8: Theses and Dissertations about the Feeding of the Five Thousand | 126

Table 9: Books about the Feeding of the Five Thousand | 127

Foreword

THE HYPOTHESIS OF UNDESIGNED Coincidences (HUC), first proposed in the 18th century, has recently received new attention as an apologetic argument for the historical reliability of the Bible, thanks in large measure to a modern defense of it by Lydia McGrew. At its heart, the argument is an appeal to probabilities, to wit, that we find in the Bible independent narratives that report seemingly identical events, often insignificant, whose similarity can only be plausibly explained by historicity. It is an argument that, by eliminating other explanations of the coincidence as extremely improbable, leaves one with two alternatives: that of agreement between independent witnesses on the occurrence of the event, or sheer coincidence—itself wildly improbable. So, it is an argument for historical veracity that, perhaps ironically, turns on an appeal to the *non*-occurrence of a miracle.

The most obvious alternative explanations (to actual occurrence) are a) that one author copied, directly or indirectly, a fabricated tale found in the narrative of another, or b) that stories of the type in question existed as culturally shared tropes available to many authors at the time and place in question. In this, the argument relies upon certain intuitions about relative probabilities, intuitions that can be buttressed by means of quantifiable examples. Such quantifiably tractable examples are important because raw intuitions about probabilities are often far from accurate. The present volume is a careful and detailed re-examination of the HUC, as developed by McGrew, that arrives at a critical assessment of its apologetic power in the case of Scripture.

The idea that odd coincidences point to deeper insight into how the world works has long fascinated human imagination. The discovery of certain tropes with worldwide distribution in myth traditions led to culture diffusionist theories of global history, and seem to have inspired Carl Jung's theory of psychological archetypes. Closer to hand, so-called fine-tuning versions of the Argument from Design turn on similar comparisons of alternative explanations. Numerological techniques for finding hidden messages in sacred texts generated hermeneutical methods for the interpretation of those texts, such as, for example, the ancient Jewish art of gematria. But the underlying reasoning is not particularly arcane.

Consider a murder mystery set in a town in Wisconsin, say, with a reputation built upon the large variety of pies available for dessert. Various clues lead to suspicion of a regular customer. An eccentric, this man is known for an obsession with solving the ancient geometric problem of squaring the circle. Circumstances suggest that a map showing the location where the body is buried is stored on his computer, which is impounded. But access requires an eight-digit password. What are the odds of finding the right sequence of numbers? Well, there are 10⁸ such sequences of numerals; the odds of guessing the correct one at random are thus one in ten million. But our Sherlock has a hunch. She enters the first eight digits of the number—and bingo!—gains access. Clearly, her guess was not random, but how much higher were her chances of success? It is, clearly, not easy to say. However, the underlying intuition is correct and drives the HUC.

This can work in more ways than one. Suppose you have two ancient texts, A and B, which are thought on good evidence to be independently composed, but both contain narratives so similar as to ensure non-coincidence. What best explains their similarity? The natural answer is that they are products of two testimony traditions that trace back to the same actual event. This explanation entails that the event, in fact, occurred more or less as described. Now, suppose instead that there is good evidence that the author of B knew A's text and copied it. That quashes the inference to independence. But suppose, further, that one narrative includes a trivial detail that the other lacks, a detail for which there is no tendentious reason to suspect confabulation. That, too, supports a claim that both texts track the same (historical) occurrence.

In all such cases, our intuitions declare that an explanation is required for coincidence; and that such an explanation, even if rather far-fetched, is more likely true than sheer random chance. This would be so even if there were no precise way to assign a probability higher than chance—indeed, it appears legitimate to appeal to it even when there is no precise way of assigning a probability to chance coincidence—so long as the latter is clearly very small.

As the reader will discover, this kind of reasoning has been used, in several ways, to argue for the veracity of various biblical narratives—and, by extension, to justify confidence in the general historical reliability of the Bible as a window into the past. Alter tackles head-on what is perhaps the most sophisticated current deployment of such arguments for apologetic ends.

Alter examines the topic of "coincidence" from an interdisciplinary and technical perspective. He investigates the hypothesis using several strategies, such as cognitive science, literature, mathematics, probability, psychology, statistics, and biblical studies. Those strategies are not given due attention by McGrew and HUC proponents. A general aim is to show that the disparity in epistemic probability (given our actual total evidence) between "historicity" explanations and "pure chance" explanations is not large—or even that the latter might be higher than the former. However, usually, nothing so strong needs to be shown. All that needs to be made known is that *other* explanations for the target coincidences (or a disjunction of such hypotheses) have a higher probability of being true than a "historicity" explanation.

Bible scholars and individuals interested in the long-standing debates over the reliability of the Bible will find great value in exploring Alter's comprehensive analysis of the textual and other relevant data. Alter makes a forceful case that challenges the application of the HUC to biblical texts, particularly those in the New Testament, in support of their historical reliability. Notably, Alter presents readers with "a compelling cumulative argument against the hypothesis of Undesigned Coincidences and its assertion of the historical accuracy of the Gospels." Of course, many other arguments (both pro and con) exist to assess reliability. Let the trial begin.

Preface

THE HYPOTHESIS OF *UNDESIGNED Coincidences* was first proposed by William Paley (1743-1805) and later popularized by J.J. Blunt (1794-1855). More recently, Lydia and Timothy McGrew have revived this hypothesis. Lydia McGrew's text, *Hidden in Plain View*, is especially noteworthy. McGrew defines an *undesigned coincidence* as "a notable connection between two or more accounts or texts that doesn't seem to have been planned by the person or people giving the accounts. Despite their apparent independence, the items fit together like pieces of a puzzle."[1] Advocates use undesigned coincidences to argue that the Gospels are a compilation of independent and reliable sources. However, these advocates do not engage with biblical criticism and overlook relevant research on coincidences and casualness. The feeding of the five thousand is a prominent example discussed by proponents who point to details such as the green grass, the location of Bethsaida, and the question posed by Jesus to Philip. These episodes are thoroughly reviewed and analyzed.

The Hypothesis of Undesigned Coincidences: A Critical Review is divided into five chapters.

Chapter 1—The Hypothesis of Undesigned Coincidences: It examines various topics. Select examples include the following:

The Importance and Relevance of *Hidden in Plain View* and Undesigned Coincidences

Who Is Lydia McGrew?

The Credentialism Controversy

Definitions and Quotations

The Methodological Problem of Casualness

Critical Remarks on Undesigned Coincidences

---

1. McGrew, *Hidden in Plain View,* 12.

Excerpts From and Responses to Dr. Lydia McGrew's General Introduction

Chapter 2—The Hypothesis of Undesigned Coincidences: How Well Does It Explain the Gospel Accounts of the Feeding of the Five Thousand? This chapter investigates a frequently claimed fact: feeding of the five thousand. It scrutinizes several topics:

Sources for the gospel accounts of the feeding of the five thousand.

Logistical factors relating to the feeding of the five thousand.

Why does Mark mention the green grass in his miracle account?

Chapter 3—The Philip Controversy: This section discusses several issues related to the Philip Controversy. Answers to many questions and topics are unverifiable and unfalsifiable. Experts and pundits can only offer arguments from silence.

Why does John mention Philip in his account?

Background on the Apostle Philip

Background on Bethsaida

Was Jesus' Question to Philip a Literary Device?

Speculations: Why Mention Philip?

Why Philip from Bethsaida Does Not Explain Why Jesus Asked Him Where to Buy Food

Chapter 4—Summary of Problems with the Hypothesis of Undesigned Coincidences. This part of the text engages several crucial topics. Noteworthy are:

Eyewitness Testimony and Maximal Data

Explaining the Differences between the Gospel Narratives

Six Criteria in Transcending Horizons

Critical Thinking

The Scientific Method

Chapter 5—Conclusion: The Cumulative Argument against the Hypothesis of Undesigned Coincidences. This section of the text explores the cumulative argument against the hypothesis of Undesigned Coincidences. Noteworthy it presents:

Lengthy arguments and observations that undermine and refute the hypothesis of undesigned coincidences

Provides an overview of the Cumulative Case Methodology

This text presents a robust review of the hypothesis of Undesigned Coincidences. Notably, advocates do not engage with biblical criticism and overlook relevant research on coincidences and casualness. The upshot of this review is that arguments from Undesigned Coincidences suffer from a critical flaw. There needs to be a methodology for identifying a coincidence, deciding what counts as one, or determining what is and is not designed. This text holds significance as it systematically reviews and analyzes the hypothesis of Undesigned Coincidences.

Acknowledgments

VIRTUALLY ALL BOOKS ARE a team project. There is no letter "I" in the word team. *The Hypothesis of Undesigned Coincidences: A Critical Review* is no different. This text was made possible through the efforts of many people. Alphabetically, I also wish to recognize the contribution of three external readers:

David Austin was a crucial external reader from Down Under (Australia). He is a rationalist and skeptic about Jesus' resurrection. David has published several guest essays about the resurrection online at Patheos.com (A Tippling Philosopher). This Aussie contributed ideas and textual matter to the content. In addition, David caught several errors that slipped through multiple draft readings.

Gerald Sigal is a member of the Orthodox Jewish community and a long-time Jewish counter-missionary. He has published numerous texts that serve as a "vaccination" against proselytizing Klal Yisrael. His noteworthy texts include *The Jew and the Christian Missionary: A Jewish Response to Missionary Christianity* (1981); *Trinity Doctrine Error: A Jewish Analysis* (2006); *Isaiah 53: Who is the Servant?* (2007); *The Resurrection Fantasy: Reinventing Jesus* (2012); and *The Jewish Response to Missionary Christianity* (2015). I helped edit several of these works. With his forte in Torah, Gerry made suggestions that enhanced the usefulness of *The Hypothesis of Undesigned Coincidences: A Critical Review*.

Vincent J. Torley earned a PhD and MA in philosophy and teaches in Japan. He is also a Catholic who writes about apologetics. Vincent is a consummate, intellectually honest seeker of truth. He has contributed several noteworthy essays to TSZ (The Skeptical Zone). Vincent is a wordsmith—I am jealous. Once again, he smoothed out and added the human touch to my draft that several computer grammar-checks lacked. Like a prior project, he helped produce an intellectually honest analysis of the topic. With virtually every email, Vincent sent numerous criticisms and suggestions. Significantly, Vincent assisted in reordering the flow of logic and enhanced the readability and clarity of the text. He often helped me realize that key ideas needed clarification and expansion, and he helped me identify discrepancies in the text to improve the initial manuscript.

Professor Evan Fales is the author of *Causation and Universals* (1990), *A Defense of the Given* (1996), *Divine Intervention: Metaphysical and Epistemological Puzzles* (2010), and *Reading Sacred Texts: Charity, Structure, Gospel* (2021). He was also on the International Editorial Advisory Board of the GCRR Academic Society and is a welcomed contributor to this project. He earned a PhD in Philosophy at Temple University and taught at the University of Iowa before his retirement. His areas of interest include philosophy of religion, modal logic, epistemology, metaphysics, and philosophy of science. I am honored and grateful to have a distinguished scholar of his caliber agreeing to write the foreword to this text.

I also wish to acknowledge Christian Farren for copyediting and proofreading this text, as well as Kyle Lundburg for his cover design and all the other members of the Wipf and Stock staff for their helpfulness throughout the production of this text.

Abbreviations

AD	*anno Domini* ("in the year of the Lord")
ATLA	American Theological Library Association
BC	Before Christ
BCE	before the common era
c.	century; common
CE	Common Era
cf.	[Lat.] *confer*, compare
ed(d).	edition(s)
e.g.	*exempli gratia*, for example
esp.	especially
ESV	English Standard Version
f(f).	and the following one(s)
i.e.	*id est*, that is
JSTOR	Journal Storage
LXX	Greek Septuagint
MT	Masoretic text
n(n).	note(s)
NIV	New International Version
NT	New Testament
OT	Old Testament [Hebrew Bible]
p(p).	page(s)
PhD	Doctor of Philosophy
v(v).	verse(s)

BIBLICAL BOOKS OF THE HEBREW BIBLE

Gen	Genesis	Song	Song of Songs
Exod	Exodus	Isa	Isaiah
Lev	Leviticus	Jer	Jeremiah
Num	Numbers	Lam	Lamentations
Deut	Deuteronomy	Ezek	Ezekiel
Josh	Joshua	Dan	Daniel
Judg	Judges	Hos	Hosea
Ruth	Ruth	Joel	Joel
1–2 Sam	1–2 Samuel	Amos	Amos
1–2 Kgs	1–2 Kings	Obad	Obad
1–2 Chr	1–2 Chronicles	Jonah	Jonah
Ezra	Ezra	Mic	Micah
Neh	Nehemiah	Nah	Nahum
Esth	Esther	Hab	Habakkuk
Job	Job	Zeph	Zephaniah
Ps(s)	Psalms	Hag	Haggai
Prov	Proverbs	Zech	Zechariah
Eccl	Ecclesiastes	Mal	Malachi

NEW TESTAMENT

Matt/Mt	Matthew	1–2 Thes	1–2 Thessalonians
Mk	Mark	1–2 Tim	1–2 Timothy
Lk	Luke	Titus	Titus
Jn	John	Phlm	Philemon
Acts	Acts	Heb	Hebrews
Rom	Romans	Jas	James
1–2 Cor	1–2 Corinthians	1–2 Pet	1–2 Peter
Gal	Galatians	1–3 Jn	1–2–3 John
Eph	Ephesians	Jude	Jude
Phil	Philippians	Rev	Revelation
Col	Colossians		

1

The Hypothesis of Undesigned Coincidences

Introduction, Key Terms and Definitions, Methodological Problems, and a General Critique of the Hypothesis

1.1 INTRODUCTION

SELF-PROCLAIMED "ANALYTIC PHILOSOPHER" DR. Lydia McGrew's text, *Hidden in Plain View: Undesigned Coincidences in the Gospels and Acts*, has received accolades and endorsements by many of the foremost evangelical conservative Christian apologists, philosophers, scholars, theologians, and others.[1] McGrew, whose PhD is in English literature,[2] first learned about undesigned coincidences from her husband, Professor Timothy McGrew, a Christian apologist and chair of the Department of Philosophy at Western Michigan University. (Note: Throughout this text, the terms "McGrew" are intended to refer to Lydia McGrew, and "Professor McGrew" to refer to her husband.)

McGrew's text "resurrects" a long-forgotten Christian apologetic argument: the argument from "undesigned coincidences"—a term coined by

---

1. Endorsements have come from the following individuals: William Lane Craig, Craig L. Blomberg, Gary R. Habermas, Paul Maier, Craig Keener, C. Stephen Evans, Craig A. Evans, Sean McDowell, J. Warner Wallace, Darrell Bock, Greg Boyd, Paul Rhodes Eddy, Abdu Murray, C. John Collins, Timothy McGrew, David Marshall, Frank Turek, Robert M. Bowman, Tom Gilson, and John Warwick Montgomery.

2. McGrew, "Edmund Spenser's Defense of Love in a Moral Universe."

the 18th-century Anglican clergyman and apologist William Paley, which appears no less than six times in his highly popular book, *Horae Paulinae: Or The Truth of the Scripture History of St. Paul Evinced*. It appears in multiple editions.[3] Additionally, the term is in collections of Paley's works and is under discussion in numerous texts and journal articles.

McGrew describes how the term "undesigned coincidences" entered common usage:

> The phrase received further popularity from the work of 19th-century Anglican priest John James Blunt, who began in 1828 to publish a series of lectures that made use of the argument. These came together in 1847 in Blunt's book *Undesigned Coincidences*, which uses this type of argument to support the reliability of the Old Testament as well as the New.[4]

A literature review finds that Blunt's text went through seven editions until 1890. In her book, McGrew provides a broad definition of an undesigned coincidence:

> An undesigned coincidence is a notable connection between two or more accounts or texts that doesn't seem to have been planned by the person or people giving the accounts. Despite their apparent independence, the items fit together like pieces of a puzzle.[5]

Related to this, McGrew advocates the Maximal Data strategy for defending the resurrection of Jesus on historical grounds. This tactic differs from the Minimal Facts approach, which was originated and developed by Gary Habermas. Proponents of the "Maximal Data" approach argue that the Gospels are not documents written forty to sixty years after Jesus' death. Instead, they are either eyewitness reports of Jesus' life, death, and resurrection (e.g., John's Gospel) or (in the case of the Synoptic Gospels written by Matthew, Mark, and Luke) biographical reports, written only about twenty-five to thirty years after Jesus' death. Moreover, the Gospels focus on interviews with eyewitnesses who personally knew Jesus. Therefore, the Gospel authors are presenting reportage of actual historical events. "An undesigned coincidence provides reason to believe that both (all) of the statements that contribute to it are truthful."[6] Consequently, the presence of "undesigned

---

3. In the 1822 publication, the phrase appears on pages 3, 11, 18, 25, 173, and 174. The word "coincidences" appears twenty-nine times.
4. McGrew, *Hidden in Plain View*, 21.
5. McGrew, *Hidden in Plain View*, 12.
6. McGrew, *Hidden in Plain View*, 13.

coincidences" in the Gospels validates the Maximal Data approach by providing evidence that the Gospels are a composition of independent and reliable sources that fit together like pieces of a puzzle.

The Importance and Relevance of *Hidden in Plain View* and Undesigned Coincidences

An undesigned coincidence, a vital tool for Christian fundamentalists, is an internal indicator. It supports the claim that the New Testament writers (especially the Gospel authors) were *not* copying from each other but engaging in historical reportage. This claim is significant in apologetics as it counters the view of scholars, critics, and skeptics who argue that the gospel writers drew from each other's sources and showed limited independence. The proponents of undesigned coincidences use it as evidence to discredit this belief.

In an interview with Jonathan Petersen of Bible Gateway, McGrew makes several remarks that explain the importance of the hypothesis of Undesigned Coincidences (and her book, *Hidden in Plain View*). The numbering below is not hers:

1. When we start seeing again and again that the accounts fit together in these subtle ways, we're reasonably confident that they're reliable.

2. We learn first of all that they [the authors of the books] knew what they were talking about. These accounts aren't made up of rumors and legends. In some cases, like the Gospels of John and Matthew, the authors may have been eyewitnesses themselves. I think undesigned coincidences support the conclusion that the author of Acts was a companion of Paul.

3. We also learn that they intended to be truthful in a normal sense of the word.

4. Sometimes one reads that ancient people didn't care very much about accuracy in reporting and that such a concern, applied to the books of the Bible, is anachronistic. I think that's false, and undesigned coincidences show that it's false.

5. What we can say is that even a single undesigned coincidence is evidence for the truth of the accounts involved.

6. I'd like it to give them confidence when people suggest that we have no idea where the Gospels and Acts came from, or whether they're just

late and legendary. I'd like to think that after reading *Hidden in Plain View*, you'll have something to say when you hear that accusation.[7]

Aim of the Research

This five-chapter review aims to define, examine, and critique the hypothesis of Undesigned Coincidences elaborated in Lydia McGrew's book, *Hidden in Plain View*. An earlier nineteenth-century text, *Undesigned Coincidences*, written by John J. Blunt, and contemporary writings in the field are further subjects of inquiry. This text integrates current research on casualness, coincidence, and biblical criticism.

Review of the Literature

The Hypothesis of Undesigned Coincidences: A Critical Review began with a literature review, including the bibliography of *Hidden in Plain View*. Standard research tools include ATLA, *Index Theologicus*, JSTOR, Google search, Google Books, Wikipedia, WorldCat, YouTube, and the bibliography accompanying books, journal articles, blogs, and podcasts. Additionally, Google Scholar is used to identify scholarly literature in the field.

Investigative Obstacles and Limitations

A comprehensive review of undesigned coincidences and *Hidden in Plain View* would include sources written in all languages. This text will focus exclusively on English language sources, primarily sources dating from its publication and older material interacting with the topic if undesigned coincidences exist. A significant obstacle to this research was a lack of adequate peer-reviewed articles that critiqued McGrew's text in book reviews, journal articles, and chapter entries. Remarkably, the *ATLA religion database, Index Theologicus, and JSTOR only managed to locate two relevant articles* about the text, or undesigned coincidences, that had been composed since 1990. One of these articles was by McGrew herself. Virtually all articles, blogs, and podcasts are by apologists and evangelical Christians who support the hypothesis of Undesigned Coincidences. An examination of sources dating back in time reveals that discussion of undesigned coincidences almost died out from 1920 to 1990, while authors writing before 1920 engaged with John J. Blunt's text, *Undesigned Coincidences*. Virtually all reviews were superficial and supportive of the hypothesis.

---

7. McGrew, "How the Bible's Obscure 'Coincidences' Demonstrate Its Reliability."

Who Is Lydia McGrew?

The best way to introduce Dr. McGrew is to examine what she says about herself in her curriculum vitae, where she puts her cards on the table squarely. The following excerpts are from a post on May 14, 2021.

> I am a wife, homemaker, mother, emeritus home schooler, and scholar. (My youngest daughter has recently graduated.) My husband is Timothy McGrew, full professor in the Department of Philosophy at Western Michigan University and a well-known scholar and apologist. As a scholar, I'm an analytic philosopher with a fairly hefty publication record in such areas as testimony, independence, probability theory, etc. More recently my work has extended to New Testament studies. *Here* is my curriculum vitae.
>
> My undergraduate degree was from a Bible college, without much literature background, so I prepared myself to apply for graduate studies in English by self-teaching. That work paid off, and I received a Department of Education fellowship to take a graduate degree. I received my PhD in English Literature from Vanderbilt University in 1995. Subsequently I began publishing in epistemology (the theory of knowledge) in co-written works (articles and a book) with my husband, Timothy McGrew, after he was teaching at Western Michigan University. Tim and I branched off on my own and continued building my publication record with peer-reviewed articles written alone in both classical and formal epistemology. This was the second scholarly field that I "broke into" without taking formal courses, but my publication record, continued up to the present, speaks for itself.
>
> Around 2013 to 2014 Tim introduced me to the argument from undesigned coincidences, which he was reviving as part of his work on the history of ideas—specifically the history of the deist controversy and responses to David Hume's argument against miracles in the 18th century. As it happened, I "ran with" that argument and wrote a book-length manuscript on it on my own, though I learned of it originally from Tim. In 2017 I published a book on the argument from undesigned coincidences, which supports the reliability of the Gospels and Acts. *Hidden in Plain View: Undesigned Coincidences in the Gospels and Acts* was released in the spring of 2017 by DeWard Publishing. This was the beginning of my move into a third field of scholarly work, once again carried out in a non-traditional manner. In December, 2019, I published *The Mirror or the Mask: Liberating the Gospels from Literary Devices*. In March, 2021, I published my

third book in New Testament studies—this one on the Gospel of John: The Eye of the Beholder: The Gospel of John as Historical Reportage. See the main page of this website for samples of this third book and for its endorsements. I hope that these three books will be used by laymen and scholars alike.

I'm very interested in the intersection of issues in biblical studies and epistemology (theory of knowledge), and there are many ways in which knowledge about independence, testimony, and evidence can be helpful in biblical studies. This sort of crossover work is desperately needed in a field such as biblical studies that has become, unfortunately, rather inward looking...

I am (as readers of my various blog posts and my Facebook posts know) politically and socially very conservative. The murder of the innocent, born and unborn, seems to me a crux of our time. Another crux is the sanctity of marriage, the nature of male and female, and the nature of human sexuality, and on those issues, too, the skies are very dark in the West. I have also been extremely concerned during 2020 and 2021 about the loss of civil liberties and religious liberties resulting from government responses to Covid. I think it's very important for Christians and conservatives to be willing to speak up for what we believe and stand for.

I'm an entirely traditional and theologically conservative Christian—deity of Christ, resurrection, the whole works. Raised a fundamentalist Baptist, I'm now a member of a *continuing Anglican church*. Continuing Anglicans use the 1928 Prayer Book and do not ordain women...[8]

The Credentialism Controversy

The credentials of Lydia McGrew and Professor Tim McGrew have been the subject of discussion. Does a PhD in English literature or Philosophy qualify someone to engage in New Testament studies? McGrew confronts the topic head-on in a 2018 post:

> I dislike credentialism intensely...
>
> In my current work in NT studies, I ask people, even beg people, to consider the arguments and the information, first and foremost....
>
> A recent meme (as one might call it) is that neither I nor Tim is qualified to address these issues of literary devices in the Gospels at all because we lack relevant credentials... I have

---

8. McGrew, "About Me." Last updated May 14, 2021 and February 5, 2024.

also argued explicitly that the field of NT studies in particular is inbred, subject to perpetuating epistemic pathologies, and needs an outsider perspective.... Most of the explicit claims that we are unqualified or that I am unqualified are being made in public by the followers of prominent scholars rather than by the scholars themselves.[9]

Next, McGrew interacts with her critics and discusses her credentials afterward. Readers are encouraged to examine the entire article and her curriculum vitae. It speaks volumes, attesting to her scholarly credentials. McGrew's works appear in several peer-reviewed journals.

Michael Alter and Darren Slade addressed the question of who counts as a scholar in a SHERM publication[10]:

> To be categorized as a "scholar" in the field, an obvious problem is relevant qualifications. In 2017, one reader asked Bart Ehrman, Can biblical scholars be historians? His response was, "*I would say that most biblical scholars in fact are not historians. But some are. It depends on what their interests and expertise are.*"[11] (Bold, italics, and underline in Ehrman's original.)

The fairest and most unbiased response to credentialism is that the degree earned is irrelevant. What matters is whether the article or book is:

1. Truthful.
2. Factual (i.e., it presents facts, not "alternative facts").
3. It cites "substantial" peer-reviewed evidence supporting its findings and interpretations.
4. Engages and interacts with ideas, pros, and cons about the topic.
5. Presents a broad scope about the topic (discussing numerous topics, authors, agendas, dating, apologetics, controversial issues, and current discussion.).
6. Depth of insight and knowledge.
7. Can withstand critical analysis
8. Frankly admits when it is presenting an argument from silence.[12]

Ad hominem arguments have no place in academia. This text will engage with McGrew's arguments purely on their merits.

9. McGrew, "On Credentials, Philosophy, and NT Studies."
10. Alter and Slade, "Dataset Analysis of English Texts," 380–81.
11. Ehrman, "Biblical Scholars Don't Typically Call Themselves Biblical Historians."
12. Alter, "An Author Based Analysis of Resurrection Texts," 13 (modified).

1.2 THE HYPOTHESIS OF UNDESIGNED COINCIDENCES: SOME DEFINITIONS AND QUOTATIONS

McGrew incorporates two key terms into her argument: "undesigned" and "coincidence," before defining what she means by an undesigned coincidence on page twelve of her book. It is important to note that the two key terms she employs have a symbiotic relationship: the former functions as a qualifier, while the latter, as readers will see, is a loaded term. Before proceeding to analyze McGrew's arguments and hypotheses, however, it is necessary to define the terms "designed," "undesigned," and "coincidence."

Definitions

a. *Undesigned* means *not planned beforehand, unpremeditated*, or *unintentional*.

Words related to and synonymous with "undesigned" include the following list: accidental, aimless, casual, chance, erratic, extemporaneous, fortuitous, haphazard, inadvertent, involuntary, purposeless, random, unconscious, undevised, unexpected, unforeseen, unintended, unmeant, unplanned, unpremeditated, unthinking, unthought, unwitting.

b. In contrast, words related to and synonymous with the verb "*design*" include the following lists:

plan, draw, sketch, outline, map out, plot, block out

Or

delineate, draft, depict, invent, originate, create, think up, come up with

Or

devise, form, formulate, conceive, make, produce, develop, fashion

Or

fabricate, forge, hatch, coin, dream up

Or

plan, delineate, devise, fabricate, draft, form, forge, draw, depict, formulate, hatch, sketch, conceive,

Or

intend, aim, devise, contrive, purpose, plan, tailor, fashion

Or

adjust, adapt, fit, gear, equip, mean, destine, orient

c. The term "coincidence" is defined by *Oxford Languages*, a gold standard, as follows:

1. a remarkable concurrence of events or circumstances without apparent causal connection: "they met by coincidence."
2. correspondence in nature or in time of occurrence: "the coincidence of interest between the mining companies and certain politicians."[13]

Another definition, taken from *The Cambridge English Dictionary* says:

An occasion when two or more similar things happen at the same time, especially in a way that is unlikely and surprising.[14]

Notable Quotations About Coincidences

"In fact, coincidences *do* happen, and when they do, we take note. Any particular coincidence is indeed an extremely rare event; however, as we'll soon see, what is rarer yet is for us to experience *no* coincidences at all. Basically, the moral is to expect the unexpected."—Edward P. Burger[15]

"Every single moment is a coincidence."—Douglas Coupland[16]

"Statisticians who study coincidences are fond of saying that ordinary people don't know how to estimate the probabilities of coincidences."—Bernard D. Beitman[17]

"It's hard to believe in coincidence, but it's even harder to believe in anything else."—John Green[18]

---

13. *Oxford English Dictionary*, "Coincidence."
14. *Cambridge English Dictionary*, "Coincidence."
15. Burger and Starbird, *Coincidences, Chaos, and All That Math Jazz*, 4.
16. Coupland, *Girlfriend in a Coma*.
17. Beitman and Osman, "Can You Accurately Estimate Coincidence Probabilities?"
18. Green and Levithan, *Will Grayson, Will Grayson*, 72.

"But really, there are no coincidences."—Elise Broach[19]

"When a coincidence seems amazing, that's because the human mind isn't wired to naturally comprehend probability and statistics."—Neil deGrasse Tyson[20]

"Coincidence is the word we use when we can't see the levers and pulleys." —Emma Bull[21]

"The human mind delights in finding pattern—so much so that we often mistake coincidence or forced analogy for profound meaning."—Stephen Jay Gould[22]

"We are swimming in an ocean of coincidences."—Persi Diaconis and Frederick Mosteller[23]

"Just think of all the billions of coincidences that don't happen."—Dick Cavett[24]

"The synchronicity principle asserts that the terms of a meaningful coincidence are connected by *simultaneity* and *meaning*."—Carl Jung[25]

"There is always room for coincidence."—Alva Noto[26]

"Coincidence may be described as the chance encounter of two unrelated causal chains which miraculously, it seems merge into a significant event." —Arthur Koestler[27]

19. Broach, *Shakespeare's Secret*, 65.
20. Tyson, "When a Coincidence Seems Amazing."
21. Bull, *Bone Dance: A Fantasy for Technophiles*, 22.
22. Gould, *The Flamingo's Smile: Reflections in Natural History*, 199.
23. Diaconis and Mosteller, "Methods for Studying Coincidences," 860.
24. Cavett, "Dick Cavett Quote."
25. Jung, "Synchronicity: An Acausal Connecting Principle," *The Structure and Dynamics of the Psyche*, para. 916.
26. Nicolai (Alva Noto), "Alva Noto Quote". Alva Noto is his musical pseudonym.
27. Koestler, *Janus: A Summing Up*, 144.

"Coincidence, if traced far enough back, becomes inevitable."—Inscription on a Hindu temple near New Delhi and quoted by Charles Gustav Jung.[28]

"If there were no coincidence, it would be the greatest coincidence of all."
—G.K. Chesterton[29]

"There can be no doubt that, however unlikely an event may be, if we (loosely speaking) vary the circumstances sufficiently, or if in other words, we keep on trying hard enough, we shall meet with such an event at last."
—John Venn[30]

"That's too coincidental to be a coincidence."—Yogi Berra[31]

Books on Coincidences

Numerous books exist on the topic of coincidence. A few examples follow below.

David Peat, *Synchronicity: The Bridge Between Matter and Mind*, New York: Bantam, 1987.
Allan Combs, *Synchronicity; Through the Eyes of Science, Myth, and the Trickster* 3rd ed. New York: Marlowe, 2001.
Bernard Beitman, *Connecting with Coincidence: The New Science for Using Synchronicity and Serendipity in Your Life*, Deerfield Beach, FL: Health Communications, 2016.
David J. Hand, *The Improbability Principle: Why Coincidences, Miracles, and Rare Events Happen Every Day*, New York: Scientific American, 2014.
Edward B. Burger and Michael Starbird, *Coincidences, Chaos, and All That Math Jazz: Making Light of Weighty Ideas*, New York: Norton, 2006.
Joseph Mazur, *Fluke: The Maths and Myths of Coincidences*, New York: Basic, 2016.

Additional sources are available under the Library of Congress Subject Heading classification, Coincidence theory (Mathematics), and Coincidence/Chance.

The Word "Coincidence": Some Technical Definitions

Coincidence is a diverse, interdisciplinary topic. It encompasses many fields: Anthropology, Biology, Cognitive Science, Mathematics, Parapsychology,

---

28. obstinateguy (@obstinateguy), "Coincidence if traced far enough back, becomes inevitable."
29. Chesterton, "The Human Will and the Decline of Empire."
30. Venn, *The Logic of Chance*, 274.
31. Berra, "Quotesweekly.Com."

Philosophy, Probability, Psychology, and Statistics, to mention a few. This topic is also a subject of exploration in the field of Religion. So, what makes a coincidence? Thomas Griffiths and Joshua Tenenbaum write, "Coincidences arise when there is a conflict between the evidence an event provides for a theory and our prior beliefs about the plausibility of that theory."[32] Before analyzing the hypothesis of "Undesigned Coincidences," it is vital to examine the topic of "coincidence" from an interdisciplinary field and technical perspective. A working definition is essential. Afterward, the definition(s) interact with the hypothesis of Undesigned Coincidences.

1. Jane Henry proposes, "A coincidence experience may be defined as the occurrence of two (or more) odd, surprising, out-of-the-ordinary or personally meaningful events connected in the mind of the observer."[33]

2. Persi Diaconis and Frederick Mosteller: "Let us begin with a working definition. A coincidence is a surprising concurrence of events, perceived as meaningfully related, with no apparent causal connection."[34]

3. Mark Johansen and Magda Osman: "[C]oincidences are surprising pattern repetitions that are observed to be unlikely by chance but are nonetheless ascribed to chance since the search for causal mechanisms has not produced anything more plausible than mere chance."[35]

Johansen and Osman point out that while definitions of coincidence differ widely, they share one or more of the following key components:

1. Definitions emphasizing connected mental states.
2. Definitions emphasizing low probabilities.
3. Definitions emphasizing causal phenomena.
4. Definitions emphasizing pattern repetition.[36]

The Subjective Element of Surprise in a Coincidence

Definitions of "coincidence" share vital components that necessitate investigation. First, they include the word *surprising*. One notable fact about coincidences is that they tend to be surprising.[37] However, surprising events are *not* necessarily experienced as coincidental: for instance, an unexpected

---

32. Griffiths and Tenenbaum, "From Mere Coincidences," 189.
33. Henry, "Coincidence Experience Survey," 97.
34. Diaconis and Mosteller, "Methods for Studying Coincidences," 853.
35. Johansen and Osman, "Coincidences," 36.
36. Johansen and Osman, "Coincidences," 35–36.
37. Falk and MacGregor, "The Surprisingness of Coincidence," 489–502.

bang from a firecracker may induce surprise but it does *not* warrant further investigation about its cause. Moreover, research substantiates that "Coincidences are also fairly rare events, but rare events need not be coincidental."[38] Readers, therefore, need to ask themselves: is it surprising to find "undesigned coincidences" in the Bible?

What determines if an event is surprising? In a 2015 paper, Meadhbh Foster and Mark Keane inquired why some surprises are more surprising than others. Their paper contained several important observations:

1. The authors argue that "surprise is a graded experience that depends fundamentally on explanation. Surprise seems to necessarily be about explanation; an event is not surprising if it can be explained easily, and becomes more surprising the harder it is to explain."

2. Moreover, surprise is highly context-dependent: "Surprise is a graded experience; it is not all-or-nothing, we experience different degrees of surprise depending on the situation."[39]

Readers need to ask about the hypothesis of Undesigned Coincidences: are the undesigned coincidences identified in the New Testament by McGrew, Blunt, or others *surprising*? That answer is personal, depending on the person exposed to the coincidences. For the detractor and skeptic, it may not be surprising at all. However, some believers in Scripture may be amazed, especially if they lack knowledge of the Bible, statistics, and other variables. On the other hand, for apologists and evangelical Christians, the proposed undesigned coincidences may be personally meaningful and support the New Testament's historical reliability.

Furthermore, as previously mentioned, an undesigned coincidence may not be surprising if it is open to an easy explanation. For example, while the miracle of feeding the 5,000 is in all four Gospels, Mark exclusively mentions that the grass was green, while John mentions that the event occurred right before the Passover (which falls in the spring, when the grass is green). For McGrew, these two details appear unrelated to readers yet dovetail neatly. However, biblical commentators on the Gospel of Mark argue that it is logical to assume that the author of Mark's Gospel included the word "green" because he was deliberately tying the event to Psalm 23—a hypothesis we will explore. In Mark 6:34, Jesus takes pity on the crowd of people following him because they are "like sheep without a shepherd" (ESV), while Psalm 23:1 declares, "The Lord is my shepherd; I shall not want. He makes me lie down in green pastures" (ESV). Readers knowledgeable about the

---

38. Johansen and Osman, "Coincidences," 36.
39. Foster and Keane, "Why Some Surprises are More Surprising," 81, 74.

twenty-third psalm may experience a lesser degree of surprise than readers who are not so well-informed.

The Element of Meaningfulness

A second common element in the definitions listed above was *meaningful*. This element is personal, depending on the person exposed to the coincidence. What is meaningful for one person may be irrelevant for another. In an article in the *Journal of the American Statistical Association*, authors Persi Diaconis and Frederick Mosteller remark, "What we perceive as coincidences and what we neglect as not notable depends on what we are sensitive to."[40] Griffiths and Tenenbaum point out that the definition of coincidences as unlikely events neglects one of the critical components of coincidences: their apparent meaningfulness.[41] Dovetailing the previous remarks, Catherine Watt, writing in the *European Journal of Parapsychology*, asked, "What makes some concurrences of events remarkable and not others"? At the end of her paper, she concludes, "It seems clear that beliefs, expectations and personal involvement play a large role in our amazement at coincidences."[42]

The proposed undesigned coincidence is significant for "believers" listening to or reading McGrew or other Christian apologists. The reason is apparent and elaborated by its advocates: Undesigned Coincidences' hypothesis supports the New Testament's historical reliability. In McGrew's podcasts, viewers can see the emotional connection expressed in her body language and hear her spoken words. She is a devoted and sincere believer in Christianity. The hypothesis of Undesigned Coincidences is an apologetic tool that defends her theological beliefs.

The Third Element: Absence of Causal Connection

A third key component, shared by the two definitions listed above, is that the coincidences have *no* apparent causal connection/mechanism. David Marks and Richard Kammann describe "unseen cause" as "the second root of coincidence,"[43] the first being probability. In this connection, Caroline Watt points out two crucial facts:

1. A coincidence is not surprising if we discover a simple reason for it.

---

40. Diaconis and Mosteller, "Methods for Studying Coincidences," 859.
41. Griffiths and Tenenbaum, "From Mere Coincidences to Meaningful Discoveries," 186.
42. Watt, "Psychology and Coincidences," 82.
43. Marks and Kammann, *The Psychology of the Psychic*, 171.

2. Other surprising coincidences can have perfectly straightforward hidden causes, which we have just not yet discovered.[44]

For McGrew and her fellow Christian apologists, a coincidence may appear undesigned. However, Bible commentators, detractors, and skeptics can argue that the coincidence is *not* undesigned and that a causal connection exists behind the alleged "undesigned coincidence." A prime example is the presence of "green grass" in Mark's description of the miracle of the feeding of the 5,000 (they are comparable in Mark as sheep without a shepherd), its alleged connection to the Fourth Gospel (which mentions that the miracle took place shortly before the Passover when the grass in the Holy Land is green), and Psalm 23 (which likens God to a good shepherd, who makes His sheep lie down in green pastures). Many New Testament scholars argue that the shepherd motif in Mark implicitly appeals to Psalm 23. This alleged undesigned coincidence with green grass is subject to the analysis below.

Undesigned Coincidences: A Definition and Some Illustrations

In an interview with Ian Paul (IP) on his Psephizo blog, McGrew (LMcG) defines the term "undesigned coincidence" as follows:

> IP: Can you explain what the term 'undesigned coincidence' means?
>
> LMcG: An undesigned coincidence is an incidental interlocking that points to truth. The coming together of two statements has an appearance of casualness. The word "undesigned" means, for example, that the author(s) do not appear to be trying to explain one another or allude to one another by giving the facts. And the word "coincidence" means co-incidence—coming together. A classic kind of undesigned coincidences occurs when two different writers or speakers give details of an incident and one of them explains the other without appearing to be doing so intentionally.[45]

The last word in McGrew's prior paragraph demands attention: intentionally. However, she omits any discussion about that loaded term. Numerous texts, journal articles, and encyclopedia entries exist about "intention."[46] Crucially, writers distinguish between (1) intending as doing, (2) intention

---

44. Watt, "Psychology and Coincidences," 67.
45. Paul and McGrew, "What Do Interlocking 'Coincidences.'"
46. Alonso, "Planning on a Prior Intention, 813–50; Anscombe, *Intention*; Ehrman, "How Can We Possibly Know?"; Setiya, "Intention."

in action, (3) intention and the good, (4) intentions as plans and intention, and (5) belief. A brief example will suffice.

> In this connection we may be helped by considering a categorical distinction made by philosophers of intention. A classic work in the field is G. E. M. Anscombe, *Intention*. At the outset of her study, Anscombe indicates that "we may be inclined to say that 'intention' has a different sense when we speak of a [person's] intentions *simpliciter*—i.e., what he intends to do—and of his intention *in* doing or proposing something—what he aims at." That is to say, there's a key difference between what one intends to do and what one intends to achieve. If I say, "I'm planning to go into town today," it is clear what I am intending to do, but it is not clear what my intention is in doing it, that is, what I am going into town *for*.[47]

In her book on the subject, McGrew tersely defines the undesigned coincidence as follows:

> An undesigned coincidence is a notable connection between two or more accounts or texts that doesn't seem to have been planned by the person or people giving the accounts. Despite their apparent independence, the items fit together like pieces of a puzzle.[48]

McGrew illustrates her definition with a homely example, in which two friends, Alan and Betty, separately relate to you, the reader, a distressing conversation they just had with a third friend, Carl, in a coffee shop. Carl allegedly confessed to a serious wrongdoing during the conversation, but he now denies having the conversation. Your task is to sort out what happened by separately interviewing Alan and Betty, who claim to have heard Carl's confession. Alan says, "The place was so crowded that we could hardly find a spot for all three of us to sit." Later, Betty adds another detail: "While we were talking, Alan accidentally knocked his coffee into my lap." Although Alan does not mention the accident and Betty says nothing about the coffee shop being crowded, the two accounts buttress one another nicely. If the coffee shop were crowded, then they would have been cramped in a small space, making the accidental spillage of the coffee more likely. For that reason, you will be more inclined to credit their accounts and conclude that the conversation likely took place.

---

47. Ehrman, "How Can We Possibly Know?"
48. McGrew, *Hidden in Plain View*, 12.

In an interview with Christian apologist Sean McDowell, McGrew cites what she claims is an example of an undesigned coincidence in the Gospels of Luke and John:

> In John 13 we're told that Jesus got up after eating the Last Supper and washed the disciples' feet. It just sort of happens out of the blue. Reading only John, you might think that Jesus thought of this idea for no special reason, and it does raise the question, "Why did he do that just then?" If you go over to Luke 22, though, there is an explanation: It says that the disciples had been bickering at that very meal about who would be greatest in the kingdom. So the foot-washing in John is explained. Jesus was giving them an example of humility and service when they had just been competing and fighting. Luke never mentions the foot-washing, and John never mentions the argument. Those same two passages have a coincidence in the other direction. In Luke, Jesus scolds the disciples for bickering and says, of himself, that though he is their master, "I am among you as the one who serves." This is a slightly weird expression in Luke, because he hasn't done anything especially servant-like. But if you read about the foot-washing in John, you see that he has just dressed himself like a servant and washed their feet. He has *literally* been among them as one who serves. So the two passages fit together extremely tightly because of what each one contains and each one leaves out. Luke explains John, and John explains Luke.[49]

The above example is a plausible instance of an undesigned coincidence, and it might be one. However, a few general remarks are necessary before proceeding further.

1.3 THE METHODOLOGICAL PROBLEM OF CASUALNESS

The concept of *casualness* is crucially significant to the idea of an undesigned coincidence. It is precisely because the connection between two different accounts of the same event is *unplanned* that they can reinforce one another's veracity. This section will analyze whether it is inherently unlikely that the Gospels' authors, who knew they were writing for a mass audience, would have employed their words casually when composing their narratives. Additionally, the vast number of biblical quotations and deliberate allusions to Hebrew Bible verses in the New Testament constitute robust

---

49. McDowell, "Unique Evidence for the New Testament."

evidence against the hypothesis that the details in their accounts were casual. Here, readers must be the final judge and jury. Finally, currently, there is no satisfactory methodology for distinguishing casually recorded details in the Gospels from deliberately inserted ones. These arguments pose difficulties for McGrew and other contemporary defenders of the hypothesis of Undesigned Coincidences.

Casualness and Biblical Criticism

Lydia McGrew writes about the concept of casualness in the General Introduction to her book. Her words on this subject must be properly understood: "The casualness of undesigned coincidences is worth stressing and is also closely connected to the concept of *subtlety*."[50] She then discusses an example before continuing, "It is a connection that many people would not notice explicitly and that some might not even notice subconsciously. This is all the more reason to believe that it is not deliberate."[51]

In her General Introduction, McGrew adds, "Sometimes the gist of that exposition follows a line of argument given by Blunt, Paley, or McGrew [Timothy], and I strongly encourage readers to read other sources."[52] Unfortunately, McGrew does not elaborate. The question must be answered in the eyes of Bible commentators and skeptics: Why is McGrew reluctant to encourage her readers to examine *identified sources* that explicitly challenge or refute the hypothesis of Undesigned Coincidences despite her words, "and I strongly encourage readers to read other sources"?

In an earlier passage, McGrew declares, "I suggest that we take this hypothesis for a test drive while setting aside the apparatus of critical scholarship."[53] Unfortunately, McGrew does not define the term "critical scholarship." This text assumes that she is referring to biblical criticism. Robert L. Plummer (PhD in New Testament, The Southern Baptist Theological Seminary) is the Collin and Evelyn Aikman Professor of Biblical Studies at The Southern Baptist Theological Seminary. In question 37 from his book, *40 Questions About Interpreting the Bible*, 2nd ed., Professor Plummer directly interacts with the topic of *biblical criticism*, immediately dispelling a popular misconception about the term: "When people hear the word *criticism*, most think of a disparaging remark. In reality, biblical criticism or

---

50. McGrew, *Hidden in Plain View*, 16.
51. McGrew, *Hidden in Plain View*, 16.
52. McGrew, *Hidden in Plain View*, 22.
53. McGrew, *Hidden in Plain View*, 17.

various critical approaches to the Bible are not about attacking the Bible but rather relate to the careful, academic study of it."[54]

Harper's Bible Dictionary entry on biblical criticism includes the following definition:

> *biblical criticism*, the study and investigation of biblical writings that seeks to make discerning and discriminating judgments about these writings. The term 'criticism' is derived from the Greek word *krino*, which means 'to judge,' 'to discern,' or to be discriminating in making an evaluation or forming a judgment. It has come to refer to a form of inquiry whose purpose is to make discriminating judgments about literary and artistic productions. Thus, we speak of literary criticism, art criticism, music criticism, or film criticism as disciplines or fields of inquiry whose purpose is to review productions in their respective areas in order to discuss and appraise their significant features and judge their lasting worth.[55]

Writing in *Oxford Bibliographies*, Daniel Harrington defines the term as follows:

> The term "biblical criticism" refers to the process of establishing the plain meaning of biblical texts and of assessing their historical accuracy. Biblical criticism is also known as higher criticism (as opposed to "lower" textual criticism), historical criticism, and the historical-critical method. The word "criticism" need not be interpreted negatively, as if the task were mainly criticizing the Bible or pointing out its errors. Rather, "criticism" indicates the effort at using scientific criteria (historical and literary) and human reason to understand and explain as objectively as possible the meaning intended by the biblical writers.[56]

By its acknowledgment, biblical criticism holds the Bible under scrutiny.

Baird, Clines, O'Neill, and Plummer identify and discuss several types of biblical criticism:

1. Textual Criticism
2. Historical Criticism
3. Form Criticism
4. Source criticism

---

54. Plummer, *40 Questions About Interpreting the Bible*, 299.
55. Holladay, "Biblical Criticism," 129.
56. Harrington, "Biblical Criticism".

5. Redactional Criticism
6. Tradition Criticism
7. Literary Criticism
8. Rhetorical Criticism[57]

Additional categories in the literature include (9) Religious studies, (10) Classical studies, (11) Critical realism, (12) Statistical Criticism, and (13) Canonical Criticism. Admittedly, some skeptical authors skewer biblical scholarship for failing to allow for alternative opinions, thereby misleading their readers. Curiously, many advocates make an identical accusation of undesigned coincidences. Therefore, contrary to McGrew's advice, this text will employ biblical criticism to evaluate her assertion that the "casualness of undesigned coincidences is worth stressing and is also closely connected to the concept of subtlety."[58]

Can biblical criticism provide tools that challenge McGrew's working hypothesis that the New Testament passages containing alleged undesigned coincidences were composed casually? One good place to start is biblical quotations, surprisingly common in the New Testament. Dr. W. Hulitt Gloer offers some highly informative remarks on this subject in an article in *The Holman Bible Dictionary* (edited by Trent C. Butler) on "Old Testament Quotations in the New Testament":

> Indirect quotations or allusions form the most difficult type of Old Testament quotation to identify. The gradation from quotation to allusion may be almost imperceptible. An allusion may be little more than a clause, phrase, or even a word drawn from an Old Testament text which might easily escape the notice of the reader...
> ...In summary, the New Testament writer quoted or alluded to the Old Testament in order to demonstrate how God's purposes have been fulfilled and are being fulfilled in Jesus.[59]

Roger Nicole, a former president of the Evangelical Theological Society, expresses similar opinions: "The New Testament contains an extraordinarily large number of Old Testament quotations. It is difficult to give an accurate figure since the variation in use ranges all the way from a distant allusion to a definite quotation introduced by an explicit formula stating the citation's

---

57. Baird, "New Testament Criticism," 730–36; Clines, "Historical Criticism: Are its Days Numbered?", 542–58; O'Neill, "Biblical Criticism," 725–30; Plummer, *40 Questions About Interpreting the Bible*, 299–303.

58. McGrew, *Hidden in Plain View*, 16.

59. Gloer, "Old Testament Quotations in the New Testament," 1047.

source. As a result, the figures given by various authors often reflect a startling discrepancy."[60]

In her podcasts, McGrew argues that the Gospel of John includes multiple undesigned coincidences based on specific words or phrases used in the Gospel. According to her, these phrases are used casually, indirectly, or artlessly. Readers are urged to consider: How can an investigator verify or falsify the intentions of an author who wrote almost 2,000 years ago and is presumably anonymous? How can a researcher determine what the author was unaware of? What knowledge did the author possess while writing the Gospel, and what were the sources?

One methodology is to examine biblical commentaries written by Bible commentators with varying beliefs, from liberal to conservative. This text quotes almost thirty commentators. As this text shows, many Bible commentators reject McGrew's notion. For example, McGrew claims that Mark 6:39, with its seemingly casual reference to the green grass, is an instance of an undesigned coincidence. However, numerous Bible commentators and theologians argue that this passage has a theological foundation: Psalm 23. This position is in several doctoral dissertations on Mark's Gospel.

Another tool to assess McGrew's assertions on casualness is to examine the biblical passages employed by the Gospel authors. Careful students of the Bible have often observed that many Hebrew Bible passages are in the New Testament. In the above-cited article from *The Holman Bible Dictionary*, W. Hulitt Gloer observes, "The New Testament writers included approximately 250 express Old Testament quotations, and if one includes indirect or partial quotations, the number jumps to more than 1,000."[61] Roger Nicole provides some even more staggering figures:

> The present writer has counted 224 direct citations introduced by a definite formula indicating the writer purposed to quote. To these must be added seven cases where a second quotation is introduced by the conjunction "and," and 19 cases where a paraphrase or summary rather than a direct quotation follows the introductory formula. We may further note at least 45 instances where the similarity with certain Old Testament passages is so pronounced that, although no explicit indication is given that the New Testament author was referring to Old Testament Scripture, his intention to do so can scarcely be doubted. Thus a very conservative count discloses unquestionably at least 295 separate references to the Old Testament. These occupy some

---

60. Nicole, "New Testament Use of the Old Testament, 137–51.
61. Gloer, "Old Testament Quotations in the New Testament," 1047.

352 verses of the New Testament, or more than 4.4 per cent. Therefore one verse in 22.5 of the New Testament is a quotation.

If clear allusions are taken into consideration, the figures are much higher: C. H. Toy lists 613 such instances, Wilhelm Dittmar goes as high as 1640, while Eugen Hühn indicates 4105 passages reminiscent of Old Testament Scripture. It can therefore be asserted, without exaggeration, that more than 10 per cent of the New Testament text is made up of citations or direct allusions to the Old Testament.[62]

Nicole (1915–2010) was a Swiss Reformed Baptist theologian and founding member of the International Council of Biblical Inerrancy and the Evangelical Theological Society.

Gleason Archer and Gregory Chirirchigno, who are both esteemed Christian apologists, identify five categories of quotations:

1. These quotations consist of reasonably or completely accurate renderings from the Hebrew of the Masoretic Text (MT) into the Greek of the Septuagint (LXX), and from there (apart from word order, which sometimes deviates slightly) into the New Testament passage in which the Old Testament text is cited.

2. This category includes instances where the New Testament quotation quite closely adheres to the wording of the LXX, even where the LXX deviates somewhat (though not so seriously as to distort the real meaning of the Old Testament passage as given in the MT) from the received text in the Hebrew Bible.

3. These are the citations in which the New Testament adheres more closely to the MT than the LXX does, indicating that the apostolic author may have consulted his Hebrew Bible directly in the preparation of his own account or letter.

4. These consist of passages in which the New Testament quotation adheres quite closely to the LXX rendering, even when it deviates somewhat from the MT.

5. This category of quotations consists of those that give the impression that unwarranted liberties were taken with the Old Testament text in the light of its context. In this class of quotations, we have found many

---

62. Nicole, "New Testament Use of the Old Testament" 137–38. Referencing Eugene Hühn, *Die alttestamentlichen Citate und Reminiscenzen im Neuen Testamente*. Available at archive.org.

between tween the Old Testament source and the New Testament application.⁶³

Another crucial and relevant topic, and a focal point of this text, is whether the New Testament material contains scriptural allusions. In a recent South African journal *Conspectus* article, McGrew defines the term *allusion* as follows: "An unexplained allusion occurs in a document when a speaker or the narrator refers to something that, within that document, remains a 'loose end.' It appears that the speaker or narrator has something in mind, but he does not gloss it."⁶⁴

The field of biblical criticism has extensive literature on allusions, including books, theses, journal and chapter articles, and encyclopedia entries. However, in her work, McGrew does not elaborate on this critical subject to benefit her readers or engage with biblical scholars in the field. This text addresses that deficiency by quoting a few pertinent passages from Rev. Dr. Neil Parker's scholarly work, titled *"The Marcan Portrayal of the 'Jewish' Unbeliever: A Function of the Marcan Reference to Jewish Scripture in Studies in Biblical Literature."* The page numbers of the quoted passages are in brackets:

1. Those scholars who have detected evidence of the influence of OT texts in various contexts of the NT generally assign it to three different categories, viz. quotation (or citation), allusion and reminiscence. The identification of a passage as a quotation presupposes a significant degree of verbal contact between that passage and the source from which it is said to be a quotation. Quotations may be formal or informal. A formal quotation of scripture includes some kind of citation formula; an informal quotation does not include a citation formula. [13]

2. An allusion is somewhat different. The degree of verbal correspondence between a given passage and the source to which it is said to allude is somewhat less than that of a quotation and may, in fact, be virtually absent. Here again allusions may be formal or informal. A formal allusion to scripture includes some kind of introductory formula; an informal allusion includes no introductory formula. [14]

3. Since the degree of verbal correspondence between a text and its alleged source or sources is less than that of a quotation it is sometimes difficult, if not impossible, to ascertain which of several possible sources were used. [14]

---

63. Archer and Chirichigno, *Old Testament Quotations in the New Testament*, ix–xii.
64. McGrew, "Is Jesus John's Mouthpiece," 53.

4. The terms *quotation* and *allusion* both denote conscious deliberate use of external documents. This, of course, would have to be established from the context. Yet one has to exercise caution here. Firstly, verbal correspondence between earlier and later compositions in and of itself is not a sufficient condition to establish a direct literary relationship between them. [15]

5. Reminiscences of OT texts constitute a different phenomenon altogether. A reading of a passage in the NT simply reminds a given reader of another passage in the OT. The identification of reminiscences would therefore involve an element of subjectivity. . . . Reminiscences of texts in the OT may or may not, therefore, be literary phenomena of genuine theological import. [16]

6. A complete investigation of the manner in which a writer has made use of earlier literary sources would ideally require a knowledge of the texts and versions of those literary sources which were available to him. This piece of information would afford some standard for comparison. However, this information may be virtually beyond recovery. On the one hand, extant texts and versions may or may not have preserved certain readings which were contained in earlier manuscripts. The relationship between the Septuagint Version and the Masoretic Text is an illustration of what we mean by this. No official text of the Hebrew Bible enjoyed undisputed authority during the first century AD. Nor did the NT writers in fact recognize one. Yet a thorough revision of the Hebrew Bible, presumably under the official direction of the Jewish authorities, must have taken place at some time between the completion of the LXX (third century BC) and the work of Aquila (early second century AD). [20–21][65]

Readers are encouraged to examine dictionary or encyclopedia entries to broaden their knowledge. Further reading about allusions may explain, in part, why, in the eyes of skeptics, McGrew was so reluctant to engage and interact with biblical criticism.

If the material in John's Gospel (or the other Gospels) contains biblical allusions, were they casual or designed? McGrew claims many coincidences are undesigned and casual, often almost like an allusion. Other scholars may disagree. How can researchers answer this question? Absolute certitude in this field is unattainable since the authors of these Gospels have been dead for a long time. Nevertheless, one (limited) research tool allows laypeople to identify passages in the New Testament deriving from the Hebrew Bible:

65. Parker, *The Marcan Portrayal of the "Jewish" Unbeliever*, 13–16, 20–21.

internet searches. Readers are encouraged to employ an internet search engine and delve into the following topics.

1. Mark/Old Testament quotes in the New Testament.
2. Matthew/Old Testament quotes in the New Testament.
3. Luke/Old Testament quotes in the New Testament.
4. John/Old Testament quotes in the New Testament.
5. Bible: Old Testament Quotations in the New Testament
6. Synoptics/Old Testament quotes in the New Testament.
7. Table of Old Testament Quotes in the New Testament.
8. Imagery in the Bible.

Blueletterbible.org, a Christian Bible study tool, has published an extensive list of biblical allusions on its website. Blueletterbible.org says, "The list contains not only the direct or indirect citations but also the allusions which are particularly worthy of attention."[66] They identify two categories of allusions: mere allusions and possible allusions. The strength of the allusion is subjective. Similarly, on his blog, Kristan Marotta has identified at least fourteen biblical quotations and sixteen allusions in the Fourth Gospel. Table 1, "John's Use of the Hebrew Bible," presents information on using biblical references in the Fourth Gospel.

Table 1. John's Use of the Hebrew Bible: Biblical Quotations and Allusions in the Fourth Gospel

Verse from John	ESV translation	Hebrew Bible Source	Classification
1:23	He said, "I am the voice of one crying out in the wilderness, 'Make straight the way of the Lord,' as the prophet Isaiah said."	Isa. 40:3	Quotation
1:51	And he said to him, "Truly, truly, I say to you, you will see heaven opened, and the angels of God ascending and descending on the Son of Man."	Gen. 28:12	Allusion
2:17	His disciples remembered that it was written, "Zeal for your house will consume me."	Ps. 69:9	Quotation

66. "Parallel Passages in New Testament Quoted from Old Testament: Part II"

Verse from John	ESV translation	Hebrew Bible Source	Classification
3:14	And as Moses lifted up the serpent in the wilderness, so must the Son of Man be lifted up,	Num. 21:8–9	Allusion
4:37	For here the saying holds true, 'One sows and another reaps.'	Micah 6:15	Allusion
5:46	For if you believed Moses, you would believe me; for he wrote of me.		
6:31	Our fathers ate the manna in the wilderness; as it is written, 'He gave them bread from heaven to eat.'"	Ps. 78:24; Exod. 16:4, 15	Quotation
6:45	It is written in the Prophets, 'And they will all be taught by God.' Everyone who has heard and learned from the Father comes to me—	Isa. 54:13	Quotation
6:49	Your fathers ate the manna in the wilderness, and they died.	Exod. 16:15	Allusion
7:22	Moses gave you circumcision (not that it is from Moses, but from the fathers), and you circumcise a man on the Sabbath.	Lev. 12:3	Allusion
7:38	Whoever believes in me, as the Scripture has said, 'Out of his heart will flow rivers of living water.'"	Zech. 13:1; 14:8; Prov. 18:4; Isa. 12:3; 44:2	Allusion
7:39	Now this he said about the Spirit, whom those who believed in him were to receive, for as yet the Spirit had not been given, because Jesus was not yet glorified	Isa. 44:3	Allusion
7:42	Has not the Scripture said that the Christ comes from the offspring of David, and comes from Bethlehem, the village where David was?"	Ps. 132:11; Micah 5:1–2; 1 Sam. 16:1f	Allusion
8:5	Now in the Law, Moses commanded us to stone such women. So what do you say?"	Lev. 20:10; Deut. 19:15	Quotation
8:17	In your Law it is written that the testimony of two people is true.	Deut. 19:15; Num. 35:30	Quotation
9:31	We know that God does not listen to sinners, but if anyone is a worshiper of God and does his will, God listens to him.	Ps. 82:6	Quotation
10:34	Jesus answered them, "Is it not written in your Law, 'I said, you are gods'?	Ps. 82:6	Allusion

Verse from John	ESV translation	Hebrew Bible Source	Classification
12:13	So they took branches of palm trees and went out to meet him, crying out, "Hosanna! Blessed is he who comes in the name of the Lord, even the King of Israel!"	Ps. 118:26	Allusion
12:14–15	And Jesus found a young donkey and sat on it, just as it is written, "Fear not, daughter of Zion; behold, your king is coming, sitting on a donkey's colt!"	Zech. 9:9	Quotation
12:34	So the crowd answered him, "We have heard from the Law that the Christ remains forever. How can you say that the Son of Man must be lifted up? Who is this Son of Man?"	Ps. 89:30; 89:37; 110:4; Isa. 9:7	Allusion
12:38	so that the word spoken by the prophet Isaiah might be fulfilled: "Lord, who has believed what he heard from us, and to whom has the arm of the Lord been revealed?"	Isa 53:1	Quotation
12:40	"He has blinded their eyes and hardened their heart, lest they see with their eyes, and understand with their heart, and turn, and I would heal them."	Isa. 6:9, 10	Quotation
12:49	For I have not spoken on my own authority, but the Father who sent me has himself given me a commandment—what to say and what to speak.	Deut. 18:18	Allusion
13:18	I am not speaking of all of you; I know whom I have chosen. But the Scripture will be fulfilled, 'He who ate my bread has lifted his heel against me.'	Ps. 41:9	Quotation
15:25	But the word that is written in their Law must be fulfilled: 'They hated me without a cause.'	Ps. 69:4; 109:8; 109:17	Allusion

Verse from John	ESV translation	Hebrew Bible Source	Classification
16:21	When a woman is giving birth, she has sorrow because her hour has come, but when she has delivered the baby, she no longer remembers the anguish, for joy that a human being has been born into the world.	Isa. 13: 7–8	Allusion
16:32	Behold, the hour is coming, indeed it has come, when you will be scattered, each to his own home, and will leave me alone. Yet I am not alone, for the Father is with me.	Zech. 13:12	Allusion
17:12	While I was with them, I kept them in your name, which you have given me. I have guarded them, and not one of them has been lost except the son of destruction, that the Scripture might be fulfilled.	Ps. 41:10; 109:8; 17	Allusion
19:24	so they said to one another, "Let us not tear it, but cast lots for it to see whose it shall be." This was to fulfill the Scripture which says, "They divided my garments among them, and for my clothing they cast lots." So the soldiers did these things,	Ps. 22:19	Quotation
19:28	After this, Jesus, knowing that all was now finished, said (to fulfill the Scripture), "I thirst."	Ps. 69:21; 34:12	Allusion
19:36	For these things took place that the Scripture might be fulfilled: "Not one of his bones will be broken."	Exod. 12:46 ref. to killing the Lamb); Ps. 34:20; Num. 9:12 (ref. to the Passover Lamb)	Quotation
19:37	And again another Scripture says, "They will look on him whom they have pierced."	Zech. 12:10	Quotation
20:9	for as yet they did not understand the Scripture, that he must rise from the dead.	Ps. 16:10	Allusion

Verse from John	ESV translation	Hebrew Bible Source	Classification
20:17	Jesus said to her, "Do not cling to me, for I have not yet ascended to the Father; but go to my brothers and say to them, 'I am ascending to my Father and your Father, to my God and your God.'"	Ps. 22:22	Allusion

Sources: Blueletterbible.org; Archer and Chirirchigno, *Old Testament Quotations in the New Testament*; **Franklin Johnson**, *Quotations of the New Testament from the Old*; **Paul Fraser**, "The Use of Scripture in Saint John's Gospel"; **David Jones**, *Old Testament Quotations and Allusions in the New Testament*; **Kristen Marotta**, "John's Use of the Old Testament"; **C.H. Toy**, *Quotations in the New Testament*

These facts raise pertinent questions for the reader to evaluate.

1. When the author of Mark's Gospel was busily composing his work, was he writing casually and inattentively? McGrew assumes that the evangelist incorporated words or phrases into his Gospel casually. For instance, "green" (Mark 6:39) was casually included.

2. When the author of John's Gospel was penning his work, was he writing attentively and diligently or casually and offhandedly? Furthermore, was the Holy Spirit operating through the Gospel authors and furnishing them with an insightful commentary on the Hebrew Scriptures while they were writing? If so, the Holy Spirit must have guided the New Testament authors using interpretive techniques. McGrew assumes that John's author casually incorporated certain words or phrases into his Gospel. In particular, she claims that in John 6, John's narrative provides additional information that *casually* supports and elaborates on Mark's statement that the grass was green. However, as table 1 reveals, at least three verses in John 6 are either biblical quotations or allusions. Given this information, is McGrew's hypothesis prudent, or is it merely wishful thinking designed to support a theological apologetic that the New Testament is historically reliable?

Data varies from sources depending on the text (Hebrew, Greek, and Septuagint), the translation, and subjectively interpreting that a verse contains an allusion. Just as an inkblot can mean one thing to one person and something entirely different to another, the same applies to interpreting allusions in art, music, literature, or poetry. Why is Scripture held to a different standard? McGrew and Professor McGrew are entitled to their opinion that certain verses from the New Testament contain undesigned allusions.

However, that is just their opinion. The question bears repeating: when the author of John's Gospel composed his work, was he writing attentively and diligently or casually unintentionally and off-the-cuff? Let the reader judge. Do 250 or 295 biblical quotations (see Gloer and Nicole) in the twenty-seven books of the New Testament sound like the authors were composing without intent or plan? Moreover, does Eugene Hühn's tally of no less than 4,105 Old Testament allusions within the New Testament sound as if these authors were composing without intent or plan?

> There are 7,957 verses in the New Testament. If a connection is made somehow (by way of citation/quotation, allusion, or echo) in say 4,000 verses, then a connection is made on average every 1.99 verses. This is a remarkably high level of intertextuality. Clearly the OT is woven into the fabric of the NT, and NT is saturated with OT language, expressions, precepts and concepts.[67]

Proponents of the hypothesis of Undesigned Coincidences must address the question: What magic number determines whether the New Testament authors composed with intent or plan?

Real World Experience Repudiates the Casualness of Undesigned Coincidences

McGrew argues that John's Gospel includes undesigned coincidences and casual information demonstrating its truth and historical reliability.[68] "The casualness of undesigned coincidences is worth stressing and is also closely connected to the concept of *subtlety*."[69] McGrew's underlying premise is that John casually, unintentionally, and offhandedly incorporated material into his gospel. Is her argument sustainable when evaluated against the following real-life cases?

3. A musical composer does *not* write a melody casually or inattentively.
4. A poet does *not* write a stanza of a poem casually or inattentively.
5. An architect does *not* design the roof of a building casually or inattentively.
6. A sculptor (e.g., Michelangelo) does *not* sculpt a statue (David, Moses, the Pieta) casually or inattentively.
7. A songwriter does *not* write a stanza of a song casually or inattentively.

---

67. Raven and Van Aarde, "The Impact of the Hebrew Scriptures," 2n4.
68. McGrew, *The Eye of the Beholder*.
69. McGrew, *Hidden in Plain View*, 16.

8. A doctor does *not* write a prescription casually or inattentively.

9. A presidential speech writer does *not* compose a sentence for a State of the Union Address casually or inattentively.

10. A minister, pastor, preacher, priest, rabbi, or imam does *not* compose a sentence for a funeral eulogy casually or inattentively.

The author of the Scripture does not write inattentively or casually. Although John did not know that his writing would be considered Scripture, he undoubtedly recognized that his work was of supreme theological importance for the followers of Jesus. Therefore, it is unlikely that he would have written his Gospel casually or carelessly. This text challenges the McGrews to explain why they believe that John differs from the eight categories of people mentioned above, who all concentrated diligently on their chosen field while working. There is no reason why John or the other Gospel authors would have been any different when composing their Gospels.

John's Theological Agenda Repudiates the Casualness of Undesigned Coincidences

McGrew argues that John's Gospel includes undesigned coincidences and casual information demonstrating its truth and historical reliability. "The casualness of undesigned coincidences is worth stressing and is also closely connected to the concept of *subtlety*."[70] McGrew's underlying premise is that John incorporates in his Gospel material that is casually unintentional and unplanned. Readers must bear in mind John's words at the end of his Gospel and ask themselves: does McGrew's argument appear compatible with the avowedly theological agenda of the Gospel's author?

> 30 Now Jesus did many other signs in the presence of the disciples, which are not written in this book; 31 but these are written so that you may believe that Jesus is the Christ, the Son of God, and that by believing you may have life in his name (John 20:30–31, ESV).

From the above, readers see that John is deliberately writing his gospel for a threefold purpose:

1. So that readers may believe that Jesus is the Messiah;
2. So that readers may believe that Jesus is the Son of God; and
3. So that through believing, they may have life through his name.

---

70. McGrew, *Hidden in Plain View*, 16.

Do proponents of undesigned coincidences believe that the writer of John's Gospel would write in a casually unintentional and offhand manner with such a vital agenda at stake for his readers?

John wrote his gospel about thirty years after the death of Paul and forty years after the composition of 1 Corinthians 15. This text, therefore, assumes that the writer of John had access to and knew of the existence of 1 Corinthians 15. In that epistle, Paul writes words that John must have taken to heart when composing his Gospel:

1. For I delivered to you as of first importance what I also received: that Christ died for our sins in accordance with the Scriptures,[4] that he was buried, that he was raised on the third day in accordance with the Scriptures (1 Cor. 15: 3–4, ESV).

2. And if Christ has not been raised, your faith is futile and you are still in your sins. [18] Then those also who have fallen asleep in Christ have perished. [19] If in Christ we have hope in this life only, we are of all people most to be pitied (1 Cor. 15: 17–19, ESV).

If John 20:31 accurately reports the author's goals, it is inconceivable that he would have been writing casually, unintentionally, and slapdash, as proponents of undesigned coincidences envisage. The reader must evaluate the merits of this counterhypothesis. The question that requires asking: Do proponents of undesigned coincidences believe that the author of John's Gospel would have written in a casually unintentional and offhand manner with such a vital agenda at stake for his readers?

1.4 SOME CRITICAL REMARKS ON UNDESIGNED COINCIDENCES

Exegesis Versus Eisegesis

When evaluating an explanation or interpretation of a text, the writer's methodology is of utmost importance. Two methodologies stand in stark contrast: exegesis and eisegesis. *Exegesis*, a precise and reliable approach, is employed when a person interprets a text based solely on what it says. This method ensures that the reader extracts what is there from the text rather than reading what is not there. The rules for proper exegesis are straightforward: read the immediate context, related themes, and word definitions crucial for correctly understanding the text. Exegesis is a theological term used to describe an approach to interpreting a passage in the Bible by critical analysis. Proper exegesis consists of the following:

1. Using the context around the passage,
2. Comparing it with other parts of the Bible, and
3. Applying an understanding of the language and customs of the time of the writing to understand clearly what the original writer intended to impart.

In other words, it is trying to "pull out" of the passage the meaning inherent in it. In contrast, *eisegesis* evolves when a person interprets and reads information *into the text that is not there*. For example, in its online *Dictionary of Theology*, under the entry for "eisegesis," CARM (Christian Apologetics and Research Ministry) cites 1 Corinthians 8:5, which declares: "For though there be that are called gods, whether in heaven or in earth (as there be gods many, and lords many) (KJV)." CARM then describes how Mormons appeal to this verse to buttress their theological claims:

> With this verse, Mormons, for example, bring their preconceived idea of the existence of many gods to this text and assert that it says there are many gods. But that is not what it says. It says that there are many that are called gods. Being called a god doesn't make something an actual god. Therefore, the text does not teach what the Mormons say and they are guilty of eisegesis; that is, reading into the text what it does not say.[71]

Putting it another way, Claude F. Mariottini of the Northern Baptist Seminary writes:

> [E]isegesis is the approach to Bible interpretation where the interpreter tries to "force" the Bible to mean something that fits their existing belief or understanding of a particular issue or doctrine. People who interpret the Bible this way are usually not willing to let the Bible speak for itself and let the chips fall where they may. They start off with the up-front goal of trying to prove a point they already believe in, and everything they read and interpret is filtered through that paradigm. Stated another way, they engage in what the Bible refers to as "private interpretation."[72]

The writer's methodology is a significant consideration when evaluating a scriptural interpretation. Christian apologists argue that detractors and skeptics employ eisegesis when interpreting the Bible. Similarly, skeptics contend that Christian apologists, who are, more often than not,

---

71. CARM, "Eisegesis."
72. Mariottini, "Republicans v. Democrats."

fundamentalists, employ eisegesis. In reality, both are guilty. The reader must ask themselves whether Christian apologists advocating undesigned coincidences also employ eisegesis.

General Remarks on Undesigned Coincidences

Vincent Torley offers the following methodological observations on the subject of undesigned coincidences:

> First, let us admit at the outset that Dr. McGrew is correct when she argues that the presence of an undesigned coincidence between two accounts provides us with at least a *prima facie* reason to believe that both (or all) of the statements that fit together are truthful. However, a *prima facie* reason is not necessarily a powerful one. Allegedly undesigned coincidences are defeasible: new information may remove the element of surprise or establish the existence of a causal connection between two accounts where there was formerly thought to be none.
>
> Second, it bears pointing out that by Dr. McGrew's own admission, undesigned coincidences are conspicuously absent from the accounts of Jesus' resurrection, with a solitary exception: the appearance of Jesus to seven of his disciples while they were fishing by the Sea of Tiberias in John 21. Among the forty-seven alleged undesigned coincidences listed in her book, this is the only one which bears any relation to the resurrection. Dr. McGrew claims to find two undesigned coincidences in this account: (a) the fact that the Gospel specifically mentions that the net was *not torn* when the disciples miraculously caught 153 large fish after following Jesus' advice to cast their nets, despite failing to catch a single fish all night long (which is alleged to be a deliberate contrast with another miraculous catch of fish described in Luke 5, where the nets broke), and (b) the fact that Jesus asked Peter, "Do you love me?" no less than three times (which is said to refer back to Jesus' warning to Peter at the Last Supper that he would deny him three times, recorded in Matthew and Mark's Gospels). However, Dr. McGrew fails to adequately explore the possibility that John 21 and Luke 5 are simply different retellings of the *same* miracle, and that in the time between the writing of Luke's and John's Gospels, the story grew in the telling, so that the torn net in Luke's account is said to be miraculously *untorn* in John's narrative. And although John's Gospel does not record Jesus' prediction of Peter's triple denial, found only in Matthew and Mark, it *does* record the triple denial itself, and it also ascribes to Jesus an intimate

knowledge of each man's heart (John 2:24), including Peter's, as well as explicit foreknowledge of the fact that Judas was going to betray him (John 6:64), so it is hardly surprising that John 21:17 relates that Peter was grieved when Jesus asked him for the *third* time, "Do you love me?" On John's account, Jesus was hinting to Peter that he *knew* what Peter had said. Surely that is a sufficient explanation in itself. Finally, Dr. McGrew fails to mention the fact that the resurrection appearance in John 21 is a late account that was appended to John's Gospel, probably around 90 to 100 AD, making it the *least* likely of any of the resurrection accounts to contain the genuine recollections of a (by now long-dead) eyewitness. Given that the sole alleged instance of an undesigned coincidence in the gospel accounts of Jesus' resurrection turns out to be a doubtful case at best, one can only conclude that the presence of undesigned coincidences in the Gospels lends no evidential support whatsoever to the resurrection of Jesus from the dead.

Third, undesigned coincidences cannot establish the occurrence of miracles—a point conceded by Professor Tim McGrew in an online debate with New Testament scholar Bart Ehrman ("Do Undesigned Coincidences Confirm the Gospels?" on Justin Brierley's talk show, *Unbelievable*, March 7, 2016, at https://www.youtube.com/watch?v=Gm-nx8yNK3o, from 34:31). At best, what they establish is the general reliability of the Gospels—in particular, that they are based on accounts by people who were "close up to the facts."

Fourth, instances of undesigned coincidences are considerably weakened by any evidence of *literary dependence* between the two accounts they link, as the alleged independence of the two testimonies they provide is contaminated by the presence of a connection between the two. Christian apologist and homicide detective J. Warner Wallace, who is himself a fan of Dr. Lydia McGrew's argument from undesigned coincidences, emphasizes this point in his 2013 best-seller, *Cold-Case Christianity*. In his book, he writes:

> I learned many years ago the importance of separating witnesses. If eyewitnesses are quickly separated from one another, they are far more likely to provide an uninfluenced, pure account of what they saw... I can deal with the inconsistencies; I expect them. But when witnesses are allowed to sit together (prior to being interviewed) and compare notes and observations, I'm likely to get one harmonized version of the same event... The apparent contradictions

are usually easy to explain once I learn something about the witnesses and their perspectives (both visually and personally) at the time of the crime.[73]

As the reader will see below, virtually all scholars agree that Matthew and Luke were familiar with Mark's Gospel, and some would also argue that John was familiar with some or *all* of the Synoptic Gospels.[74] This familiarity means that the alleged "eyewitness testimonies" are nothing like Dr. McGrew's original example, in which the reader converses separately with two people, Alan and Betty, whose accounts dovetail neatly, and who both claim to have been present at a conversation with Carl. It bears pointing out that the Gospels were not written by eyewitnesses but by people who were one or more steps removed from them. (Virtually no biblical scholar today believes that the apostles Matthew and John wrote the Gospels named after them.)

Fifth, undesigned coincidences weaken with time as people's memories get distorted. Cognitive psychologists Christopher Chabris and Daniel Simons document the phenomenon of memory distortion with a wealth of examples in their 2009 classic text, *The Invisible Gorilla*. On pages 72 and 73 of their book, they cite research conducted by psychologists Ulric Neisser and Nicole Harsch, who asked a class of Emory University undergraduates to record their memories of the explosion of the space shuttle *Challenger*, the morning after it happened on January 28, 1986, and to answer a detailed questionnaire about how they heard about it, what time they heard about it, what they were doing at the time, who was with them, how they felt about the disaster, and so on. Two and a half years later, the researchers asked the same students to complete a questionnaire that again covered almost the same points. As Chabris and Simons tell it, the results were striking:

> The memories the students reported had changed dramatically over time, incorporating elements that plausibly fit with how they could have learned about the events, but that never actually happened ... That is, years after the event, some of them remembered hearing about it from different people, at a different time, and in different company.
>
> Despite all these errors, subjects were strikingly confident in the accuracy of their memories years after the

---

73. Wallace, *Cold-Case Christianity*, 75.

74. Bauckham, *The Gospels for All Christians*; Barker, *John's Use of Matthew*; Smith, *John Among the Gospels*; Lindars, "John and the Synoptic Gospels," 287–94.

event, because their memories were so vivid—the illusion of memory at work again.⁷⁵

The explosion of the space shuttle *Challenger*, a publicly televised event, had a powerful impact on the American national psyche when it took place in 1986. It created incredibly vivid, detailed memories in the minds of those who saw the event on TV. Such memories are known as *flashbulb memories* in the psychological literature. Despite their vividness, however, these memories are liable to distortion over a period as short as two years, even among subjects who took the trouble to record their original memories in writing. The story's relevance to Lydia McGrew's "undesigned coincidences" proposal should be readily apparent. Elements of a story that may have dovetailed perfectly when freshly remembered are liable to do so only awkwardly (if at all) after years have elapsed and critical details have been distorted in witnesses' memories. The Gospels were composed not two years but over *thirty* years after the events they describe. How likely is it that two accounts of the same event in the life of Jesus, written at such a late date, will still retain interlocking coincidences that fit together like pieces of a puzzle? The short answer is: not very. It is far more likely that the pieces will not fit together at all.

Finally, it bears repeating that an undesigned coincidence can only be said to exist when there is no alternative explanation that eliminates the element of surprise. Putting it another way: even *one* plausible surprise-busting explanation is enough to deflate any alleged instance of an undesigned coincidence, robbing it of its force. Defenders of the "undesigned coincidences" need to be reasonably certain that no such explanations exist for the cases they cite, or their apologetic fails.⁷⁶

Is Evidence of Literary Dependence Between the Gospels Fatal to Lydia McGrew's Enterprise?

McGrew is well aware of the objection that the four Gospels are not independent accounts. She has responded to it at length in two comments attached to a post titled "Undesigned Coincidences" on her blog, Extra Thoughts. In a comment dated January 27, 2011 (9:09 a.m.), she explains

---

75. Chabris and Simons, *The Invisible Gorilla*, 72–73.
76. Personal e-mail.

that one account of an event may depend on another yet still have access to its unique sources:

> The great thing about undesigned coincidences, though, is that they show that whatever dependence there was of that kind was conjoined with a significant amount of independence in sources—for example, Luke was probably interviewing people other than the writers of the other synoptics.[77]

Years later, McGrew responded to a reader's query, proposing a variant of her original example concerning Alan, Betty, and Carl. Alan tells the same story in this example, but with two added details: "I got into a fender-bender on the way here" and "I paid for our coffee." You also stumble across a written account of the conversation by someone called Diana, who was not actually present. Diana's story is partly based on Alan's, but it includes the following additional comments: "Alan walked in in a bad mood," "Carl was visibly shaken the whole time—he couldn't even find his wallet," and "Alan accidentally knocked coffee into Betty's lap." The two accounts dovetail nicely: Diana's explains Alan's (the reason why Alan paid for the coffee is that Carl couldn't find his wallet), and Alan explains Diana (Alan was in a bad mood because he had been in a car accident). Should we credit Diana's account, even though it depends on Alan's? McGrew argued that we should, in a comment dated March 8, 2019 (11:36 a.m.):

> There would be no reason for Diana to write in just the fact that Carl couldn't find his wallet but not the fact that Alan paid for the coffee *because* she had read Alan's account. How would that even work? It would be extremely implausible to think that Diana read Alan's account and decided to *make up* the idea that Carl couldn't find his wallet, hoping that readers would notice that this explains why Alan paid for the coffee, but hyper-subtly neglect to include the fact that Alan paid for the coffee. . .
>
> The sort of subtle putting-in-fake-things-and-leaving-things-out behavior I sketch above for Diana is simply not how fakers behave.[78]

In the above case, readers would probably be justified in crediting Diana's account despite its not being an eyewitness report and its dependence on Alan's report. However, what if we are trying to determine what happened in the coffee shop some decades *after* the alleged incident of Carl's embarrassing confession? Moreover, what if we can no longer interview

---

77. McGrew, "Undesigned Coincidences."
78. McGrew, "Undesigned Coincidences."

either Alan or Betty? What if we are unsure whether an eyewitness wrote *any* of the accounts we possess of what happened? Finally, what if two of our accounts show evidence of copying (with only slight alterations) *whole slabs of material* from what we believe to be the earliest account? At the same time, we suspect our remaining account may have also had access to it. Now, the task of identifying undesigned coincidences becomes infinitely trickier. This identification is precisely the situation we are in concerning the Gospels of Mark (which is agreed by virtually all scholars to be the oldest), Matthew and Luke (who both borrow heavily from Mark), and John (who may have read Mark as well). *All* of these accounts date from three to six decades after Jesus' death, and *none* is considered by the majority of scholars to have been written by an eyewitness. Looking for undesigned coincidences becomes a perilous task, indeed.[79]

Illustrating this counterargument, the late, widely respected, conservative New Testament scholar Richard Bauckham writes that a significant majority of New Testament scholars reject the eyewitness/associate eyewitness authorship of the Gospels:

> The argument of this book [*Jesus and the Eyewitnesses* (2017)]– that the texts of our Gospels are close to the eyewitness reports of the words and deeds of Jesus–*runs counter to almost all recent scholarship*. As we have indicated from time to time, the prevalent view is that a long period of oral transmission in the churches intervened between whatever the eyewitnesses said and the Jesus traditions as they reached the Evangelists [the authors of the Gospels]. *No doubt the eyewitnesses started the process of oral tradition, but it passed through many retellings, reformulations, and expansions before the Evangelists themselves did their own editorial work on it.*[1] (Italics added)[80]

This strategy is the investigative tool McGrew proposes readers use to establish the general reliability of the Gospels. Should readers trust such a tool? Readers can decide for themselves.

John Nelson's Critique

John Nelson, who writes under the pseudonym Thomas Horatio, is a Christian, a student of Christian origins, and a believer in undesigned coincidences. However, in a blog post, he argues that "a closer examination of the gospels reveals that 'undesigned coincidences' are often easily explained

---

79. Personal communication and input from Torley.
80. Bauckham, *Jesus and the Eyewitnesses*, 240.

by the kind of redactional interests, compositional practices, or points of context which have been traditionally highlighted by gospel scholars."[81] He provides several rationales that challenge the hypothesis of Undesigned Coincidences. The nine points in the summary below are excerpts from various paragraphs in his review.

1. Some 'undesigned coincidences' fade when the interests of the evangelists in the way they have compiled their sources and shaped their narratives—their 'redactional' interests—are considered.
2. Other 'undesigned coincidences' fall away once the processes of oral tradition are considered.
3. Some coincidences can be explained regarding the use of literary *imitation*.
4. Other undesigned coincidences disappear when the *assumed knowledge of an audience* is brought into view.
5. McGrew interprets some phenomena in the gospels as 'undesigned coincidences,' but they only fit by expanding the definition so broad as to negate its significance.
6. Other 'undesigned coincidences' do not concern two reports of the *same event*.
7. Even if the gospels possessed many undesigned coincidences, it would not support the conclusion that eyewitnesses were the direct source.
8. We have four authors working with different source materials, with their redactional interests and compositional techniques, writing to different audiences, sometimes decades apart. Unsurprisingly, the complex 'writing a gospel' process should give rise to apparently 'undesigned' coincidences. This reality was one of the reasons why John Henry Newman was cautious about Paley's 'courtroom' apologetic. The evidence is slim. The unknowns are great. Moreover, this history will not often bend to the courtroom's demands.
9. One of the reasons why [apologist Peter J.] Williams', and to a greater extent, McGrew's presentation of undesigned coincidences will seem so compelling is because they are interested in the text as an apologetic. In this apologetic work, they are not factoring in the much more difficult work that historians of the text and exegetes do in theirs.[82]

---

81. Nelson/Horatio, "Some Thoughts on 'Undesigned Coincidences' in the Gospels." His real name is John Nelson.

82. Nelson/Horatio, "Some Thoughts on 'Undesigned Coincidences' in the Gospels."

Chris Sandoval's Critique

In an Amazon book review, Chris Sandoval elaborates that McGrew's argument from undesigned coincidences is vulnerable on account of three flaws:

1. The most recent common source for an undesigned coincidence may be well-known stories about Jesus and his disciples that circulated among many Christians.
   a. The similarities derive from popular stories, and the differences arise from the evangelists' creativity (or carelessness) or their sources.
   b. Stories about Jesus found in the Q source or Mark, which were well-known and repeated, would hardly be independent, playing a significant role in the formation of the narratives.
   c. An evangelist may have intentionally omitted minor details, knowing his Christian audience knew the story well enough to fill in the gaps.
2. The evangelists were as careless and forgetful as any other author. An undesigned coincidence between two Gospels may result from two sloppy authors accidentally omitting minor details, one evangelist recording a detail neglected by his counterpart.
3. Each Gospel had to be short enough to fit into one standard papyrus scroll approximately thirty feet long. This constraint forced the evangelists to edit their works.[83]

Jeffrey M. Tripp's Critique

Jeffrey M. Tripp received a New Testament and Early Christianity doctorate from Loyola University Chicago and now teaches at Rock Valley College. He is also the author of a text titled *Direct Internal Quotation in the Gospel of John*. He often incorporates statistical methods into his biblical research, focusing on the New Testament narratives and their reception. Tripp critiques Lydia McGrew in her book, *Hidden in Plain View*, in the podcast MythVision. He says

1. McGrew's book is a reaction to biblical studies. It's it [sic] you need biblical studies there first highlighting these problems for her to then come in and say this is how I can solve it.[84] [34:50 timestamp]

---

83. Sandoval, "Amazon Book Review of *Hidden in Plain View*."

84. Tripp and Lambert, "The FAILURE of 'unDESIGNED Coincidences,'" timestamp 34:55.

2. Fundamental Problems
    a. The argument is circular (assumes the narratives are reliable history) [40:00]
    b. McGrew ignores contradictions/inconsistencies [50:00]
    c. A failure of Bayesian reasoning [57:00]
3. What has McGrew shown overall?
    - That the Gospels take place in the same basic narrative universe (if you ignore the contradictions and inconsistencies)
    - That Paul's genuine letters and Acts take place in the same basic narrative universe (but doesn't prove the miraculous, visionary events took place in the universe of Paul's letters)
    - That Acts and the disputed letters take place in the same basic narrative universe (stacking hypotheses, tautological argument)
    - Wants a maximalist conclusion, but demonstrates only minimal reliability even if we grant her all her arguments. [timestamp 1:55]

The three-hour-plus podcast requires watching.

A General List of Counter-Apologetics

A literature review finds that few critical analyses and evaluations of McGrew's book exist, compared to copious positive reviews. Below is a partial listing of criticisms of the hypothesis of Undesigned Coincidences:

1. There is no methodology to help us decide what counts as a coincidence.
2. No criteria exist to determine what is and is not designed.
3. An undesigned coincidence is harmonization under a different name.
4. There are far more apparent discrepancies between the Gospels than apparent undesigned coincidences. McGrew fails to address this point.
5. The accounts connected by an undesigned coincidence may describe two completely different events.
6. Undesigned coincidences can be found even in fictional stories like *Star Trek* and *Star Wars*.
7. Coincidences are things we all experience. Those who believe they have had a 'meaningful coincidence' in their lives choose to ascribe a form of grander meaning to the occurrence via fate, divinity, or

existential importance. The skeptic may be correct, but he cannot deny the power of the experience.⁸⁵

8. Undesigned coincidences, even when considered cumulatively, fail to demonstrate that the writers were well-informed about their subject. Nor do they show that the writers were habitually truthful. Besides, even habitually truthful people may sometimes be wrong and may unintentionally pass along inaccurate information.

9. A lack of adequate numbers of peer-reviewed articles on McGrew's book exists in mainstream academic journals. [see ATLA, JSTOR, and *Index Theologicus*]

10. Most of McGrew's book's featured reviewers are committed evangelical Christians, fellow apologists, and conservative theologians. "They are writing to the choir."

11. McGrew and proponents decline to engage with possible causal connections between alleged undesigned coincidences.

12. McGrew's approach is tantamount to reviving a pre-critical view of the Gospels. She lacks interest in source criticism or even consulting significant commentaries on the undesigned coincidences (e.g., the green grass in Mark 6 and the Passover in John 6).

13. McGrew refuses to interact and engage with the abundant academic literature on cognitive science, literature, mathematics, probability, psychology, and statistics.

McGrew's Theological Presuppositions: The Historical Reportage Hypothesis

In an August 21, 2022 podcast, McGrew argues that the authors of the four Gospels are narrating "historical reportage." However, this claim is unverifiable. It reflects a theological mindset and belief. McGrew contrasts the position of detractors, who promote that the Gospel authors wrote "non-reported symbolic alternatives," with her position that the authors "reported reality." McGrew criticizes detractors for arguing that "sometimes the Gospel authors did make up things, and sometimes they just reported the facts." She categorizes this approach as a "schizophrenic author model" and strongly urges her listeners not to follow this model. At the end of the podcast, she puts her cards on the table:

1. The authors were reporting reality,

85. King and Plimmer, *Beyond Coincidence*, 7.

2. The authors did not make things up, and

3. The authors were writing in good faith.

In response, skeptics would claim McGrew's beliefs are naive and theologically motivated. The inconvenient truth is that the hypothesis of Undesigned Coincidences, the Maximal Fact hypothesis, and their accompanying "cottage industry" are sandy foundations. The hypothesis is like a house built on sand (see Matt 7:26).[86]

Michael Licona and the Compositional Devices Hypothesis

New Testament scholar, Christian apologist, and advocate of "compositional devices," Michael Licona, has engaged Lydia McGrew and the hypothesis of Undesigned Coincidences. McGrew has sharply criticized Licona in lengthy blogs and two articles in evangelical journals, one of which she sells as a PDF on Amazon.[87] Before continuing, it is necessary to explain the concept of compositional devices. Licona's text, *Why Are There Differences in the Gospels?: What We Can Learn from Ancient Biography* presents to his readers an array of nine apologetics that presumably account for "differences" in the Gospels. His approach differs from McGrew's. These apologetics, Licona terms "compositional devices," which he claims are "practically universal in ancient historiography."

> *Transferal*: When an author knowingly attributes words or deeds to a person that actually belonged to another person, the author has transferred the words or deeds.
>
> *Displacement*: When an author knowingly uproots an event from its original context and transplants it in another, the author has displaced the event. Displacement has some similarities with telescoping, which is the presentation of an event as having occurred either earlier or more recently than it actually occurred. Plutarch displaces events and even occasionally informs us he has done so. In *Cat. Min.* 25.5, having told the story of Hortensius's request of Cato that he be allowed to marry Cato's wife, Marcia, Plutarch adds, "All this happened later, but as I had mentioned the women of Cato's family it seemed sensible to include it here."
>
> *Conflation*: When an author combines elements from two or more events or people and narrates them as one, the author has

---

86. McGrew, "The Green Grass: Undesigned Coincidences vs. Symbolic Invention," 2.

87. Licona, "Lydia McGrew Answered."

conflated them. Accordingly, some displacement and/or transferal will always occur in the conflation of stories.

Compression: When an author knowingly portrays events over a shorter period of time than the actual time it took for those events to occur, the author has compressed the story.

Spotlighting: When an author focuses attention on a person so that the person's involvement in a scene is clearly described, whereas mention of others who were likewise involved is neglected, the author has shined his literary spotlight on that person. Think of a theatrical performance. During an act in which several are simultaneously on the stage, the lights go out and a spotlight shines on a particular actor. Others are present but are unseen. In literary spotlighting, the author only mentions one of the people present but knows of the others.

Simplification: When an author adapts material by omitting or altering details that may complicate the overall narrative, the author has simplified the story.

Expansion of Narrative Details: A well-written biography would inform, teach, and be beautifully composed. If minor details were unknown, they could be invented to improve the narrative while maintaining historical verisimilitude. In many instances, the added details reflect plausible circumstances. This has been called "creative reconstruction" and "free composition."

Paraphrasing: Plutarch often paraphrased using many of the techniques described in the compositional textbooks. I had initially considered creating a synopsis of Plutarch's parallel pericopes that we will be examining in the next chapter, which would be arranged in a manner similar to Kurt Aland's *Synopsis of the Four Gospels*. However, I decided against including a synopsis because Plutarch paraphrases so often; plus we do not observe in his *Lives* anything close to the near "copy and paste" method that is very often employed by Matthew and Luke.[88]

Licona says, "In my opinion, undesigned coincidences are legitimate phenomena in the Gospels. Of course, some are stronger than others."[89] Later, he clarifies, adding, "Unfortunately, her [Lydia McGrew] black & white concept of truthful reporting leads her to create a false "either/or" scenario when it comes to compositional devices."[90]

88. Licona, *Why Are There Differences*, 17–21.
89. Licona, "Lydia McGrew Answered," 47.
90. Licona, "Lydia McGrew Answered," 47.

Licona adds,

> In short, ancient authors of historical literature would adapt their sources to varying degrees. However, there was a limit. Good historians did not fabricate events out of nothing. Acknowledging that ancient historians often adapted details and on rare occasions narrated an actual historical event in a context they had created could potentially frustrate McGrew's efforts to identify undesigned coincidences and overturn some of those she puts forth as examples . . .

Therefore, McGrew's "all or nothing" reasoning is problematic.[91]

He adds several critical responses to McGrew that deserve diligent consideration.

1. McGrew's criticisms are saturated with her black & white concept of truthful reporting, while literary sensitivity is given very little attention, if any.[92]
2. It's also clear that, in her mind, compositional devices pose a serious threat to undesigned coincidences.[93]
3. In summary, McGrew's black & white concept of truthful reporting leads her to read into the New Testament literature something its authors never intended, just as she does with literature written by other ancient historians. Her method fails to appreciate the varied degrees of strength by which something can be implied. And it inappropriately insists on an either/or approach to understanding Gospel differences.[94]

How Independent Are the Gospels, and Why Does It Matter?

Readers are invited to assiduously peruse and contemplate the significance of McGrew's working definition of an "undesigned coincidence." Two concepts, in particular, demand the reader's attention.

1. The notable connection between the two accounts does *not* seem planned.
2. The accounts or texts are apparently *independent*.

When we apply these criteria to the gospels, we find that the first criterion possibly holds true, but it cannot be proven or disproven (discussed later).

---

91. Licona, "Lydia McGrew Answered," 50.
92. Licona, "Lydia McGrew Answered," 51.
93. Licona, "Lydia McGrew Answered," 51.
94. Licona, "Lydia McGrew Answered," 52.

The second criterion, however, is empirically false. It is evident that some gospel accounts (Matthew and Luke) depend on the earliest gospel account (Mark), which can be easily demonstrated.

The Synoptic Problem and Markan Priority Controversy

The literature on the subject of the relationships between the Gospels is extensive. Biblical scholars overwhelmingly agree that Matthew and Luke copied and edited Mark. This hypothesis that the Gospel of Mark was composed as the first of the three Synoptic Gospels and that afterward, it was a source by the other two gospel writers (Matthew and Luke) is known as Markan Priority. The "Synoptic Problem" is the question of the specific literary relationship among the three Synoptic Gospels—the question as to the source or sources upon which each Synoptic Gospel was based when it was composed. The Synoptic Problem attempts to explain how the first three Gospels agree yet disagree in content, wording, and order.

Understandably, copies and re-edited works *focus on the same people and events as the original works*. Robert Stein makes the following observation in his book, *Studying the Synoptic Gospels: Origin and Interpretation*: "Of the 11,025 words found in Mark, only 304 have no parallel in Matthew and 1,282 have no parallel in Luke. This data means that 97.2 percent of the words in Mark have a parallel in Matthew and 88.4 percent have a parallel in Luke."[95] William Barclay confirms this observation in *Barclay's Guide to the New Testament*: Mark has 661 verses; Matthew has 1,068 verses; and Luke has 1,149 verses. Matthew reproduces at least 606 of Mark's verses, and Luke reproduces 320. Of Mark's fifty-five (55) verses, which Matthew does not reproduce, Luke reproduces thirty-one (31). Consequently, only twenty-four (24) verses in Mark are not reproduced somewhere in Matthew or Luke.[96]

Is it rational to suppose that Matthew, writing some ten to fifteen years after Mark independently and employing only purported eyewitnesses, would have penned almost word-for-word 11,025 words found in Mark? In comparison, there are only 304 words in Mark's Gospel without parallels in Matthew. Beyond that, how can it be claimed that Luke is independent of Mark and Matthew if he penned almost word-for-word an identical text? On the other hand, these similarities are readily explicable if Luke was copying and editing their works. While scholars continue to debate the sources Luke used to compile his Gospel, what is undisputed is that both Matthew and Luke draw upon the anonymous author of Mark's Gospel.

95. Stein, *Studying the Synoptic Gospels*, 52.
96. Barclay, *Barclay's Guide to the New Testament*, 2.

Readers must answer the following questions. Presume the four Gospel authors provide reportage of the feeding or resurrection episodes. The people involved in the episode spoke Aramaic, as did the witnesses. Nevertheless, the Gospel authors composed a report virtually word for word in sophisticated Greek about thirty to seventy years later on the alleged translation of the Aramaic conversations. Is it probable that the Gospel authors could *report almost word for word on the Aramaic conversation translated into Greek decades later*? Do you think the authors' compositions were independent works?

The data presented above requires readers to ask the following questions about Matthew's Gospel:

1. If Matthew copied Mark, would not a special connection between the two gospels be understandable?
2. Second, how could Matthew's Gospel be independent if Matthew copied Mark?
3. Third, if Matthew copied Mark, how could he independently corroborate Mark's claims?
4. Fourth, why would Matthew, an alleged apostle, eyewitness, and "presumably" an independent writer, need to borrow as much as eighty percent of the material in the Gospel of Mark, a non-eyewitness, to compose his gospel?
5. If Matthew copied Mark, would not the items in the two gospels appear to fit together like pieces of a puzzle?

In a similar vein, the following questions about Luke's Gospel need addressing:

1. If (as some scholars think) Luke copied both Mark *and* Matthew, would not a notable connection between the three gospels be understandable?
2. Second, how could Luke's Gospel be an independent source if Luke copied Matthew and Mark?
3. Third, if Luke copied Matthew and Mark, how could he corroborate Matthew or Mark's claims?
4. Fourth, how could Luke, who claims to be a thorough investigator of everything from the beginning, determine whether Mark or Matthew's reportage was factual? Presumably, he was writing about ten to twenty years later and in a different location. How would Luke determine that what Mark or Matthew reported was factual? How would Luke treat material omitted by Matthew yet appearing in Mark, and why? How

would Luke deal with information in Matthew yet omitted in Mark, and why?

5. If Luke copied Mark and Matthew, would the items in the three Gospels not appear to fit together like pieces of a puzzle?

The Fourth Gospel creates a further dilemma for proponents of the hypothesis of Undesigned Coincidences. It is not one of the Synoptic Gospels (Mark, Matthew, and Luke) because its contents differ dramatically from these gospels. Academics debate whether the author John had access to the Synoptic Gospels.[97] The question requires asking: is it possible that the author of John did not have access to the written versions of the Synoptics but was nevertheless familiar with the oral accounts found in these gospels? Researchers cannot answer this question. Assuming that the author of the Fourth Gospel had access to the oral traditions, several vital questions require answering:

1. First, if John had access to oral traditions found in the Synoptic Gospels, would not a connection between accounts narrated in the four gospels be expected?

2. Second, how could John's Gospel be considered an independent source if John reported the oral traditions utilized by Mark, Matthew, and Luke?

3. Third, if John reported the oral traditions utilized by Mark, Matthew, and Luke, how could John's gospel independently corroborate Mark, Matthew, or Luke's claims?

4. Fourth, how could John have determined whether what Mark, Matthew, or Luke reported was factual? John was writing around 90 to 110 CE, presumably in Ephesus, in Asia Minor. How would John have treated material omitted by Matthew yet appearing in Mark, and why? How would John have dealt with information found in Matthew yet omitted in Mark, and why? How would John deal with information found in Luke yet omitted in Mark and Matthew?

5. If John incorporated known oral traditions narrated in Mark, Matthew, or Luke, would the items in the four Gospels not appear to fit together like pieces of a puzzle?

---

97. Several commentators and scholars argue that John was *not* composed independently of the Synoptic Gospels. See Barker, *John's Use of Matthew*; Barrett, *The Gospel According to St. John*; Bauckham, *The Gospels for all Christians*; Lindars, "John and the Synoptic Gospels," 287–94; Moloney, *The Gospel of John*; North, *What John Knew and What John Wrote*; Smith, *John Among the Gospels*; von Wahlde, *The Gospel and Letters of St. John*.

Finally, there are two cautionary excerpts for readers to contemplate. D.A. Carson and Douglas Moo issue the following reminder to their readers:

> Redaction criticism reminds us that the evangelists wrote with more than (though not less than) historical interest. They were preachers and teachers, concerned to apply the truths of Jesus' life and teaching to specific communities in their own day. This theological purpose of the evangelists has sometimes been missed, with a consequent loss of appreciation for the significance and application of the history that the evangelists narrate.[98]

The late Helmut Koester (1926—2016), an American scholar who specialized in the New Testament and early Christianity at Harvard Divinity School adds

> The quest for the historical kernel of the stories of the Synoptic narrative materials is very difficult. In fact such a quest is doomed to miss the point of such narratives, because these stories were all told in the interests of missions, edification, cult, or theology (especially Christology), and they have no relationship to the question of historically reliable information.[99]

1.5 EXCERPTS FROM AND RESPONSES TO DR. LYDIA MCGREW'S GENERAL INTRODUCTION

The following are some key excerpts from McGrew's General Introduction to her book, *Hidden in Plain View* (pages 11–24), with brief responses.

McGrew:

> Notice, too, that these sorts of details are not likely to be the result of collusion.
> An undesigned coincidence provides reason to believe that both (all) of the statements that contribute to it are truthful.[100]

Response: Truthfulness does not correlate with accuracy. Witnesses making "true" testimony in court and elsewhere can and do make errors.

McGrew:

---

98. Carson and Moo, *An Introduction to the New Testament*, 107.
99. Koester, *Introduction to the New Testament*, 64.
100. McGrew, *Hidden in Plain View*, 12–13.

THE HYPOTHESIS OF UNDESIGNED COINCIDENCES: INTRODUCTION   51

> Different passages in a work by the same author can also fit together in this special, puzzle-like way, especially when they are far apart in a document.[101]

Response A: What criterion determines whether "a work by the same author can also fit together in this special, puzzle-like way"?

Response B: McGrew fails to define "far apart."

Response C: [Example] John testifies to John in the piercing episode (John 19:34–35 and John 20:27–29). It need not be an undesigned coincidence. Logically, it is a "designed" coincidence. Verses 27–29 serve at least two functions: apologetic and theological.

McGrew:

> I should say at the outset that there are gray areas when it comes to the question of whether something counts as an undesigned coincidence argument.[102]

Response: This statement is an honest and vital caveat that readers must continually be on their best guard to remember. More succinctly, there is no methodology or standard for how anyone identifies and decides what is an undesigned coincidence. The presence of a coincidence or undesigned coincidence is subjective. What makes an undesigned coincidence good or poor, stronger or weaker than others? How does a reader grade or quantify the appearance of casualness in the text?

McGrew:

> [Why are they important?]
> The big picture is this: The occurrence of multiple undesigned coincidences between and among these documents supports the conclusion that the Gospels and Acts are historically reliable and that they come from people close to the facts who were attempting to tell truthfully what they knew. The big picture of the Gospels and Acts stands in sharp contrast to alternatives that would make the Gospels much less reliable.
>
> 1. The idea that the Gospels were written at many removes from the events that they chronicle,

---

101. McGrew, *Hidden in Plain View*, 13.
102. McGrew, *Hidden in Plain View*, 13.

2. The idea that they are so full of contradictions that we cannot trust them,
3. The idea that they are full of legendary accretions, or
4. The idea that the Gospels contain statements that are contrary to fact but that were included as literary or theological embellishments or alterations.

I am suggesting that the reader consider the question of the historical reliability of the Gospels and Acts from a new angle. Instead of getting involved in the specifics of alleged contradictions and proposed resolutions to them (not a bad enterprise in itself), instead of tackling these books from the perspectives of source and redaction criticism with the assumption that they represent multiple redactors, layers, and "developments," instead of thinking and speaking of Jesus or Paul as if they are literary characters in fictional works, I suggest that the reader take seriously the hypothesis that they are what they appear to be *prima facie* and what they were traditionally taken by Christians to be-historical memoirs of real people and events, written by those in a position to know about these people and events, either direct eyewitnesses or friends and associates of eyewitnesses, who were trying to be truthful. I suggest that the reader take seriously the hypothesis that they are what they appear to be *prima facie* and what they were traditionally taken by Christians to be—historical memoirs of real people and events, written by those in a position to know about these people and events, either direct eyewitnesses or friends and associates of eyewitnesses, who were trying to be truthful. I suggest that we take this hypothesis for a test drive while setting aside the apparatus of critical scholarship. Suppose that these were such memoirs. What might they look like? How does the occurrence of coincidences that appear casual and unrehearsed between and among these documents support that hypothesis? When all you have is a hammer, everything looks like a nail. I suggest that we expand our toolkit.[103]

McGrew:

I suggest that we take this hypothesis for a test drive while setting aside the apparatus of critical scholarship.[104]

---

103. McGrew, *Hidden in Plain View*, 15.
104. McGrew, *Hidden in Plain View*, 15.

Response A: Is McGrew willing to employ a contra-test drive? If not, she needs to explain why.

Response B: Is McGrew willing to test drive the hypothesis of Undesigned Coincidences employing the apparatus of critical scholarship? If not, she should explain why.

McGrew:

> Casual comments, allusions, and omissions that *fit together* are not what one would find in different fictional or fictionalized works written by different people.[105]

Response: McGrew's claim is incorrect. Casual comments, allusions, and omissions that fit together are in the *Star Trek* franchise.

1. The Original Series (1966–1969)
2. The Animated Series (1973–1974)
3. The Next Generation (1987–1994)
4. Deep Space Nine (1993–1999)
5. Voyager (1995–2001)
6. Enterprise (2001–2005)
7. Discovery (2017–2024)
8. Short Treks (2018–2020)
9. Six Star Trek movies (1979, 1982, 1984, 1986, 1989, 1991)

Viewers familiar with the franchise see characters, events, and technology fit together in a unique, puzzle-like way:

1. Vulcans' ability to mind-meld
2. Spock's family: relationship and siblings
3. Khan Noonien Singh
4. The Federation's relationship with the Klingon Empire.
5. Starship design and capabilities
6. Time travel

Undesigned coincidences are also apparent in the *Star Wars* franchise. Similarly, do *West Side Story* and *Romeo and Juliet* fit together? Or do the *Lion King* and *Hamlet* fit like a puzzle?

---

105. McGrew, *Hidden in Plain View*, 15.

McGrew:

> A further word is in order here about alleged contradictions. It might seem surprising that I do not do more in these pages to address alleged contradictions...
>
> (a) Entire books have been written on the subject of alleged contradictions in the Gospels, and this is not one of those books.
> (b) I believe that an understanding of the case from an undesigned coincidence helps us to see the forest and not get lost in the trees.[106]

Response: Skeptics and detractors beg to differ. They argue that apologists like McGrew are lost in the "trees of apologetics" and possess an *a priori* theological mindset, and for many apologists, a belief in inerrancy and a tendency to harmonize at all costs. (McGrew is not an inerrantist but strongly tends to harmonize discrepant New Testament texts.) These apologists do not see the surrounding forest, waterfalls, clouds, butterflies, rabbits, and birds because they choose not to see them.

McGrew:

> [A] focus on the alleged discrepancy creates a false impression that the question of [the miracle's] location [a point on which the Gospels appear to differ] is a point *against* their reliability.[107]

Response: Consider the following scenario. A criminal detective decides that the boyfriend, butler, husband, or lover is guilty at the onset of the investigation. Therefore, he ignores additional facts and leads. Specifically, he declines to follow up on leads and interview other viable witnesses. Consequently, an innocent person is found guilty, and the guilty party escapes punishment. Project Innocence has confirmed that hundreds of innocent people were convicted and sentenced in the criminal justice system because of a similar strategy employed by McGrew.

McGrew:

> Here I must emphasize two important further points about the argument from undesigned coincides, which are related to each other.

---

106. McGrew, *Hidden in Plain View*, 17–18
107. McGrew, *Hidden in Plain View*, 18.

> 1) The argument is cumulative...When, in instance after instance, these documents fit together just as truthful testimony fits together, there is a strong cumulative case for the documents.[108]

Response: This argument works both ways:

a. Embellishments, aggrandizing, and legendary growth fit together; there is a strong cumulative case for embellishments, aggrandizing, and legendary growth in the New Testament.
b. Truthful testimony can be wrong. The criminal justice system demonstrates eyewitness testimony and technical forensic experts can and do make mistakes.
c. There exists no positive relationship between truthful testimony and correct testimony.

McGrew:

> 2) The argument is varied in strength... If you think a particular argument is extremely weak, I will of course disagree with you.[109]

Response: This reaction works both ways.

McGrew:

> In this book I take an argument that has unfortunately and inexplicably fallen out of favor and present it to a new audience, and in a new century, in a new voice.[110]

Response: McGrew is correct on this point. A literature review finds that up to about 1920, Paley and Blunt's works were frequently cited and that the phrase "undesigned coincidences" appeared hundreds of times in books and journals. From 1920 to about 1980, it seldom appeared. The reason for its abandonment is subject to scholarly debate. Craig Keener offers two reasons why scholars may have come to dismiss some of the earlier apologists' arguments.

1. Through developments in philosophy and

---

108. McGrew, *Hidden in Plain View*, 20.
109. McGrew, *Hidden in Plain View*, 20–21.
110. McGrew, *Hidden in Plain View*, 24.

2. Probably a more influential factor in the neglect of the undesigned coincidences argument, at least in biblical studies, has been our appropriate but often myopic focus on a single source.[111]

In a 2020 interview, Ian Paul asked McGrew why the undesigned insights approach was lost or forgotten. She offered three hypotheses:

> First, the rise of higher criticism itself made too many Christians diffident about this type of argument. They may have thought that they could not make it any longer because the higher critics had called so many things into question–traditional authorship of the Gospels, for example. If "all the scholars now know" that these documents are factually embellished and corrupted, written long after the events and at many removes, don't represent eyewitness testimony, then there's no point in looking for undesigned coincidences. We can just assume that any such appearance of mutual explanation is an illusion or a coincidence in the pejorative sense. So I think a kind of chronological snobbery kicked in very quickly during and after the rise of higher criticism, so that everything that came before was regarded as permanently obsolete. You just "couldn't" do this sort of argument anymore, simply because the critics would sneer at it. Of course, that obviously doesn't tell us anything about the real strength of the argument . . .
>
> The second cause may have been the emphasis upon inerrancy in the twentieth century in response to the higher criticism. I want to be clear that I am not saying that inerrancy is incompatible with the argument from undesigned coincidences. Far from it. But it was just a different emphasis and tended to supersede a more evidential, bottom-up defense of the reliability of the documents.
>
> The third cause, late in the 20th century, for no one's noticing this argument was the emphasis upon a "minimalist" approach to defending the doctrines of Christianity and the fact of the resurrection. In this minimalist approach, one doesn't really make any kind of "root and branch" challenge to the assumptions of higher criticism. Instead, one tries to use the critically approved "criteria of authenticity" to "mine out" passages from the Gospels that one thinks even skeptics will grant are authentic—i.e., historical. Then one tries to use just those passages to defend conclusions such as that Jesus thought that he was divine or that Jesus rose from the dead. It's really a very different approach from what is represented by using undesigned coincidences.

---

111. Keener, Foreword, in *Hidden in Plain View*, 7–8.

When one uses undesigned coincidences, one is often going for the "big picture." What kind of authors were these? What kind of documents are these? It looks like these are really strongly reliable whole documents, written by people close to the facts, and it looks like these authors were very honest. I'm always trying to draw those larger, stronger conclusions in *Hidden in Plain View*. That's a bold defiance of higher critical approaches, an attempt to refute them completely, that has not been popular in Christian circles, not even evangelical apologetic circle . . .[112]

To sum up, the sudden disappearance of the argument from undesigned coincidences from the literature reflects a change in the methodology employed by scholars in the field.

McGrew:

How can we know that the Gospels are historically reliable? . . .
First, it is contained in the text itself and can usually be seen just by reading and making notes.
Second, evidence from undesigned coincidences would be difficult to fake, and it would be even more unlikely to come about by sheer chance in non-factual or manipulated stories.
Third, undesigned coincidences create an "Aha!" moment for the person who gets a particular argument.[113]

Response:
First, detractors can compose an identical counterargument: We can know that the Gospels are *un*reliable by reading them *horizontally* and carefully noting the discrepancies.

Second, the evidence from undesigned coincidences is unlikely to come about by sheer chance in non-factual or manipulated stories. Notably, Matthew quotes Mark, and Luke quotes Mark and Matthew. It remains open to academic debate whether John had access to the Synoptic Gospels or, perhaps, their oral traditions. However, perceived "coincidences" are likely to occur in stories about stories, stories deliberately written by authors to embellish or aggrandize the reading, or stories written to evangelize or serve as an apologetic.

---

112. Paul and McGrew, "What Do Interlocking 'Coincidences.'"
113. McGrew, *Hidden in Plain View*, 27.

Third, an "Aha!" moment exists for skeptics and detractors when they uncover new insights. For example, the piercing episode recorded in John, the tearing of the Temple veil at Jesus' death, and Jesus' appearance to Paul:

1. How could John possibly have known that not a bone of Jesus' body was broken (John 19:27) without the luxury of an X-ray machine or a CAT scan? Indeed, John was employing theology when he wrote this verse.

2. How could Matthew 27:54 have reported that the centurion saw the tearing of the Second Temple's veil if he was standing on Golgotha, where it is not visible? Robert Gundry explains why:

   > Since the traditional site of Golgotha lies to the west end of the temple, whereas the east end was veiled (not to mention intervening obstacles to view), whether tradition has misplaced Golgotha or the centurion's seeing of the veil-rending lacks historical substance.[114]

3. In the Acts of the Apostles, Jesus tells Paul *in Hebrew* while lying on the ground: "Saul, Saul, why do you persecute me? It is hard for you to kick against the goads." Christian apologists posit that this statement was a well-known Greek proverb of its day. However, Uta Ranke-Heinemann, a German theologian and former chair of the history of religion at the University of Duisburg-Essen in Essen, makes the following pertinent observation:

   > This [verse] is a quotation from *The Bacchae* by Euripides (d. 406 B.C.). It's no surprise to find a quotation from ancient literature; *the only peculiar thing is that Jesus should quote a Greek proverb to Paul while speaking Aramaic ("in the Hebrew language"). But the really strange thing is that with both Jesus and Euripides we have the same "familiar quotation" and the same situation.* In both cases, we have a conversation between a persecuted god and his persecutor . . .
   > Quite obviously, the author of Acts borrowed the episode "Dionysus" and relocated it near Damascus. Paul even used the plural form of the noun (*kentra*) required by Euripides for the meter of this line (italics in the original).[115]

Quoting *The Bacchae* is not a meaningless trapping or coincidence of imagery. Luke, the assumed author of Acts, had a designed purpose when he

---

114. Gundry, *Mark: A Commentary on His Apology for the Cross*, 970.
115. Ranke-Heinemann, *Putting Away Childish Things*, 163.

THE HYPOTHESIS OF UNDESIGNED COINCIDENCES: INTRODUCTION   59

quotes *The Bacchae*. Neil Godfrey of Vridar discusses this topic on his web page.[116] He makes the following remarks.

1. Readers should expect Luke to have written like this.
2. Readers should acknowledge the chances of the author of Acts using this Greek play: For centuries, it was a popular tragedy.
3. Readers should expect Luke's audience to have recognized the allusions.
4. Readers should understand and expect Luke to use a Greek play in a work of history. Richard Pervo and Dennis MacDonald demonstrate the characteristics of the Hellenistic novel and Homer's influence in Acts.
5. The Dionysiac parallels highlight elements in Acts.[117]

John Moles' article, "Jesus and Dionysus," published in 2006 in *Hermathena*, identifies numerous parallels between these two works.[118] This topic is of further exploration at length in Alter.[119] Why, then, would Luke employ a pagan source? The answer is open to speculation and equivalent to an argument from silence. However, possibilities suggest themselves: (a) entertainment, (b) humor, (c) as a literary device, and (d) Luke understood that these literary "fabrications" did not bother the early Christians, as they knew that such embellishments were perfectly acceptable in a Greco-Roman biography.

> McGrew:
>
> [Conclusion] Here I have shown that John explains various aspects of the Synoptic Gospels but does it in so casual a way and with so little appearance of attempted harmonization between his own accounts and the earlier accounts that any theory of design on the part of the author of John is overwhelmingly implausible. (p. 73)
>
> *Response*:
> 1. McGrew's phrase, "does it in so casual a way," reflects her subjective opinion. The question arises: how can a reader objectively measure the degree of "casualness"?

---

116. Godfrey, "The Point of the Dionysiac Myth, #1."
117. Alter, *The Resurrection and Its Apologetics Vol 2*, forthcoming.
118. Moles, "Jesus and Dionysus," 65–104.
119. Alter, *The Resurrection and Its Apologetics Vol 2*, forthcoming.

2. McGrew's opinion that John writes his account "with so little appearance of attempted harmonization between his accounts and the earlier accounts" is subjective.

3. McGrew has no methodology to determine whether John deliberately harmonized the accounts in a style he chooses for reasons known only to himself.

Conclusion

Undesigned Coincidences is a hypothesis advocated and popularized by J.J. Blunt and William Paley in the nineteenth century. Lydia McGrew and Professor McGrew have resurrected this hypothesis. Noteworthy is Lydia McGrew's text, *Hidden in Plain View*. An undesigned coincidence is a notable connection between two or more accounts or texts that do *not* seem to have been planned by the person or people giving the accounts. Despite their apparent independence, the items fit together like pieces of a puzzle. Proponents failed to engage and interact with biblical criticism, nor relevant research about coincidence and casualness.

Biblical criticism is the study and investigation of biblical writings that seek to make discerning and discriminating judgments about them. This chapter identified at least thirteen types of biblical criticism. Proponents of the hypothesis of Undesigned Coincidences fail to engage and interact with biblical criticism or relevant research about coincidence and casualness. Notably, *no* existing methodology exists for how anyone can identify and decide what a coincidence is, and there are *no* criteria to determine what is and is not designed.

The feeding of the five thousand is often cited as a prime example of an undesigned coincidence, a topic extensively discussed by advocates and analyzed in Chapter 2. However, a significant issue with this hypothesis is the absence of a definitive methodology for identifying coincidences. This lack of a defined process raises questions about determining what is and is not a coincidence. In the eyes of skeptics and detractors, the hypothesis of Undesigned Coincidences is a form of traditional apologetics, repackaged to defend the historical reliability of the Christian Bible. It is essentially harmonization under a different name.

2

The Hypothesis of Undesigned Coincidences

How Well Does It Explain the Gospel Accounts of the Feeding of the Five Thousand?

2.1 INTRODUCTION

MCGREW'S TEXT, *HIDDEN IN Plain View,* comprises six chapters divided into two parts: Part One focuses on undesigned coincidences in the Gospels, and Part Two focuses on undesigned coincidences between Acts and the Pauline Epistles. McGrew identifies, engages with, and discusses twenty-seven events from the Gospels in her book. These events are the subject of analysis because they frequently appear in the literature and podcasts. In Acts and the Pauline Epistles, a further twenty undesigned coincidences appear. Chapter 2 of this text will "cherry-pick" two critical details from the most widely reported miracle in the Gospels to ascertain whether these details qualify as genuine examples of undesigned coincidences. The details in question are Mark's mention of the green grass in his account of the miracle. The feeding of the five thousand is the only miracle about Jesus recorded in all four Gospels. Proponents of undesigned coincidences contend that their hypothesis best explains the similarities and differences between the gospel accounts. Below, this claim is subject to rigorous scrutiny.

Chapter 2 investigates several topics relevant to the feeding of the five thousand:

1. Sources for the gospel accounts of the feeding of the five thousand.

2. Logistical factors relating to the feeding of the five thousand.
3. Why does Mark mention the green grass in his miracle account?
4. Why does John mention Philip in his account?

Table 2 below provides a handy parallel (horizontal) reading of the four gospel accounts of the miracle.

Table 2. Parallel Gospel Accounts of the Feeding of the 5,000 (ESV)

Mark 6:30-44	Matthew 14:13-20	Luke 9:10-17	John 6:1-14
[30] The apostles returned to Jesus and told him all that they had done and taught.		10 On their return the apostles told him all that they had done.	
[31] And he said to them, "Come away by yourselves to a desolate place and rest a while." For many were coming and going, and they had no leisure even to eat.		And he took them and withdrew apart to a town called Bethsaida.	
[32] And they went away in the boat to a desolate place by themselves.	[13] Now when Jesus heard this, he withdrew from there in a boat to a desolate place by himself.		After this Jesus went away to the other side of the Sea of Galilee, which is the Sea of Tiberias.
[33] Now many saw them going and recognized them, and they ran there on foot from all the towns and got there ahead of them.	[13] But when the crowds heard it, they followed him on foot from the towns.	[11] When the crowds learned it, they followed him, . . .	[2] And a large crowd was following him, because they saw the signs that he was doing on the sick.
			[3] Jesus went up on the mountain, and there he sat down with his disciples. [4] Now the Passover, the feast of the Jews, was at hand.

THE HYPOTHESIS OF UNDESIGNED COINCIDENCES: HOW WELL DOES IT EXPLAIN

Mark 6:30–44	Matthew 14:13–20	Luke 9:10–17	John 6:1–14
[34] When he went ashore he saw a great crowd, and he had compassion on them, because they were like sheep without a shepherd. And he began to teach them many things.	[14] When he went ashore he saw a great crowd, and he had compassion on them and healed their sick.	. . . and he welcomed them and spoke to them of the kingdom of God and cured those who had need of healing.	[5] Lifting up his eyes, then, and seeing that a large crowd was coming toward him,
			Jesus said to Philip, "Where are we to buy bread, so that these people may eat?" [6] He said this to test him, for he himself knew what he would do.
[35] And when it grew late, his disciples came to him and said, "This is a desolate place, and the hour is now late. [36] Send them away to go into the surrounding countryside and villages and buy themselves something to eat."	[15] Now when it was evening, the disciples came to him and said, "This is a desolate place, and the day is now over; [15] send the crowds away to go into the villages and buy food for themselves."	[12] Now the day began to wear away, and the twelve came and said to him, "Send the crowd away to go into the surrounding villages and countryside to find lodging and get provisions, for we are here in a desolate place."	
[37] But he answered them, "You give them something to eat." And they said to him, "Shall we go and buy two hundred denarii worth of bread and give it to them to eat?"	[16] But Jesus said, "They need not go away; you give them something to eat."	[13] But he said to them, "You give them something to eat."	[7] Philip answered him, "Two hundred denarii worth of bread would not be enough for each of them to get a little."
			[8] One of his disciples, Andrew, Simon Peter's brother, said to him,

Mark 6:30–44	Matthew 14:13–20	Luke 9:10–17	John 6:1–14
³⁸ And he said to them, "How many loaves do you have? Go and see." And when they had found out, they said, "Five, and two fish."	¹⁷ They said to him, "We have only five loaves here and two fish." ¹⁸ And he said, "Bring them here to me."	They said, "We have no more than five loaves and two fish—unless we are to go and buy food for all these people.	⁹ "There is a boy here who has five barley loaves and two fish, but what are they for so many?"
³⁹ Then he commanded them all to *sit down in groups on the green grass.*	¹⁹ Then he ordered the crowds *to sit down on the grass* . . .	¹⁴ For there were about five thousand men. And he said to his disciples, "*Have them sit down* in groups of about fifty each."	¹⁰ Jesus said, "Have the *people sit down.*" Now there was much *grass in the place.* So the men sat down, about five thousand in number.
⁴⁰ So they sat down in groups, by hundreds and by fifties.		¹⁵ And they did so, and had them all sit down.	
⁴¹ And taking the five loaves and the two fish, he looked up to heaven and said a blessing and broke the loaves and gave them to the disciples to set before the people. And he divided the two fish among them all.	¹⁹ . . . and taking the five loaves and the two fish, he looked up to heaven and said a blessing. Then he broke the loaves and gave them to the disciples, and the disciples gave them to the crowds.	¹⁶ And taking the five loaves and the two fish, he looked up to heaven and said a blessing over them. Then he broke the loaves and gave them to the disciples to set before the crowd.	¹¹ Jesus then took the loaves, and when he had given thanks, *he distributed them to those who were seated. So also the fish, as much as they wanted.*
⁴² *And they all ate and were satisfied.* ⁴³ And they took up twelve baskets full of broken pieces and of the fish. ⁴⁴ And those who ate the loaves were five thousand men.	²⁰ And they all ate and were satisfied. And they took up twelve baskets full of the broken pieces left over.	¹⁷ And they all ate and were satisfied. And what was left over was picked up, twelve baskets of broken pieces.	¹² *And when they had eaten their fill,* he told his disciples, "Gather up the leftover fragments, that nothing may be lost." ¹³ So they gathered them up and filled twelve baskets with fragments from the five barley loaves left by those who had eaten.

Mark 6:30–44	Matthew 14:13–20	Luke 9:10–17	John 6:1–14
			[14] When the people saw the sign that he had done, they said, "*This is indeed the Prophet who is to come into the world!*"

2.2 SOURCES FOR THE GOSPEL ACCOUNTS OF THE FEEDING OF THE FIVE THOUSAND

Several particularly compelling details surround the story of the miraculous feeding of the 5,000, which is present in all four gospels. The narratives parallel the image of the Exodus experience, Psalm 23, and parts of 2 Kings 4:38–44. Suzanne Henderson writes, "In fact, such a variety of allusions need not be mutually exclusive."[1] In particular, the details do not need to be precisely 100 percent accurate (e.g., the number of people and the amount of food produced). It is the overall picture that matters. Suppose the Gospel authors successfully evoke an image of the Exodus experience in their readers' minds. In that case, we may conclude that the narratives are a deliberate design and not coincidental. The causal factor is readily understandable.

As a general rule, analogies are imperfect. Dissimilarities will appear. The crucial point is recognizing the overall motif/parallel. Here, the resonance with Psalm 23, the Exodus motif, and Elisha's multiplication of the loaves is open for the reader to judge. A question for readers to ponder is why McGrew does "not" want her readership to examine the entire Bible and judge for themselves the viability of these motifs.

In *Through the Looking Glass*, Lewis Carroll makes a thoughtful observation relevant to the hypothesis of Undesigned Coincidences.

> "Alice laughed. 'There's no use trying,' she said. 'One *can't* believe impossible things.'
> I daresay you haven't had much practice,' said the Queen. "When I was your age, I always did it for half-an-hour a day. Why, sometimes I've believed as many as six impossible things before breakfast. There goes the shawl again!"[2]

---

1. Henderson, *Christology and Discipleship in the Gospel of Mark*, 196.
2. Carroll, *Through the Looking Glass*, 102–3.

Was Mark 6 Adapted from 2 Kings 4:38–44?

Several authors have discussed the parallels between the Markan story of the feeding of the 5,000 and the story in the second book of Kings of the prophet Elisha multiplying the loaves, citing "biblical echoes."[3] For this reason, Bible commentators suggest that significant themes, structure, and narrative details in the Markan story were drawn directly from the books of Exodus, Isaiah, and 2 Kings. Another speculation in the literature is that Mark conflated his narrative with 2 Kings 4:38–44 and possibly other literary sources (Exod. 18:25; Num. 27: 15–18; Psalm 23; and 1 Sam. 21: 1–6). Michael Turton has developed a helpful summary (see table 3 below).[4]

Table 3. A Comparison of 2 Kings 4: 38–44 and Mark 6: 30–44.

2 Kings 4: 38–44	Mark 6: 30–44.
Elisha went to a place where there was a famine in the land.	Jesus went with his disciples to a deserted place where there was no food.
The followers ('sons') of the prophets were sitting before Elisha.	All who recognized Jesus went out to him, and in the course of the story he had them all sit down.
Elisha wishes to feed them.	Jesus commands that his servants feed them.
They have small quantities of 2 types of food: 20 barley loaves and newly ripened grain.	They have small quantities of 2 types of food: 5 loaves and 2 fish.
His servants protest that they have too little.	His disciples protest that they must send them away to find food for themselves.
Elisha overrides their objections and orders his servants to feed the crowd with the little they have.	Jesus overrides their objections and has his disciples feed the crowd with the little they have.
Elisha said God had promised there would be more than enough.	Jesus prayed to God to bless the food.
They all ate.	They all ate.
And there was some left over.	And there was much left over.
100 men were fed.	5000 men were feed.

Eddy Savarimuthu, a priest of the Archdiocese of Madurai, offers a plausible hypothesis for part of the narrative. "Mark intends to portray Jesus as a greater miracle worker than Elisha. While Elisha provided 100

---

3. Aus, *Feeding the Five Thousand*, 120; Henderson, *Christology and Discipleship in the Gospel of Mark*, 191; Mullins, *The Gospel of* Mark, 188–89.

4. Turton, "Historical Commentary on The Gospel of Mark."

THE HYPOTHESIS OF UNDESIGNED COINCIDENCES: HOW WELL DOES IT EXPLAIN

men with 20 loaves (2kg 4:42–44), here Jesus feeds a multitude with fewer provisions."[5] Joseph Grassi expresses similar thinking. "These remarkable parallels show that the great epiphanies of God manifested through Moses, Elisha, and Elijah in the Scriptures are even exceeded by Jesus."[6] This speculation can be neither verified nor falsified. Did the author of Mark 6 adapt his narrative with 2 Kings 4:38–44 and possibly other literary sources?

Was Mark 6 Adapted from Psalm 23?

The parallels between Mark 6 and Psalm 23 "cry out for explanation." Numerous Bible commentators mention and discuss many parallels between Mark and the events of Psalm 23 (see table 4 below).[7] Biblical commentators point out that the number of parallels in just three verses is seemingly *not* coincidental but designed.

Table 4. Mark 6 and Psalm 23: A Comparison

Psalm 23	Mark 6
Ps 23:1—The Lord is my shepherd	Mark 6:34 – [Jesus] had compassion on them, because they were like sheep without a shepherd.
Ps 23:1—I lack nothing	Mark 6:42—And they all ate and were satisfied.
Ps 23:2—He makes me lie down in green pastures	Mark 6:39—Jesus told them to make all the people sit down in groups on the green grass
Ps 23:2—He leads me beside quiet waters	Mark 6:34 –When he came ashore he saw a great crowd.
Ps 23:3—He guides me along the right paths	Mark 6:34—And he began to teach them many things.

---

5. Eddy Savarimuthu, "The Feeding Narratives in Mark: Studying the Significance by a Comparative Analysis," 24.

6. Grassi, *Loaves and Fishes: The Gospel Feeding Narratives*, 29.

7. Eleven examples of commentators identifying Psalm 23 in their exegesis are France, Lane, Stein, Donahue, Boring, Garland, Bock, Black, Healy, Maloney, and Beavis.

Psalm 23	Mark 6
Ps 23:3—He restores my soul.	Mark 6:42–43—And they all ate and were satisfied. And they took up twelve baskets full of broken pieces and of the fish.

Perhaps Mark's author deliberately designed his narrative of feeding the 5,000 using a text in the Hebrew Bible as a template (i.e., literary influence): Psalm 23. On the other hand, proponents of undesigned coincidences argue that the author's incorporating "green grass" in Mark 6:39 was undesigned and coincidental. The cumulative arguments in the prior section challenge the hypothesis of Undesigned Coincidences. Readers must judge which explanation is more likely.

Was Mark 6 Adapted from an Exodus Motif?

Several authors have discussed the many parallels between Mark and the events of the exodus from Egypt, claiming to uncover an "Exodus Motif."[8] Bible commentators suggest that the Gospel of Mark's central themes, structure, and narrative details were drawn directly from the book of Exodus, Isaiah, and the Second Book of Kings.

Dennis MacDonald, the John Wesley Professor of New Testament and Christian Origins at the Claremont School of Theology in California, has put forward a list of multi-step criteria to test similarities between texts, which this text encourages its readers to employ.

1. Accessibility or availability: Did the author (of *Mark*) have access to the Hebrew Bible?

2. Density: This topic pertains to the volume of contacts between the two texts. Parallels between two texts may be numerous but trivial. In contrast, two or three weighty similarities may suffice.

3. Order: This test relates to the sequence of the parallels.

4. Distinctiveness: Occasionally, two texts contain distinguishing characteristics such as an unusual word or phrase. MacDonald points out: "Some interpreters consider this the best test of dependence."[9] A remarkably similar context hardly seems accidental (p. 41).

---

8. Aus, *Feeding the Five Thousand*, 142–60; Davies and Allison, *A Critical and Exegetical Commentary*, 655; Derrett, "Daniel and Salvation History," 62–68; Montefiore, *The Synoptic Gospels*, 1:93–104, 353; Towner, *Daniel*, 84–87; Henten, "Daniel 3 and 6 in Early Christian Literature," 158; Wright, *The Resurrection of the Son of God*, 640–41.

9. MacDonald, *Homeric Epics and the Gospel of Mark*, 8–9.

5. Interpretability or intelligibility: The capacity of the presumed original text to make sense of the later text." This reality may include the solution to a peculiar problem that has eluded other explanations (see table 5 below).

Table 5. Was Mark 6 Adapted from an Exodus Motif?

Mark	Exodus	Motifs/Thematic Parallels
Jesus is the shepherd (Mark 6:34; 10:47).	Moses is the shepherd (Exod. 3:1).	A shepherd motif (the Eschatological Davidic Shepherd Messiah).
Jesus was a teacher (Mark 6:1–2).	Moses was a teacher (Exod. 3:16).	A teacher motif.
Jesus appoints his twelve disciples (Mark 1:14–20; 3:13–19).	Moses was instructed to assemble the elders of Israel (Exod. 3:16).	The assemblage of leaders motif.
Jesus performed miracles and wonders (Mark 6:5).	Moses performed miracles with God's assistance (the Ten Plagues and accompanying miracles in the wilderness) (Exod. 4:21; 7:14—11:10).	The performance of miracles motif.
Jesus assembles twelve disciples for a mission (Mark 6:7–11).	Moses assembles the elders of Israel (Exod. 4:29; 18:25).	Assembling leaders for a mission motif.
Jesus sends the twelve disciples on a mission (6:7–13, 30) to Galilean villages (Mark 6:7–11).	Twelve chieftains, one from each of the Twelve Tribes, were sent by Moses to scout out the Land of Canaan (Num. 13:1–33).	A mission motif.
Jesus was testing the twelve disciples (Mark 6:7–11).	God was, in effect, testing the Twelve chieftains (two passed the test) and, later, the Twelve Tribes of Israel (Num. 13:1–33).	A testing motif.
Jesus forbids his disciples to take any provisions. Take nothing for the journey except . . . but wear sandals and not to put on tunics (Mark 6: 8–9).	Israelites had not prepared any provisions for themselves (Exod. 12:39).	Limited provisions motif.

Mark	Exodus	Motifs/Thematic Parallels
The twelve disciples travel to a deserted area (Mark 6:31–32).	Moses requests Pharaoh to go three days into the wilderness (Exod. 5:1; 8:27).	A deserted/remote area motif.
The flock is the approximate 5,000 Children of Israel (6:44).	The flock are the 600,000 plus Children of Israel (Exod. 12:37).	A flock motif.
Mark envisions the new exodus.	The Bible narrates the exodus from Egypt.	An exodus motif.
The twelve disciples went by boat to a solitary place (Mark 6:32).	The Children of Israel passed through the Sea of Reeds to reach the wilderness (Exod. 14:1–31).	A water scene motif.
People travel to a deserted/remote area (Mark 6:32). [To be sure, as in v. 31, Mark purposely wants his audience to evoke the memories of the wandering of the Israelites in the wilderness and the wondrous feedings that happened there (Exod. 16:1–35; Num. 11:1–9; Pss. 78:20b–29; 105:40–41)].	The Children of Israel wander forty years in the (Sinai) wilderness being refined to atone for the sin of the Golden Calf and preparation for conquering the land of Israel (Exodus).	The wilderness motif: a person, people, or nation has to be isolated and refined by trial in a desolate area.
The events typify the journey of the twelve disciples, from being appointed by Jesus, recreated and reconstituted as Israel and its leadership.	The events typify the journey of the twelve leaders of the twelve tribes, from being appointed, and designated the leadership (Exod. 18:25).	Twelve designated leaders as a motif.
"You give them something to eat." Jesus was testing the twelve disciples (Mark 6:37).	"Why are you crying out to Me? Tell the Israelites to move on." God was, in effect, testing the Twelve Tribes of Israel (Exod. 14: 10–12, 15).	A testing motif.
The disciples respond with a lack of faith (Mark 6:37).	The people complain, demonstrating a lack of faith (Exod. 14:12–14).	The lack of faith motif.
Jesus encounters a lack of faith (Mark 6:37).	Moses also encounters rejection (cf. e.g., Exod. 15:24. 16:2–3; 17:3).	The lack of faith motif.

Mark	Exodus	Motifs/Thematic Parallels
Jesus sees the people as being sheep without the shepherd (v34). This recalls to mind the wilderness wanderings after the Israelites left Egypt. Jesus challenges the disciples who respond with a lack of faith (Mark 6:37).	Moses tells the people do not be afraid. He has compassion on his flock (Exod.14:13–14).	The shepherd has compassion on his flock motif. [Sheep without a "shepherd" reflects a Hebrew Bible image of Israel. See Num. 27:17; 1 Kgs. 22:17; Ezek. 34:5.]
Jesus has the people sit in groups of hundreds and fifties (Mark 6:39).	First, Moses arranged the Israelites in groups of 10, 100, 500, and 1000. Exodus 18: 25–26 Moses sets appointed officers and judges over thousands, hundreds, fifties, and tens. Second, the groups of hundreds and fifties imagine the Mosaic camp-formation in the wilderness, Exodus 18:21.	Arranging in groups motif.
The miraculous feeding of the 5,000 takes place in a deserted or remote place (Mark 6:32)	The miraculous feeding of the 600,000 Children of Israel takes place in a deserted or remote place (Exod. 16).	Miraculous feeding motifs.
Jesus feeds a large crowd with a bread and fish (Mark 6:38, 43–44; 8:5, 9).	The feeding miracles associated with Moses in the Exodus journey to the Promised Land in the unending supply of manna and the two times it rained quail (Exod. 16:4–13, 35; Num. 11:31–33). In Numbers 11:44, the people complain there is no fish.	The bread and fish motifs.
The disciples picked up twelve baskets containing pieces of bread and fish (Mark 6:44).	The Twelve Tribes and the Twelve chieftains (Exod. 18:25).	The number twelve motif [The number twelve has symbolic references to the twelve tribes of Israel and their leaders.

Mark	Exodus	Motifs/Thematic Parallels
At the end of each meal all the people are satisfied and there is an abundance of leftover food (Mark 6:42–43; 8:8).	Then the Lord said to Moses, "I will rain down bread from heaven for you. The people are to go out each day and gather enough for that day.... Everyone had gathered just as much as they needed.... However, some of them paid no attention to Moses; they kept part of it until morning, but it was full of maggots and began to smell (Exod. 16:4, 17, 20; Num. 11:31–32).	Enough food motif.
Jesus feeds five thousand people (Mark 6:44).	Moses, through God's assistance feeds the Children of Israel (Exod. 16:15–19; Num. 11:31–34)	Jesus is the Lord of Hunger
The 5000 men ate, filled up, with more left over (Mark 6:42; John 6:12–13; see also Isaiah 25:6)	The Israelites received as much food as necessary. Those who took more than needed, the manna spoiled (Exod. 16:17–18, 20; Also see Num. 11:31–34)	The Feeding of the 5000 as a Foretaste of the Messianic Banquet
The loaves of barley bread are part of the first fruits (6:42) brought as the 'omer offering on the second day of Passover. Additionally, Jesus celebrated the Passover meal after dark on the 15th of Nisan.	The Passover seder and the firstborn's death led to the Israelites' redemption from slavery occurring on the 15th of Nisan.	Redemption Through the Messiah at Passover

2.2 LOGISTICAL FACTORS RELATING TO THE FEEDING OF THE FIVE THOUSAND

Logistics of Walking About Three Miles

Mark 6:44 says, "And they that did eat of the loaves were about five thousand men."

Matthew 14:21 reports that those who had eaten numbered "about five thousand men, *besides* women and children."

Luke 9:14 remarks, "For there were about five thousand men."

John 6:10 states, "So the men sat down, in number about five thousand."

The Gospels supplement the miracle of Jesus Feeding the Five Thousand with additional details:

> Mark 6:42–43 And they all ate and were satisfied. [43] And they took up twelve baskets full of broken pieces and of the fish.
>
> Matthew 9:20 And they all ate and were satisfied. And they took up twelve baskets full of the broken pieces left over.
>
> Luke 9:17 And they all ate and were satisfied. And what was left over was picked up, twelve baskets of broken pieces.
>
> John 9:12–13 And when they had eaten their fill, he told his disciples, "Gather up the leftover fragments, that nothing may be lost."[13] So they gathered them up and filled twelve baskets with fragments from the five barley loaves left by those who had eaten.

To sum up:

1. Jesus fed *over* 5,000 people.
2. Not only were the people fed, but they were also *satisfied*.
3. Moreover, there was food *left over that was placed in twelve baskets*.

Roger Aus comments, "Strangely, the question is almost never asked: Where did the twelve baskets suddenly come from?"[10]

Playing the "undesigned coincidences" card, one could suggest that Matthew 14:21 enlarges Mark's narrative by adding the crucial phrases "besides women and children." Curiously, Mark, Luke, and John omit the women and children from their narratives. However, Matthew is unequivocal. In addition to "about five thousand men," there were also women and children. Is this information historical, accurate, and reliable reportage? Does Matthew's narrative seem plausible? First, the reader should examine Professor N.S.L. Fryer's "Grammatico-Historical Exegesis of Matthew 14:14—21." His commentary bears careful consideration:

> *Verse 21. And there were about five thousand men who ate, aside from women and children*
>
> 'about five thousand men.' 'About' (*hosei*) taken as a round number. The arrangement of the crowds by hundreds and fifties

---

10. Aus, *Feeding the Five Thousand*," xv.

(Mk 6: 40) would doubtless facilitate the numbering. 'men,' i.e. adult males.

'aside from women and children.' 'Aside' *(chōris)*—'without', 'exclusive of'. It was the custom that men 'recline at their repasts, while the women and children ate apart from them in ordinary sitting posture' (Alexander 1980:170). It is possible, then, that the groups of hundreds and fifties on this occasion would be composed of men alone and that they alone could be counted with facility. It is also possible that the men constituted so overwhelming a majority that they alone were counted (cf. Hendriksen 1973:596 on this latter option). Be it as it may, the total number of those fed must remain unknown.[11]

However, the reportage in Matthew, if historically reliable, raises important questions.

1. How many people were in the crowd pursuing Jesus?

    a. About 5,000

    b. Less than 5,000

    c. More than 5,000

    d. About 10,000

    e. About 20,000

2. What was the crowd's composition?

    a. Men—how many or what percentage of the walkers did they make up altogether? (unknown)

    b. Women—how many or what percentage of walkers did they make up altogether? (unknown)

    c. Children—how many or what percentage of walkers did they make up altogether? (unknown)

    d. Adolescents—how many or what percentage of walkers did they make up altogether? (unknown)

    e. Unhealthy individuals—how many or what percentage of walkers did they make up altogether? (unknown)

    f. Sedentary individuals—how many or what percentage of walkers did they make up altogether? (unknown)

    g. Pregnant women—how many or what percentage of walkers did they make up altogether? (unknown)

11. Fryer, "Matthew 14:14–21."

How many people were in the crowd? The only honest response is that nobody knows. Any number proposed by exegetes is neither verifiable nor falsifiable. (See photo of The July 4, 2023 Independence 5 K Run.) Conservative Christian commentators suggest *ten to twenty thousand*, and possibly more, probably in the neighborhood of the actual number. A review of six leading conservative Bible commentaries on Matthew 14:21 substantiates this view.

Craig Blomberg, *Matthew: An Exegetical and Theological Exposition of Holy Scripture*

> But Jesus provides enough food for well over five thousand people (the women and children could easily have more than quadrupled the size of the crowd)[12]

D.A. Carson, *Matthew 13–28*

> Matthew omits many details—the greenness of the grass, the groups of fifty and one hundred—but points out that all ate and were satisfied (v.20), perhaps an anticipation of the messianic banquet, and at least evidence that there was lots to eat! The twelve baskets of leftovers . . . and the size of the crowd (which might have been fifteen or twenty thousand total, if there were five thousand "men," v. 21) also support the latter point.[13]

R.T. France, *The Gospel of Matthew*

> All four gospel accounts of feeding miracles draw attention to the numbers involved. In this incident the four evangelists agree not only on the number 5,000 but also on describing these 5,000 as "men," using *andres*, which normally applies to adult males rather than to people in general (though the distinction is not hard-and-fast). Matthew, however, underlines the masculinity of the number estimated by adding "apart from women and children." This would normally be understood to mean that women and children were also present, and the number fed was thus considerably higher than five thousand. But the Greek phrase ("*without* women and children") could also be taken to mean "and there were no women and children," thus indicating an exclusively masculine gathering, as the use of *andres* in all the other gospels might also imply . . . .
>
> What then of Matthew's "without women and children"? A simpler explanation is that he is merely following OT

---

12. Blomberg, *Matthew An Exegetical and Theological Exposition*, 223.
13. Carson, *Matthew 13–28*.

> convention: in Exod 12:37 the tally of the people who left Egypt is given as 'six hundred thousand men, besides children,' where the term "men" is firmly masculine (literally, "feet of males"), not inclusive. Such numbering in the OT generally of the men rather than of the whole population, even where no such explicit rider is added. If that is the pattern Matthew is following, the number actually fed must be seen as well over 5,000 (unless only the men received the food, which is hardly likely!). When such large numbers are involved, however, it is pedantic to attempt to calculate them; the traditional term "feeding of the five thousand" serves well enough.[14]

Craig S. Keener, *A Commentary on the Gospel of Matthew*

> If it was impossible to feed the crowds, it was *nearly* impossible to imagine perhaps ten thousand people (five thousand men plus women and children—14:21) fending for themselves in the countryside (pace Freyne 1988: 144–45, who wrongly compares this with the emergency situation of supporting insurgents).[15]

In footnote 24, Keener elaborates:

> Against the charge that the Gospels devalued women and children, they may have simply been reticent to *invent* a number for women and children that their tradition did not supply. It was customary in many circles to number only men (e.g., Ps-Philo 5:7; 14:4) ... The proposed allusion to Ex 12:37 (France 1985: 237) is possible, but it actually reads only "besides children", ... emphasizing the inclusiveness of this assembly.[16]

Grant R. Osborne, *Matthew*

> Matthew wants the reader to know this is not an exact number but an approximate count (ὡσεί; how could one begin to count that size of crowd in the ancient world?). This is an astounding number and also points to the multitudes to be present at the messianic banquet. Matthew follows Jewish practice by giving the number of adult males, but then adds that women and children were also present. This means the total there would likely be at least double that.[17]

Michael J. Wilkins, *The NIV Application Commentary: Matthew*

---

14. France, *The Gospel of Matthew*, 563–65.
15. Keener, *A Commentary on the Gospel of Matthew*, 404.
16. Keener, *A Commentary on the Gospel of Matthew*, 404.
17. Osborne, *Matthew*, 567.

Matthew is the only evangelist to note that the number five thousand associated with the feeding counts only men, not women and children. The total number may have stretched to ten thousand or more, far larger than the populations of most villages surrounding the Sea of Galilee.[18]

Aus elaborates on this controversy. He points out that the noun in Mark 6:44 literally means "men" and not generically as "people." In contrast, Matthew 14:21 corrects Mark's passage to "about five thousand men besides women and children." Aus continues, "This increases the total feed to at least 20,000, exaggerating the miracle even more. Yet, strangely, this is an all male meal in Mark. For him, no women and children have come along to the wilderness."[19]

Assume that there were approximately 10,000 people who were walking from Capernaum to catch up with Jesus at Bethsaida (a distance of about three miles) and subsequently fed. Logistically, does that number seem plausible? Readers must begin by considering the following variables:

1. Variables affecting walking time:
   a. Men are generally taller, walk fewer steps (being taller, they have a longer stride length), and at a faster speed.
   b. Women are generally shorter than men, walk more steps (being shorter, they have a shorter stride length), and at a slower speed.
   c. Children are shorter than adolescents and adults, walk more steps (being shorter, they have a shorter stride length), and at a slower speed.
   d. Terrain.
   e. Weather.
   f. Some people walk with a short stride, others walk briskly with a moderate stride, others with a long stride, or walk fast with a very long stride.

2. Pre-walking preparations:
   a. There is no indication that the people in the crowd had previously eaten breakfast or consumed any fluid to keep them hydrated.
   b. There is no indication that they had brought food or water supplies.

---

18. Wilkins, *The NIV Application Commentary*, 515.

19. Aus, *Feeding the Five Thousand*, xvi. In support, he cites Gundry, *Mark: A Commentary*, 326.

c. There is no indication that they knew how far they would travel or for how long.

3. Walking speed: unknown.

The July 4, 2023 Independence 5K Run & Firecracker Dash in Redondo Beach, CA. Credit: Scott Christopher Stolarz Photography, SCS Photoworks, LLC

Logistics of Sitting

The four Gospels recount the feeding of five thousand. While significant in its spiritual implications, this event also raises several logistical questions that merit attention.

1. The Gospels report that a crowd of people, about five thousand, pursued Jesus and his disciples on foot. Exactly where this pursuit started is unspecified. Matthew alone reports that the people followed Jesus out of the cities on foot. Presumably, he is referring to the cities of Capernaum and Chorazin. They then followed Jesus to Bethsaida, an excursion of two to five miles. Information about whether the crowd knew where Jesus was going is unavailable. Therefore, the distance and time factors are unknown. When the crowd of five thousand chased after Jesus, presumably, they were not carrying any provisions of food or water. The time required to walk from Capernaum to Bethsaida would have been approximately two to five hours, depending upon the

starting point, the weather conditions, and the crowd's composition (age, gender, health). Readers need to ask whether it seems realistic that five thousand people would have chased Jesus for several miles without provisions. Significantly, these five thousand travelers would have needed enough food and water *to return home.*

2. Five thousand people are said to have pursued Jesus and arrived at Bethsaida. Would this village have had sufficient resources in the first century to feed five thousand people?

3. Imagine the scene: Five thousand people, driven by their faith and curiosity, chase after Jesus. They arrive near Bethsaida, where Jesus imparts his teachings (Mark 6:34) and performs miraculous healings (Matt. 14:14). Eventually, the five thousand are instructed to sit down on the grass. This command, seemingly simple, raises intriguing logistical questions. How much space would each person have required to sit on the grass?

   a. Their legs would have needed enough space to extend comfortably: approximately four feet.

   b. Their arms and the width of their bodies would have required approximately three feet.

   c. Extra space would have been required to separate the groups by hundreds and by fifties (Mark 6:40).

   d. Four feet times three feet would equal twelve square feet per person. Twelve square feet per person times five thousand people is approximately 60,000 square feet. For comparison, an American Football field is about 57,000 square feet (109.728 meters long by 48.768 meters wide). Conservative Christian commentators have suggested that about 10,000 to 20,000 people were present, including women and children.[20] Question: How would Jesus' voice have been audible even to 5,000 travelers (let alone 10,000 or 20,000) in an area the size of a stadium when he taught them?

Research by Braxton Boren sheds light on this topic. He earned a PhD at the Music and Audio Research Laboratory at New York University. Boren specializes in the physics of sound and computational simulation techniques. He investigated the claim that George Whitefield, a famous preacher, drew thousands of people during the First Great Awakening in

---

20. Blomberg, *Matthew: An Exegetical and Theological Exposition*, 223; Carson, *Matthew 13–28*; France, *The Gospel of Matthew*, 563–65; Keener, *A Commentary on the Gospel of Matthew*, 404; Osborne, *Matthew*, 567; and Wilkins, *The NIV Application Commentary*, 515.

Britain and America. According to data from Benjamin Franklin about an outdoor assembly with thousands of attendees in the Market Street area, "Whitefield had a maximal intelligible area of 25,00 to 30,000 square meters under optimal conditions." The article on The Gospel Coalition Council.org website and the chapter entry in the text are informative, engaging, and relevant to Jesus instructing the people in Bethsaida.[21] Readers must evaluate the article, chapter entry, and gospel accounts of feeding the five thousand. Would Jesus' voice have been audible even to 5,000 travelers (let alone 10,000 or 20,000) in an area the size of a stadium when he taught them?

The story of Jesus feeding the five thousand stands or falls on the trustworthiness of the Gospels. The McGrews, J.J. Blunt, and others propose that undesigned coincidences can explain the alleged details (factoids) omitted by the other New Testament writers. Furthermore, they argue that with the help of these coincidences, many alleged inconsistencies can be easily answered. Christian apologists, Bible commentators, and theologians argue that the details of this event (feeding the five thousand) given in each Gospel are essentially the same if readers examine parallel passages. The four Gospels mention incidental independent details that explain each other in a non-contrived way (without collaboration). They posit that while one Gospel may add specific details that the others omit, none of the extra details are contradictory. Proponents argue this is a clear example of one event being independently described in all four Gospels. Therefore, there are no contradictions between the Gospels, and the events narrated in each Gospel are the same. The Gospels—Matthew, Mark, Luke, and John—focus on particular elements of Jesus' ministry.

Consequently, a writer can adapt or tailor a message to a specific audience in his inimitable style without subjecting to compromise the core of that message—in this case, the details relating to Jesus' life. Proponents of undesigned coincidences also argue that this feature is a distinctive characteristic of reports of historical events based on eyewitness accounts. A typical example is when four people witness the same car accident yet report different facts. This occurrence happens because the various witnesses report different features that stand out in their minds. This phenomenon occurs only in the four canonical gospels.

In contrast, skeptics and detractors argue that proponents of the hypothesis of Undesigned Coincidences cannot determine *why* the New Testament writers decided to include, edit, redact, or omit specific details found in other books they used as sources. Proponents can only offer their best guess, hunch, opinion, or speculation to explain the inconvenient reality of

---

21. Kidd, "The Science of Sound," and Boren, "Whitefield's Voice," 167–89.

existing contradictions, differences, or omissions. Employing good-natured humor, detractors counter that there are curious parallels between the collection of undesigned coincidences put together by leading proponents of the hypothesis and the terrifying monster whose body parts were "collected and assembled" by its creator in Mary Shelley's novel *Frankenstein*:

> Victor Frankenstein's passion for chemistry was unparalleled, and he delved into the depths of this scientific field.
>
> Likewise, proponents of undesigned coincidences have an attachment to and love for theology and Jesus.
>
> A deep-seated curiosity about the nature of life that propelled Victor Frankenstein on his path. His relentless studies eventually revealed a miraculous discovery that allowed him to breathe life into inanimate matter.
>
> Likewise, proponents of undesigned coincidences are curious about Jesus' life and the New Testament's reliability. Their studies in Scripture led them to a "wondrous" discovery that enabled them to provide scriptural proof that the Gospels are *not* (as commonly alleged) documents written forty to sixty years after Jesus' death. Instead, they are either eyewitness reports of Jesus' life, death, and resurrection (e.g., John's Gospel) or (in the case of the Synoptic Gospels written by Matthew, Mark, and Luke) biographical reports, written only twenty-five to thirty years after Jesus' death. Moreover, the Gospels are based on interviews with individuals who knew Jesus. Therefore, the Gospel authors present eyewitness reportage of actual historical events.
>
> Victor Frankenstein claimed to be creating his creation for the betterment of humankind.
>
> Likewise, proponents of undesigned coincidences claim to be creating a theological hypothesis for the betterment of humankind, demonstrating the reliability of the New Testament and the rationality of belief in Jesus.
>
> Victor Frankenstein created a grotesque humanoid creature by cobbling together old body parts and strange chemicals.
>
> However, in their pursuit of proving the reliability of the New Testament, the proponents of undesigned coincidences have resorted to cobbling together selected verses from Scripture. This method, while seemingly convincing, is inherently disingenuous.
>
> Victor Frankenstein created a humanoid monster.
>
> Likewise, proponents of undesigned coincidences have created a theological monster.

The reader can decide whether the humorous comparison presented above is apt.

Logistics of Jesus Breaking Loaves of Bread

Fryer comments at length on Jesus' breaking of the bread in the feeding of the 5,000:

> Verse 19. 'And ordering the multitudes to recline on the grass. He took the five loaves and the two fish, and looking up toward heaven. He blessed (the food), and breaking the loaves He gave them to the disciples, and the disciples (gave) to the multitudes.'
>
> Jesus here acts in accordance with the Jewish custom where the head of the household would take the bread, 'bless'/'give thanks'/'break' it, and distribute it to those seated at the meal. The sacramental language employed here recalls the institution of the Lord's Supper (Mt 26: 26f par), *and breaking the loaves*. The compound verb used (*kateklasen*, Mk, Lk) may point to the breaking of each loaf into pieces or fragments (Bratcher & Nida 1961:209: Swete 1909:134).
>
> *He gave (eddken) them to the disciples, and the disciples (gave) to the multitudes.* Again Mark is more vivid; '(Jesus) kept giving them to the disciples to set before them; and He divided also the two fish among them all' (6: 41).
>
> He 'kept giving (*edidou*, Mk, Lk; cf. *di-eddken*, Jn) to the disciples,' may refer to the repeated action of giving the broken pieces to each of the Twelve severally (cf. Alexander 1980:168; Swete 1909:134).
>
> 'to set before them' (Mk) (*paratithosin*). In the light of the customs of that time, the disciples probably carried from Jesus' hands the bread and fish and placed them before the various groups and not before each individually (Bratcher & Nida 1966:209; Edersheim 1962:684) . . .
>
> At what point exactly did the bread and fish multiply? We do not know. Some suggest that 'the Lord blessed, and gave the loaves and fishes to the disciples, *as they were*; and then, *during their distribution of them*, the miraculous increase took place, so that they broke and distributed enough for all (emphasis Alford's) (so Alford 1958:158f. with Meyer). Others think the miracle took place in the hands of Jesus (e.g., Hendriksen 1973 596). Probably the miracle occurred 'under His hands.' But we do not know. All we know for certain is that both the crowds

and the disciples seem to have been convinced that the miracle was connected with Jesus' act of thanksgiving (cf. Jn 6:23).[22]

The logistical problem with the narratives about the five loaves and two fish is readily apparent.

1. Envision the miracle unfolding *under the hands of Jesus.* How long would it take for the loaves and fishes to multiply, enough to feed about 5,000 to 10,000 people, *with food left over?*

2. How much time was necessary for Jesus to distribute the loaves and fish to his disciples?

3. How much time was necessary for the disciples to distribute the loaves and fish to feed about 5,000 to 10,000 people, the size of one or two stadiums, and *with abundant food left over?*

   Matthew is precise in his description of the event: "He [Jesus] gave them to the disciples, and the disciples (gave) to the multitudes." [Matt. 14:19 NKJV]

4. How many times were the disciples required to distribute the loaves and fish to feed about 5,000 to 10,000 people, spanning the area of one or two football stadiums with abundant food left over?

    a. The disciples had to receive food from Jesus.

    b. The disciples had to transport the loaves and fish to about 5,000 to 10,000 people sitting in an area the size of two football stadiums and still had abundant food left over.

    c. The disciples had to disperse the loaves and fish to the sitting crowd.

    d. The disciples had to return to Jesus to receive the next batch of food.

    e. The disciples had to transport the food to another group of unfed people sitting in an area about the size of one or two football stadiums, disperse the food, return to Jesus to receive the next lot of food, and repeat the procedure.

    f. How many loaves of bread and fish could have been carried by each disciple?

       How often would the procedure have needed to be repeated to feed a crowd of about 5,000 to 10,000 people with abundant food left over?

---

22. Fryer, "Matthew 14: 14—21," 39.

If the event was indeed historical, the logistics of the task are intriguing. The total *time* required to complete the task is open to speculation. However, it may have taken a couple of hours.

5. Logistics of Sending 5000 People to Look for Food When It Was Getting Dark

Table 6. Looking for Food

Mark [35] And when it grew late, his disciples came to him and said, "This is a desolate place, and the hour is now late. [36] Send them away to go into the surrounding countryside and villages and buy themselves something to eat."	Matthew [15] Now when it was evening, the disciples came to him and said, "This is a desolate place, and the day is now over; [15] send the crowds away to go into the villages and buy food for themselves."	Luke [12] Now the day began to wear away, and the twelve came and said to him, "Send the crowd away to go into the surrounding villages and countryside to find lodging and get provisions, for we are here in a desolate place."

Another logistical problem is the implausibility of sending 5000 people to look for food during the time indicated by the Gospel authors. (see table 6) Mark says, "It grew late," Matthew writes, "Now it was evening," and Luke declares, "Now the day began to wear away." Readers must contemplate the reality of the gospel narratives.

a. The 5000 people have been chasing Jesus: Did they bring torches for illumination?

b. Were 5000 people expected to travel at night, in a desolate place, and be expected to locate lodging and provisions?

c. The sequence of events in the Gospels presents logistical challenges. After Jesus fed the 5000, he directed the disciples to go ahead in a boat *while dismissing the crowd*. Mark 6:45 reads, [45] *Immediately* he made his disciples get into the boat and go before him to the other side, to Bethsaida, *while he dismissed the crowd* (ESV). Similarly, Matthew 14:22 says, "[22] *Immediately* he made the disciples get into the boat and go before him to the other side, *while he dismissed the crowds*" (ESV). Crucially, earlier, Matthew 14:15 reported, "*Now when it was evening*, the disciples came to him and said, "This is a desolate place, and *the day is now over*" (ESV). Considering that *it was evening* when the disciples approached Jesus, and the crowd was dismissed *after* the food distribution, it raises questions about the plausibility of the 5000 returning to their starting point in the dark, potentially without adequate clothing to stay warm and illuminated. This narrative leads to considering whether the gospel narrative holds up from a logistical perspective.

d. Joel Marcus discusses another temporal difficulty.

After it is already late, Jesus has time to arrange the huge crowd in ordered ranks, to feed them bread and fish, to have the massive amount of leftovers collected, to send the disciples away, to dismiss the crowd, to climb a mountain, and to pray-all before it gets dark! (cf. 6:47; see Brown, 1.253).[23]

---

23. Marcus, *Mark 1–8*, 406.

> M. Eugene Boring (PhD, Vanderbilt), a Protestant theologian, served as pastor for congregations in Kentucky, Indiana, and Tennessee and as professor at Phillips University (1967–1986), Texas Christian University (1987–1992), and Brite Divinity School (1992–2003). He is the author or translator of numerous books including, most recently, *Hearing Paul's Voice* (2020), *Hearing John's Voice* (2019), and *1 and 2 Thessalonians: A Commentary* (2015). He writes,
>
>> That the story does not move at the level of realistic report is indicated by several features prior to the actual miracle. A crowd of thousands is difficult to imagine in a setting in which the population of Capernaum, for example, was only two or three thousand. That such a mass of people would spontaneously follow Jesus into the wilderness without thought of what they would eat or where they would sleep is difficult to imagine. Likewise, the effort to picture the event historically has problems with their coming from "all the cities" and that they nonetheless reach Jesus' destination before he does—did word first have to be carried to the cities, from which people then formed the crowds, or had they already come to Capernaum from everywhere, yet had no provisions with them? Imagine how such an ungainly multitude outpaced the boat requires some ingenuity, and some explanation for how they knew where Jesus was going. The disciples' suggestion that local farm villages could handle an influx of five thousand hungry people would seem to be a burden even the lines of fast-food establishments that ring modern cities, and is difficult to see as a realistic suggestion in an actual historical context. That all attention is focused on food, and nothing is said of what people are to drink seems unrealistic in a hot and dry environment. It thus seems that all biblical models, not historical recollection of an actual event, provided the basic content of the story. In addition to the many shepherd imagery from biblical texts discussed above, the story has many points of contact, in both form and content with the Elisha story of 2 Kgs 4:42–44; there, too, the miracle follows the death of Elijah, the Markan John the Baptist. There, too, the prophet commands his servants to feed a large group with an impossibly small number of loaves. There, too, the objection that such a small amount is not enough for so many is overcome by the prophet's authoritative command. There, too, the miracle not only provides enough, but more than enough. The number in 2 Kgs are smaller: twenty loaves for a hundred hungry men, a proportion of one to five. In Mark, there are five loaves for five thousand, a proportion of one to a thousand: here, too, Jesus is not only "more than a prophet" (Matt 11:9); as the eschatological prophet he is *much more*.[24]

Conclusion

The upshot of the preceding discussion of the miracle of Jesus feeding the five thousand is that the size of the crowd described in the Gospels appears improbably large on purely logistical grounds. It is difficult to imagine several thousand men descending on a town the size of Bethsaida and then following Jesus for several hours to a deserted place, taking their wives

---

24. Boring, *Mark: A Commentary*, 184–85.

and children with them. Where would they have been able to buy sufficient food for the journey? How would Jesus have addressed such a large crowd? Moreover, even if he multiplied the loaves and fishes as the Gospels claim, would it not have taken hours to distribute the food to everyone in the crowd? For these reasons, readers may ask whether the gospel accounts of this spectacular miracle were intended to be literal, as defenders of undesigned coincidences assume.

Moreover, if one casts doubt on the literal accuracy of the accounts, a legitimate query could arise regarding the detail of the green grass mentioned in Mark. *Is it a factual recollection or a mere embellishment?* If it is the latter, it ceases to be an instance of an undesigned coincidence, inviting readers to consider alternative interpretations.

2.3 CONTRADICTION ABOUT THE LOCATION OF FEEDING THE 5,000

> Mark 6:45 Immediately he made his disciples get into the boat and go before him to the other side, to Bethsaida, while he dismissed the crowd (ESV).
>
> Luke 9:10 On their return the apostles told him all that they had done. And he took them and withdrew apart to a town called Bethsaida (ESV).

Christian apologists, Bible commentators, theologians, skeptics, and detractors agree that the location of feeding the five thousand is controversial. On the extreme, the narrative is contradictory. In Mark 6:45, the passage describes Jesus' disciples embarking on a boat to sail *across* the Sea of Galilee. At the same time, Jesus sends away the crowds *after* miraculously feeding the multitude with five loaves of bread and two fish. Following this event, Jesus goes up the mountain to pray alone. However, the contradiction arises when the Gospel of Luke presents a different sequence of events. Luke 9:10 portrays Jesus withdrawing with his disciples to Bethsaida *after* the miraculous feeding, where they continue to heal and preach to the crowds. This apparent inconsistency raises questions regarding the chronological order of events and the location of Jesus and his disciples after the feeding miracle.[25]

David Austin, in a private email, says,

> If the McGrews are basing their whole thesis on the Gospel writers being truthful eyewitnesses or getting their information

---

25. Strauss, *Mark*, 284–85. He offers four explanations.

directly from eyewitnesses and passing this along via the Gospels as "eyewitness testimony," then clearly, this falls apart when the witnesses cannot even agree on the location of the miracle. The whole edifice surrounding "green grass" and "why did they ask Philip?" becomes entirely moot . . . .

The text [is crucial] because it highlights that the Gospels *cannot* be eyewitness accounts by the Gospel writers or the testimony of eyewitnesses recorded by the Gospel writers.[26]

Scholars and theologians have debated this contradiction (difference?) for centuries, proposing various explanations to reconcile the two accounts. Some suggest that the discrepancy could be due to differences in the sources used by the gospel writers or the way they arranged the events to serve their theological purposes. Others argue that the discrepancy may arise from variations in oral tradition or the authors' perspectives, leading to slight differences in the details of the narratives.

New Testament scholar Michael Licona has written a concise review of the controversy. Readers must diligently examine his review. He writes,

Luke 9:10 informs us the feeding occurred at or near Bethsaida. The other three Gospels do not tell us where it occurred. However, Matthew and John appear to be in concert with Luke, because they report that Jesus and his disciples crossed the lake immediately after the feeding and landed on the northwest side (Matt. 14:34—Gennesaret; John 6:16–17, 21—Capernaum). John adds that they landed where they had intended. So, according to Luke, Matthew, and John, Jesus fed the crowd at or near Bethsaida (12:30 [being on a clock]), then the disciples crossed the lake immediately after and landed in the area of Gennesaret/Capernaum (10–11:00 [being on a clock]).

The difficulty appears after the feeding when in Mark 6:45 we read that Jesus told his disciples to cross over the lake to Bethsaida. This seems difficult to reconcile with Luke's report that the feeding had occurred at or near Bethsaida. So, what is going on here?[27]

He proceeds to examine solutions and afterwards, discusses their deficiencies. The most substantial apologetic interaction is that the Greek *pros Bethsaida* in Mark 6:45 should be translated as "toward Bethsaida." Licona points out that

---

26. David Austin, email message to author, March 26, 2024.
27. Licona, "Was Mark Confused."

THE HYPOTHESIS OF UNDESIGNED COINCIDENCES: HOW WELL DOES IT EXPLAIN   89

> In every instance, when a verb of going is followed by two accusatives of location (*eis* + accusative and *pros* + accusative), the two prepositional phrases are providing descriptions of the same location. These texts weigh heavily in favor of understanding Mark 6:45 to be reporting that Jesus instructed his disciples to go "to Bethsaida" and is another reason why that rendering is to be preferred over "toward Bethsaida." Most translators agree. Of 28 English translations, only three render *pros Bethsaidan* as "near Bethsaida" or "toward Bethsaida" (New Jerusalem Bible, New American Bible, Common English Bible).

Licona adds data supporting his view.

1. Indeed, there is an even stronger reason for preferring "to" over "toward" or "by." There are 65 occurrences of *pros* in Mark, 42 in Matthew, 166 in Luke, and 102 in John. It almost always appears in the accusative case in the Gospels, exceptions being where it appears as an infinitive (Mark 13:22 Luke 18:1; Matt. 5:28; 6:1; 13:30; 23:5; 26:12) and in the dative case (Luke 19:37; John 20:11, 12 [2x]).

2. Of 375 occurrences of *pros* in the Gospels, only 11 (or 3%) are not connected with an accusative.[28]

Aus identifies a related, dubious logistical matter.

> Although Jesus and his disciples departed from where they were and traveled by boat to a deserted place (on the Sea of Galilee) by themselves (v. 32), to get away from the many who were "coming and going," so that "they had no leisure even to eat" (v. 31), a great crowd followed them and arrived at the landing site ahead of them (vv. 33–34). This is strange because it is not stated that all were trained joggers. Normally travel by boat is much faster than walking along an irregular shoreline. The setting appears contrived.[29]

Readers should carefully consider two crucial factors: Distance and Speed. The notion that the crowd could travel faster on foot than Jesus and his disciples could by boat raises valid questions about the plausibility of the events. Although the exact distances are uncertain, it is widely believed, as Aus writes, that traveling by boat would be a quicker option than traveling on foot around the northern shore of the Sea of Galilee. Hence, the controversy revolves around reconciling the gospel accounts with practical

---

28. Licona, "Was Mark Confused."
29. Aus, *Feeding the Five Thousand*, xiii–xiv.

considerations of movement and geography. In light of this, readers must be the ultimate judge and jury.

In conclusion, Christian apologists, Bible commentators, and theologians have debated this location contradiction for centuries, proposing various explanations to reconcile the two accounts. Some suggest that the discrepancy could be due to differences in the sources used by the gospel writers or the way they arranged the events to serve their theological purposes. Others argue that the discrepancy may arise from variations in oral tradition or the authors' perspectives, leading to slight differences in the details of the narratives. The contradiction (differences?) in the chronological sequence of events between Mark 6:45 and Luke 9:10 challenges harmonizing the gospel narratives. If the location and chronology are contradictory and unreliable, this reality undermines the hypothesis of Undesigned Coincidences. Readers must decide (1) if a contradiction (difference?) exists and (2) whether the Gospels are reliable.

2.4 WHY DOES MARK MENTION THE GREEN GRASS IN HIS ACCOUNT OF THE MIRACLE?

The Undesigned Coincidence of the Green Grass: An Overview

McGrew, Professor McGrew, J.J. Blunt, and other proponents of the hypothesis of Undesigned Coincidences have argued that Mark's seemingly casual mention of green grass in his account of the feeding of the five thousand (Mark 6:39) is a genuine case of an undesigned coincidence, as it ties in with a remark in John's Gospel that the miracle took place at the time of the Jewish Passover (i.e., in spring, which was supposedly the only time of the year when the grass in that region would have been green). This text incorporates a cumulative argument challenging that claim. The arguments presented herein are multifaceted, including biblical criticism:

1. Numerous biblical commentators on Mark 6 argue that the green grass has a theological connection with Psalm 23.

2. Journal articles and doctoral dissertations argue that green grass has a theological connection with Psalm 23.

3. Biblical criticism, employing data from John's use of allusion and symbolism, provides strong evidence that the author did not write casually, unintentionally, and unplanned.

4. In its publication, *Dictionary of Biblical Imagery*, the IVP devotes an entire page to the symbolism of grass in the Bible.[30]

5. On theological grounds, *if* the gospel writers were cognizant of 1 Corinthians 15:3–4, 17–19 (where Paul emphasizes that what he received and passed on about Jesus' resurrection is "of first importance" and that if Jesus was not raised from the dead, then those who have died believing in Christ are "lost"), it is utterly inconceivable that they would have written their accounts casually, unintentionally, and unplanned.

6. John's author confirms that he composed his work based on theological motives (John 20:30–31).

7. Biblical criticism demonstrates that the later Gospel authors employed the earlier Gospels as a template. Matthew, Luke, and John could not have written independently and casually unintentionally and unplanned if they copied, edited, or redacted prior Gospels.

8. McGrew and other proponents do not interact and engage with the abundant academic literature on coincidence in cognitive science, literature, mathematics, probability, psychology, and statistics.

9. Biblical criticism cannot support the hypothesis of Undesigned Coincidences for the following reasons:

    a. No existing methodology exists for how anyone can identify and decide what is a coincidence.

    b. There are no criteria to determine what is and is not designed.

    c. No existing methodology exists for how anyone can identify and decide what an allusion is.

    d. Proponents of undesigned coincidences employ eisegesis, not exegesis: they try to make the Bible say what they want it to rather than letting it speak for itself.

    e. Proponents of undesigned coincidences assume the material in the Christian Bible is historically reliable.

    f. Writers are free to invent details at will, unlike eyewitness accounts, which require people to stick to the facts.

    g. The presumed honesty and trustworthiness of the Gospel authors have no relationship to the accuracy of their reportage.

---

30. *Dictionary of Biblical Imagery*, art. "Grass," 348–49.

h. There is no way of verifying that the Gospel authors were reporting events that happened in reality, that they did not make things up, or that they wrote in good faith.

i. There is no way of proving that the Gospel authors were truthful.

j. A lack of adequate numbers of peer-reviewed articles on undesigned coincidences in "mainstream academic journals."

k. Undesigned coincidences are traditional apologetics dressed in a new garb to defend the New Testament's historical reliability.

l. The hypothesis of Undesigned Coincidences is essentially harmonization under a different name.

Introduction to the Hypothesis of the Undesigned Coincidences and the Green Grass

Perhaps the best-known example of the many undesigned coincidences identified by McGrew in her book and subsequent internet articles and podcasts is the "green grass," which figures in Mark's description of Jesus' feeding of the five thousand. Mark tells us that Jesus got the crowd to sit on the green grass, but he does not say *why* the grass was green. The climate in that region is dry, so it would have been brown for most of the year. On the other hand, John's Gospel mentions that it was shortly before the Passover. Passover falls in spring, the only time of year when abundant rain falls in the area and the grass turns green. The information in Mark's and John's Gospels dovetails nicely, and it looks like a pretty convincing case of an undesigned coincidence.

McGrew discusses this undesigned coincidence in detail on pages 66–67 of her text. The critical verse is Mark 6:39, with the surrounding verses providing the necessary context (see table 2 at the beginning of Part 2). Jesus and his disciples travel to a remote place, not a desert. Thousands of people are following them. Jesus directs the disciples to have everyone sit in groups on the *green* grass. Mark is the *only* Gospel that records *green* grass: "Then he commanded them all to sit down in groups on the green grass" (ESV). McGrew points out that three Gospels mention that the crowds sat on the grass. She adds, "There would have needed to be quite a lot of green grass to make Mark's statement true since he implies that more than 5,000 people sat down on it." This detail is in striking contrast with the feeding of the four thousand appearing in Mark 8:1–19 and Matthew 15:29–39. No reference to grass appears in those narratives.

McGrew inquires, "Why does Mark specifically mention the grass was green?" Why does this detail about "green" exclusively in Mark matter? The most frequently given explanation is that this is not the norm. In the arid climate of Palestine, the grass is usually brown and dry, except during or just after the short rainy season. Specifically, the grass is only green in that region in the spring, just after the winter rains. Thus, this detail locates the miracle in the springtime. However, this is by no means certain.

Monsignor Charles Pope, a Catholic pastor based in Washington DC, has written a blog article arguing that the climate in Jesus' time may have been cooler and wetter than it is now. He quotes the first-century Jewish historian Flavius Josephus, who extols the fertility of the Holy Land, adding that "it supplies men with the principal fruits, with grapes and figs continually, during ten months of the year and the rest of the fruits as they become ripe together through the whole year" (*The Jewish War*, Book 3, Chapter 10:8). Additionally, Msgr. Pope cites evidence suggesting that since Jesus' time, "the overall area of the Holy Land has undergone gradual desertification."[31] If Msgr. Pope is correct, then; the grass in the area may have been green for several months of the year in Jesus' time, thus considerably weakening the force of the alleged coincidence.

Two verses later, Mark points out that big crowds tracked Jesus and his disciples everywhere. Consequently, "they had no leisure even to eat" (Mark 6:31, ESV). Moving to the Fourth Gospel, John says that this event happened around the time of the Passover: "Now the Passover, the feast of the Jews, was at hand" (John 6:4, ESV). Here, then, is the crucial link: the Passover festival falls in the middle of the growing season. Therefore, this verse from John explains why the grass was green (from Mark). McGrew elaborates that John illuminates why huge crowds were mobbing Jesus instead of being home working in their shops or fields—namely because it was the time of the Passover festival.

It is also crucial that Passover was a great feast to which hundreds of thousands of Jews traveled every year. John gives its readers, in passing, a detail that interlocks in two ways with Mark's account of the same event. McGrew observes, "So here we have a perfect fit between John's casual reference to the time of year and Mark's specification of the detail of the green grass."[32]

McGrew makes two arguments here:
1. Detractors cannot explain the undesigned coincidence.

---

31. Pope, "What Was the Climate and Weather of Israel Like at the Time of Jesus?"
32. McGrew, *Hidden in Plain View*, 66.

Response: McGrew is presenting a red herring. Skeptics and detractors are not responsible for explaining an unknown: why Mark included the word "green." Skeptics and detractors only need to say the argument is unconvincing. Of course, they can offer guesses, hunches, and speculations. However, no one can certify why Mark included "green." Any potential answer is unverifiable. Additionally, some detractors argue that this event did not occur.

2. Detractors fail to explain John's connection with John regarding the time of year (e.g., the spring and the Passover).

Response: Technically, McGrew is presenting a red herring. It is not the responsibility of detractors to explain an unknown: the connection with John about the time of year. Nobody can explain the time of year connection with absolute certainty. Detractors can offer guesses, hunches, and speculations.

Professor Dale Allison Appeals to Psalm 23 to Rebut Undesigned Coincidences

In an interview with Derek Lambert on Mythvision, Professor Dale Allison suggested that the hypothesis that the "green grass" in Mark 6:39 is a deliberate allusion to Psalm 23 is just as good an explanation as the hypothesis preferred by McGrew, that it reflects eyewitness testimony.[33] McGrew hit back on a podcast on her show, The Lydia McGrew podcast.[34] The podcast summary reads as follows:

> Green Grass: Undesigned Coincidences vs. Symbolic Invention
> 1 Aug 2022 · The Lydia McGrew Podcast
> 00:35:59
>
> Here I'm using the undesigned coincidence concerning the green grass (Mark 6) and the time of Passover (John 6) for the feeding of the five thousand as an illustration of the weakness of theological invention theories. In the course of it, I "help out" the theological theorists by presenting three suggested symbolic allusions to Old Testament passages for the pillow on which Jesus was sleeping in Mark 4:38. This is intended to show that our ability to think up a clever-sounding connection between some apparently factual, casually narrated Gospel detail and an Old Testament passage is of no epistemic value. It's much, much too easy. I'm taking the occasion from Dale Allison's recent

---

33. Derek Lambert and Dale Allison, "Challenge Dr. Dale C. Allison Jr."
34. McGrew, "The Green Grass."

discussion of this on Mythvision, where he said that it is "just as good" an explanation of the green grass in Mark that this is an allusion to Psalm 23 rather than evidence of eyewitness testimony.

Here is the exchange on Mythvision (cued up):
https://www.youtube.com/watch?v=ohvL5FoCgHA

Here is an older article by Allison where he makes this same suggestion: https://biblicalstudies.org.uk/pdf/irish-biblical-studies/05-3_132.pdf

Originally uploaded to YouTube May 1, 2022.[35]

Note: the "older article" by Allison referred to here is "Psalm 23 (22) in Early Christianity: A Suggestion," *Irish Biblical Studies* 5 (July 1983).

How Fair is Lydia McGrew's Critique of Dale Allison's Interview on Mythvision (April 5, 2022)?

McGrew dedicates a 35-minute podcast to the undesigned coincidence relating to the "green grass" while engaging with the perspectives of two notable figures: Dr. Dale Allison, a respected professor of the New Testament at Princeton Theological Seminary and a Christian, ordained elder in the Presbyterian Church (USA) and skeptic Derek Lambert, the founder of the Youtube channel Mythvision. In the interview, Lambert asks Allison about his views on the "undesigned coincidences hypothesis" defended by McGrew, explicitly focusing on the example of the "green grass." In her homepage post, McGrew responds to Allison's discussion on Mythvision, where he suggested that Mark's "green grass" could be an allusion to Psalm 23 rather than evidence of eyewitness testimony. McGrew provides a link to the podcast. The question arises: is her interpretation of Allison's interview fair, or does it potentially cast Allison in a negative light?[36]

The following points require noting at the outset:

1. Allison's discussion about green grass during his Mythvision interview spans less than three minutes (timestamp 57:15—59:35).
2. Allison modestly admits: "I honestly do not know who J.J. Blunt is."

35. McGrew, "The Green Grass."

36. McGrew, in another podcast, stated, "By the traditional creedal definition of Christianity, Dr. Allison is not in fact a Christian." Allison, in response to an interview, replied to McGrew's allegation. The transcript reads, "Question: So, for the record, do you consider yourself a Christian? Allison's response: "Yes, I do, and I deeply resent people who make such judgments without knowing me personally. I think it is unconscionable." (timestamp 2:55—3:15). Paul Ens and Dale Allison, "Apologists Turn on Christian Resurrection Scholar."

3. Allison confesses that he "is not sure what he's referring to by undesigned coincides methodology."
4. Allison says he would need some examples (i.e., of undesigned coincidences) to discuss the topic.
5. Allison inquires, "if this is like the green grass in Mark or Jesus was on a cushion in the boat in Mark?"
6. Allison admits, "I must say this: I think there are places where you can look at, say, the Gospel of John, and things that go on in the Gospel of Mark help explain what's going on in the Gospel of John. But I think myself, that's because John probably knows these texts, and he can assume certain things."
7. Allison humbly confesses, "Without an example, I'm just sort of stumbling around, so forgive me for not knowing the details of this."[37] This admission of his limited knowledge without examples underscores his honesty and encourages readers to consider the controversy from various perspectives.

Readers must adjudicate the controversy for themselves and decide whether McGrew is unfair to Allison here.

McGrew's Arguments Against a Parallel Between Mark 6 and Psalm 23

McGrew says Allison presents weak comparisons between Mark 6 and Psalm 23 (29:52). She accuses him of cherry-picking, employing sleight of hand, using disanalogies, and making an illicit move she terms *disjunction*. Specific arguments in her podcast include the following points:

1. John is more concerned with being a good shepherd than Mark.
2. John does not say that people are sheep without a shepherd.
3. There are no still waters in Mark 6.
4. In Psalm 23, the shepherd leads his flock. In contrast, Mark 6 reports that Jesus does not want the people to follow him.
5. In Psalm 23, the shepherd leads them to the green pasture (grass), whereas the people seek him in Mark 6.
6. In Psalm 23, the people do not want it, whereas Mark 6 narrates that the people want him to repeat it later.

---

37. Paul Ens and Dale Allison, "Apologists Turn on Christian Resurrection Scholar."

7. Allison says that Jesus has them sitting *or* lying on the grass (podcast).[38]
    a. Mark says nothing about lying.
    b. Psalm says nothing about sitting.
8. There is only one similarity: green grass.

Is McGrew's Argument that Allison Presents Weak Comparisons between Mark 6 and Psalm 23 Sustainable?

First, nobody, including McGrew, Professor Dale Allison, or anyone else, has ever claimed that Mark 6 and Psalm 23 *must align one hundred percent*. Such an allegation or insinuation is a phantom. *What matters is that Mark 6 contains unmistakable elements that conjure up the images of Psalm 23 that most lay people would readily recognize.* The image is of a shepherd caring for his flock, and the notable presence mention of green grass (i.e., synonymous with green pastures). McGrew enumerates the eight finely nuanced differences as anachronistic. McGrew earned a PhD in English at Vanderbilt University. Her dissertation was *Edmund Spenser's Defense of Love in a Moral Universe*. She applies modern literary standards to a time when about 95 percent of people could *not* read or write. *What matters is the image invoked by the words of the psalmist*. Presumably, Mark's author did not expect his readers to have the skills to compare and contrast words, perform literary analysis, or execute a comparison of the sentence structure. The image is unmistakable.

Second, while McGrew declares she is critiquing Allison's three-minute excerpt from his podcast interview,[39] she mainly seems to be engaging with his earlier article, "Psalm 23 (22) in Early Christianity: A Suggestion," published in *Irish Biblical Studies* 5 (July 1983), which is available online.[40] McGrew provides a link to the article on her podcast. It explains how Mark 6 directly connects with Psalm 23.

In his article, Allison remarks that commentators have long debated the importance of Mark's "green grass." For now, it requires mentioning that in her podcast, McGrew briefly engages with a single commentator, Robert Gundry, whose response she characterizes as "feeble" (18:37—18:52). She deliberately declines to engage with the multitude of biblical commentaries on the Gospel of Mark. She also declares, "I am not trying to say that Allison is the only one who advocates this idea concerning Psalm 23." However, it

---

38. This claim that Allison employs the word "or" could not be substantiated.
39. Lambert and Allison, "Challenge Dr. Dale C. Allison Jr."
40. Allison, "Psalm 23 (22) in Early Christianity," 132–37.

is vital to state that most commentaries on Mark's Gospel state that the narrative of the feeding of the 5,000 in Mark 6 parallels Psalm 23 (a point that will be subject to the discussion below).

Allison asks three questions concerning the reference to green grass in Mark 6:39:

1. Is this notice the sure trace of an eyewitness?

2. Is it perhaps an indication of the Palestinian spring, the time of the Passover (cf. John 6.4, 10)?

3. Is it a messianic sign, evidence that the wilderness has begun to bring forth miraculous bloom?[41]

Allison writes, "These questions rapidly dissolve when one discovers that allusions to Ps 22(23) are apparently imbedded in Mark 6.32–44." He strengthens his argument by providing textual parallels between Mark 6 and Psalm 23. Afterward, he remarks, "Even the Markan setting may recollect Ps 22(23):2." He elaborates that Mark 6 "contains elements which conjure up the images of Ps 22(23), and the picture in both is the same: the shepherd cares for his flock on the green grass by the water, and the sheep have no lack."[42]

Next, he reviews the literature showing that the allusion to Psalm 23 comes in an eschatological context, even "if the feeding of the five thousand should not be interpreted as an anticipation of the great messianic banquet."[43] Eduard Schweizer presents Jesus as "the one who brings salvation in the end-time."[44] Following, Allison provides a comparison.

1. The first redeemer, Moses, fed the Israelites manna in the wilderness.

2. The second redeemer, Jesus, inaugurating the new Exodus, miraculously feeds the multitude bread.

Allison concludes, "The allusions to Ps 22 (23) in Mark belong to a story whose meaning is to be discerned eschatologically."[45]

Next, Allison identifies several passages where Jesus receives the title "shepherd."

1. Mark 14: 27–28

2. John 10: 1–18

3. Heb. 13:20

---

41. Allison, "Psalm 23 (22) in Early Christianity: A Suggestion," 134.
42. Allison, "Psalm 23 (22) in Early Christianity: A Suggestion," 134.
43. Allison, "Psalm 23 (22) in Early Christianity: A Suggestion," 135.
44. Allison, "Psalm 23 (22) in Early Christianity: A Suggestion," 135.
45. Allison, "Psalm 23 (22) in Early Christianity: A Suggestion," 135.

Allison concludes, "There are also additional texts which through their imagery make it plain that Jesus was widely portrayed as being the shepherd of the Christian sheep."[46]

1. Matt. 10:6
2. Matt. 15:24
3. Luke 19:10

He demonstrates that "Jewish eschatology knew of a shepherd who would come and reign in the end of days."

1. Ezekiel 34: 23–24
2. Micah 5:3 (4)
3. Psalms of Solomon 17:45 (40)
4. Zechariah 10:3
5. Zechariah 11: 4–17[47]

Allison reiterates, "Now the NT does not lose sight of the eschatological connotation which the title "shepherd" had in Judaism." He concludes:

> No doubt it was this belief in Jesus as the Davidic shepherd which encouraged the interpretation of Ps 22(23) reflected in Revelation 7.17, 1 Clement 26 and Mark 6.32–44. As they waited for the parousia, for the shepherd who would rule over Israel and the nations, the first followers of Jesus could think of the assurances of Ps 22(23) as pertaining to the future.[48]

McGrew's Response to Dale Allison's Attempt to Explain the Green Grass by Appealing to Psalm 23

McGrew directly challenges Allison's thinking, arguing that Mark 6:39 reflects Psalm 23. In her podcast, McGrew argues this is an "illustration of the weakness of theological invention theories." She says Psalm 23 is a disanalogy compared to the Gospels. In addition to the eight points previously identified, she judges that the connection is weak—"*Mark should have made it stronger.*" Presumably, she means that if Mark intended to evoke imagery relating to Psalm 23, he should have made that point more explicit. It is also crucial that Passover was a great feast to which hundreds of thousands of Jews traveled every year. John gives its readers, in passing, a detail

---

46. Allison, "Psalm 23 (22) in Early Christianity: A Suggestion," 135.
47. Allison, "Psalm 23 (22) in Early Christianity: A Suggestion," 135–36.
48. Allison, "Psalm 23 (22) in Early Christianity: A Suggestion," 136.

that interlocks in two ways with Mark's account of the same event. McGrew observes, "So here we have a perfect fit between John's casual reference to the time of year and Mark's specification of the detail of the green grass."[49]

Her critical evaluation ("*Mark should have made it stronger.*") is reminiscent of a famous scene in the movie Amadeus, where the Austrian emperor Joseph II evaluates Mozart's [Amadeus's] composition, *The Marriage of Figaro.*

> Emperor: Well, Herr Mozart! A good effort. Decidedly that. An excellent effort! You've shown us something quite new today.
>
> [Mozart bows frantically: he is over-excited.]
>
> Mozart: It is new, it is, isn't it, Sire?
>
> Emperor: Yes, indeed.
>
> Mozart: So, then you like it? You really like it, Your Majesty?
>
> Emperor: Of course I do. It's very good. Of course, now and then—just now and then—it gets a touch elaborate.
>
> Mozart: What do you mean, Sire?
>
> Emperor: Well, I mean occasionally it seems to have, how shall one say? [he stops in difficulty; turning to Orsini-Rosenberg] How shall one say, Director?
>
> Orsini-Rosenberg: Too many notes, Your Majesty?
>
> Emperor: Exactly. *Very well put. Too many notes.*
>
> Mozart: I don't understand. There are just as many notes, Majesty, as are required. Neither more nor less.
>
> Emperor: My dear fellow, there are, in fact, only so many notes the ear can hear in the course of an evening. I think I'm right in saying that, aren't I, Court Composer?
>
> Salieri: Yes! yes! er, on the whole, yes, Majesty.
>
> Mozart: But this is absurd!
>
> Emperor: My dear, young man, don't take it too hard. Your work is ingenious. It's quality work. *And there are simply too many notes, that's all. Cut a few and it will be perfect.*
>
> Mozart: Which few did you have in mind, Majesty?[50]

Here, sarcastically (using a parody), we might say that she is comparable to the emperor Joseph II, except that McGrew is claiming there are "too few words" rather than "too many notes." Mark, equal to Mozart, would presumably refute McGrew's evaluation in an imaginary response.

49. McGrew, *Hidden in Plain View*, 66.

50. "Too Many Notes", *Amadeus*, directed by Miloš Forman, (1984; Los Angeles, CA: Orion Pictures, 1993), DVD.

Mark: I don't understand. There are just as many words as are required. Neither more nor less,

Mark: But this is absurd!

What Do Other Critics Have to Say About the Alleged Undesigned Coincidences in the Feeding of the Five Thousand?

McGrew claims to have found two undesigned coincidences in the gospel accounts of feeding the five thousand. She points out that Mark 6:31 speaks of the people "coming and going." In contrast, John 6:4 says in passing that Passover was at hand. She interprets this to mean that thousands of people were busily "coming and going" to prepare for their pilgrimage to Jerusalem to celebrate the Passover.[51] However, Chris Sandoval contends that a much more likely explanation does not involve the Passover pilgrimage. He counters that in many passages (e.g., Mark 1:28, 32–33, 35–37, 45; 2:2–4; 3:7–12, 20, 32; 4:1, 36; 5:24, 31; 8:1; 9:14–15; 10:1), the second Gospel speaks of Jesus and the disciples being mobbed by the madding crowds. Sandoval concludes that the whole point of Mark 6:31 is: "[f]or many were coming and going, and they had no leisure even to eat."[52]

Second, John Nelson, writing under the blogger name Thomas Horatio, engages with McGrew's argument that since John says this event was around Passover (6:4), Mark's note that 'many were coming and going' at that time (6:31) seems to subtly corroborate it.

1. However, it is difficult to view this as an undesigned coincidence. First, the crowd following Jesus is a Markan trope (3:7–9).

2. Second, "the Passover setting of John may simply serve to make explicit latent Passover symbolism in the early feeding accounts."

3. McGrew and Peter Williams note that the 'green grass' (Mark 6:39) corroborates a Passover setting since Passover falls in Nisan (March/April) after months of rainfall. Nelson comments, "Yet can facticity be so easily assumed from verisimilitude?"[53]

In rebuttal, Jonathan McClatchie, a Christian apologist, argues that Nelson's critique is contrived, and it does not explain why Mark and John fit together and employs a hyper-symbolic view.[54] However, McClatchie employs a red herring. It bears repeating that detractors do not need to

---

51. McGrew, *Hidden in Plain View*, 63–65.
52. Sandoval, "Amazon book review of *Hidden in Plain View*."
53. Nelson, "'Undesigned Coincidences in the Gospels.'"
54. McClatchie, "Undesigned Coincidences in the Gospels."

present speculations about why Mark and John fit together or employ a hyper-symbolic view.

Graham Twelftree, PhD, Professor of New Testament, and also on the editorial board of the *Journal for the Study of the Historical Jesus*, directly challenges the idea that the detail of the green grass found in Mark 6:39, John is an "incidental detail reflecting an eyewitness." He provides two reasons:

1. "It could have been inserted as a reminder that in the messianic age the desert will be fertile (cf. Isa. 35:1)."
2. "It may reflect the shepherd's role of leading his sheep to lie down in green pastures."[55]

The latter opinion is found extensively in the literature on the subject. In contrast, Dennis MacDonald writes, "on the 'green grass,' apparently because verdant grass offered greater comfort than the rocky shore of prickly dry grass."[56]

N.T. Wright, writing in *Mark for Everyone*, seemingly undermines the hypothesis of Undesigned Coincidences:

> The grass is green: if you've been to Galilee, you will know that this means the story is set in the springtime. Grass grows quickly in the spring, but once the rains stop in May it gets scorched with the fierce sun. This takes place, then, around Passover time. Mark will have been aware of this, and of the way in which the words he uses to describe what Jesus did with the bread fit so neatly into the pattern the early church came to use for its own regular bread-breaking new-Passover meal: he took, blessed, broke and gave it.[57]

Wright states that Mark's readers do not need to be told that it is around the time of Passover. Consequently, John 6 does not necessarily confirm that it is about the time of the Passover.[58]

Richard Carrier, a detractor, bluntly criticizes McGrew's apologetic. He argues that some of her "examples" are fabricated. He cites her attempt to argue that when Mark's account of the "feeding of five thousand" speaks of the people "coming and going," he "must" mean this was the Preparation for the Passover. Instead, the alleged undersigned coincidence about the people "coming and going" arises because when John relates the same event

---

55. Twelftree, *Jesus the Miracle Worker*, 319.
56. MacDonald, *Homeric Epics and the Gospel of Mark*, 84.
57. Wright, *Mark for Everyone*, 78–79.
58. Wright, *Mark for Everyone*, 78–79.

(he is redacting Mark's account), he adds in passing that "Passover was at hand." McGrew claims that this shows that in Mark and John's Gospels, we have the independent testimony of two eyewitnesses who must have been there—and that Mark (or rather, his eyewitness source) merely forgot or omitted to mention that the Passover was approaching.

Carrier elaborates on why McGrew's appeal to an undesigned coincidence between Mark and John fails to explain the green grass:

> Never mind that Mark places this event on the lakeshore and John places it on a mountain—a discrepancy impossible for eyewitnesses. This is fiction, not witness testimony. More to the point, there is no reason whatever to believe Mark imagined this event occurred anywhere near the Passover—in fact his narrative makes that impossible. "This is a remote place," he has the Disciples say "and it's already very late," so they recommend to Jesus that he "send the people away so that they can go to the surrounding countryside and villages and buy themselves something to eat." But *they could not do that* if the Passover was at hand: buying and selling would be illegal at sundown. And it could only be described as a "remote" place if it would take quite a long time to walk anywhere even to buy anything (Mark says Jesus and gang had to use a boat even to get there!).
>
> There is no evidence whatsoever here that Mark imagined the grass was green because it was Passover; and as we already saw, quite a lot of evidence against his doing so. In actual fact you could probably find green grass by the Sea of Galilee all year round back then; certainly for a great many months out of any given year; and Mark wasn't from there so he wouldn't know when or where grass wouldn't be green anyway (and worse, the word he chose overlaps with pale and yellow). Mark probably contrived the detail for its symbolism (such as echoing the shepherd Psalm or the same trope found across the whole Bible, or simply to evoke a pleasant scene), not because he was there or anyone told him what color the grass was. Instead, McGrew just "invents" a fact (her own reason why Mark said there was green grass), then uses that as "evidence" of an amazing "coincidence." *And this inspired her whole book* . . .[59]

---

59. Carrier, "There Are No Undesigned Coincidences."

What do the Best Biblical Commentaries Say About the Green Grass in Mark 6:39?

Do commentaries on the Gospel of Mark provide support for McGrew's hypothesis? An internet search for the best commentaries on the Gospel of Mark uncovered a consensus among various sources regarding most books comprising the top five. Fortunately, a more extensive list of top commentaries turned up at Bestcommentsaries.com. An examination of commentaries with four or five out of five stars confirms that many commentators discuss the significance of what Mark meant when he used the word "green" in Mark 6:39. Following is a list of twenty-eight commentators with four or five stars and their commentary on the word "green." They appear in the order listed on Bestcommentsaries.com.[60]

1. R.T. France:

> The χλωρῷ χόρτῳ [green grass] probably fixes the time of the incident as spring, before the grass dries up and goes brown, though Mark's motive in mentioning it after the shepherd metaphor of v. 34 may be rather to allude to the shepherd's role in leading his flock to 'green pastures' in Ps. 23:2,5–6.[61]

2. William L. Lane:

> The reference to "the green grass" is not a contradiction to the description of the locale as "wilderness." The concept of the wilderness is broad enough to include pastures sufficient for the grazing of flocks, particularly after the winter rains. Yet the vivid description is most intelligible when read in the larger context provided by the introduction to the feeding narrative. The transformation of the desert into a place of refreshment and life through the power of God is an aspect of the wilderness tradition which is prominent in the prophets. By divine intervention the land of curse will become fat pastures where the sheep will be gathered and fed by the true shepherd (Ezek. 34:26 f., 29). The Lord who causes his people to recline in green pastures (Ps. 23:1) evokes the shepherd imagery of verse 34 and implies that the wilderness is already being changed into the land of fertility and rest.[62]

3. James R. Edwards:

---

60. "Best Commentaries on Mark."
61. France, *The Gospel of Mark*, 267.
62. Lane, *The Gospel of Mark*, 229.

Particular references to the green grass, specific numbers in the story, the type of basket used, plus the populist Zealot undercurrent all testify to a historical province of the story. It is hard to conceive of all four Gospels recording a story from OT motifs, as Pesch imagines.[63]

Edwards devotes pages 192 to 196 to commenting about the green grass, feeding the 5,000, and the seating arrangements. His conclusions are as follows:

1. Moses had arranged the Israelites in groups of 1,000, 500, 100, and 10 under their respective leaders (Exod. 18:25; Num. 31:14).

2. The arrangement certainly recalls God's miraculous provision for Israel in the wilderness.

3. It may hint at the eschatological gathering of God's people on the last day.

4. Jesus presides over the multitude like a Jewish father over the family meal.

On page 228, Edwards devotes one sentence to the green grass: "The first feeding was in springtime (the word 'green grass' [G. chloros, 6:39] means the light green of spring)."

4. Adela Yarbo Collins:

The Markan Jesus commands the disciples to have the crowd recline "on the green grass" (επι τω χλωρω χορτω). This simple but adequate support for the guests is analogous to the remark of Philostratus concerning the meal at which the Indian sages hosted a king, "And the earth strewed beneath them grass softer than any mattress."

This passage suggests that the eschatological community, living already in the last days, was to be organized in groups of thousands, hundreds, fifties, and tens while they were awaiting the messiah(s). The mention of groups of hundreds and fifties in v. 40 may be a hint that the crowd around Jesus represents and anticipates the eschatological community.

That Jesus asks the disciples to distribute the bread is reminiscent of the story about Elisha and the twenty barley loaves, in which Elisha asks his servant to serve the bread to the people.[64]

---

63. Edwards, *The Gospel According to Mark*, 195n45.
64. Collins, *Mark: A Commentary*, 324-26.

5. David E. Garland

> Psalm 23 also reverberates in the account of the feeding of the five thousand. Jesus has compassion on the people because they were like sheep without a shepherd, and his actions reflect the first line of the psalm, "The LORD is my shepherd" (see Isa. 40:10–11). The principal task of a shepherd is to bring sheep to food and water. Jesus is not like worthless shepherds who do not care that the people are perishing Jer. 23:1–2; Ezek. 34:1–10, Zech 11:15–17). He is the true shepherd (Ps. 95:7; Isa. 40:10–11; Jer. 23:3–4; Ezek. 34:11–31; Pss. Sol. 17:40), who feeds his sheep so that they may "not be in want." They do not get a cracker crumb or two but a full serving, which completely satiates their hunger. Jesus makes them lie down in green pastures (Mark 6:39; cf. Ps. 23:2). Readers might be startled to read that the crowd reclines on a carpet of green when twice Mark tells us that this is a desert (6:31–32, 35). The barren desert has suddenly become green as the shepherd finds good pasture for his flock beside the waters of the sea (Mark 6:32–33, 45; cf. Ps 23:2). Most importantly, however, Jesus restores their soul and guides them in right paths by teaching them (Mark 6:34; cf. Ps. 23:3).[65]

9b. [Additional: David E. Garland]

> 290. It is not an insignificant detail that Jesus commands that the sheep be ordered in companies and made to recline on the "green grass" (6:39), which recalls Ps 23:1–2, the Lord as shepherd "makes me lie down in green pastures . . ."
>
> 465. Having them sit on "the green" (Mark 6:39, "green grass," NIV) alludes to Ps 23:2a, "He makes me lie down in green pastures." The miracle presents Jesus as the good shepherd. This imagery is absent in the second feeding.[66]

6. Robert H. Stein

> "And he ordered them [the disciples] to have all [the people recline in companies on the green grass" (6:39). To "recline" or "sit down" (ἀνακλῖναι, anaklinai) was the normal position for eating a banquet meal (Luke 12:37) and is used with respect to the messianic banquet in Matt. 8:11/Luke 13:29. Note the disciples' role in carrying out Jesus's command and later in the distribution of the miraculous food. Here, as in their mission (6:6b–13),

---

65. Garland, *Mark*, 255–56.
66. Garland, *A Theology of Mark's Gospel*, 290, 465.

they serve as extensions of Jesus's ministry. The mention of "the green grass" (τῷ χλωρῷ χόρτῳ, *to chloro chorto*) has drawn a great deal of comment. Some see this as a sign that the messianic age had arrived and the desert was now blossoming (Isa. 35:1; 2 Bar. 29.5–8; Marcus 2000: 408; contra Schweizer 1970: 139); others see it as a personal and thus historical reminiscence (V. Taylor 1952:321); still others see it as a reflection of Jesus's role as a shepherd leading his sheer to green pastures (Ps. 23:2; Pesch 1980a: 350; Guelich 1989: 341). The last interpretation encounters difficulty in that the actual verbal correspondence between "green pastures" (*Tómov xlóns, topon chloes*; Ps. 23:2 [22:2 LXX]) and "green grass" (χλωρῷ χόρτῳ) is not great. If this reference is historical, then the event must have taken place in the spring, near the time of Passover (cf. John 6:4, 10), since green grass cannot be found in the countryside during the rest of the year. Mark provides his readers with no indication as to how he wanted this reference to be interpreted. Thus, although the feeding of the five thousand should not be interpreted as a "Lord's Supper" (Pesch 1980a: 352–53; Gnilka 1978: 261), its similarities (cf. 6:41) would later bring to mind the Lord's Supper, and both would call the readers' attention to the future messianic banquet.[67]

7. John R. Donahue:

> *rest* for a while: The verb for "rest" (*anapausasthe*) may allude to the Greek text of Ps 23:2 (22:2 LXX) where the shepherd cares for the psalmist by restful waters (lit. "water of rest" [*anapauseos*]). Other possible allusions to this psalm are the green grass (Ps 23:2 [22:2]; Mark 6:39) and the provision of a meal by the shepherd (Ps 23:5 [22:5]; Mark 6:41–42). "Rest" is also used for the land promised to the people after the wilderness wandering (Exod 33:1–14; Deut 12:9–10; Josh 1:13; Jer 31:2). In Matt 11:28–29 Jesus promises rest to all who are weary, and in Heb 4:9–11 eschatological rest from toils and persecution is promised to God's people.[68]

8. Joel Marcus:

> No commentary (*Mark*, 2009)

---

67. Stein, *Mark*, 315.
68. Donahue, *The Gospel of Mark*, 204n31.

9. Robert A. Guelich:

> It may be going too far to take the "green grass" (τῷ χλωρῷ χόρτῳ; cf. John 6:10) as an allusion to the messianic age when the "desert will blossom" (Friedrich, *TZ* 20 [1964] 18–20) or as a vivid recollection of an eyewitness account.[69]

10. Robert Horton Gundry:

> Green grass implies springtime (cf. the reference to Passover in John 6:4), though grass may stay green in sheltered and well watered spots on into early summer. We should not overinterpret the green grass as symbolic of the Passover or of apocalyptic fertility. Mark gives us no reason to think of more than a suitable cushion on which to recline.[70]

11. Darrell L. Bock:

> The green grass possibly points to spring time when grass grew on the desert hills of Galilee. These are very vivid details. The scene has a serene, pastoral feel (Ps. 23:1–2), even though it is not yet clear where the food will come from . . . The gathering in fifties and hundreds partially echoes the Mosaic camp of the wilderness (Exod 18:21–1000, 500, 100, 10; also CD 13:1–8 . . . A new exodus is taking place. This is the second Moses.[71]

12. Mark L. Strauss:

> However, in the spring of the year, when this event apparently took place (cf. v.39, "green grass"), the Jordan would have had more water in it. 33–34.
>
> Mark notes the grass was green (v.39), perhaps to invoke the image of the Lord as the Shepherd who brings the sheep to feed in green pastures (Ps 32:1–2). Historically, the green grass suggests that the incident took place in the . . .[72]

---

69. Guelich, *Mark 1–8*, 341.
70. Gundry, *Mark*, 331.
71. Bock, *Mark*, 213.
72. Strauss, *Mark*, 276.

13. C. Clifton Black:

> "Green" implies lush verdancy (Deut 12:2; Song 1:16; Ezek 6:13): memorably, the pastures in which the shepherd Lord makes his sheep lie down (Ps 23:2; cf. Mark 6:34b).[73]

14. Mary Healy:

> The green grass is not an accidental detail, but an allusion to the "green pastures" in which the Lord, the Good Shepherd, gives his people repose and sets a table before them, in the well-known psalm (Ps 23:2, 5). It also evokes the prophetic promise that God would transform the desert into a place of refreshment and life (Isa 35:1; Ezek 34:25–31).[74]

0. M. Eugene Boring:

> The green grass is not, or not merely a historical reflection of the time of year, but connects both to green pastures of the Ps 23 imagery already extensively used and to the blossoming of the desert/wilderness in which the "way of the Lord" is prepared (Isa 35:1; 40:3; 51:3).[75]

16. C.E.B. Cranfield:

> The mention of the green grass may perhaps point to the spring-time, but near streams of green grass might be found as late as July.[76]

17. Donald H. Juel:

> No comment (*The Gospel of Mark*, 1999)

18. Ryle, J.C.

> No comment (*St. Mark*, 1874).

19. Francis J. Moloney:

> The starkness of Mark's story-telling seems to waver for a moment as he indicates that these companies are to sit "upon the

---

73. Black, *Mark*.
74. Healy, *The Gospel of Mark*, 128.
75. Boring, *Mark: A Commentary*, 186.
76. Cranfield, *The Gospel According to St. Mark*, 218.

green grass" (v. 39). This detail is not added for color; it recalls Ps 23:1: "The Lord is my shepherd, and nothing I shall want. In green fields he leads me." Jesus had compassion upon the crowd, regarding them as sheep without a shepherd (6:34, with its reference to Num 27:17 and Ezek 34:5–6), and now acts as shepherd to them.[77]

20. Pheme Perkins:

The vivid description of the scene, including the reference to the green grass (chloros chortos), which indicates spring time, suggests eyewitness memory.[78]

21. David Rhoads:

No commentary (*Mark as a Story*, 1999)

22. Mary Ann Beavis:

In Mark, this story is one of two where Jesus provides food for an astonishingly large crowd (cf. 8:1–10). The first feeding takes place in Jewish territory, the second in the gentile region of the Decapolis (cf. 7:31). The Jewishness of the first feeding is underlined by the exodus imagery that underlies the narrative. Like Moses, Jesus has compassion on the crowd because they are like sheep without a shepherd (cf. Num. 27:17). The phrase from Torah recalls the story of the appointment of Joshua (in Greek. Iēsous) as Moses's successor: someone "who shall go out before them and come in before them, . . . and at his word they shall go out, and at his word they shall come in, both he and all the Israelites with him, the whole congregation" (Num. 27:17a, 21b). The shepherd imagery is enhanced by the detail in Mark 6:39 that the people were instructed to recline on the green grass. For members of the audience familiar with the Palestinian climate. the reference to greenery situates the incident in the rainy season, October to early May. More than simply local color, this vivid detail evokes the "green pastures" of Ps. 23 and the blooming wilderness in the "way of the Lord," the new exodus (Isa. 35:1; 40:3; 51:3; Boring 2006, 186); in the context of a feeding miracle, it recalls the creation of the "green plants" for food in Genesis (1:30; 9:3). Most prominently, the provision of bread for a hungry crowd in the desert (Mark 6:35) echoes Exod.16;

---

77. Moloney, *The Gospel of Mark*, 131.
78. Perkins, *Mark*.

as the Israelites grumble to Moses and Aaron over lack of food (16:2–3), so the disciples urge Jesus to send the people away to buy something to eat and challenge him when he tells them to feed the crowd themselves: "Shall we leave and buy two hundred denarii worth of bread and give it to them to eat?" (Mark 6:36–37). In both stories, two kinds of food (manna and quails, bread and fish) are provided, the people's hunger is satisfied, and there is extra left over (Exod. 16:18: Mark 6:42–43).[79]

23. Ben Witherington III:

Though a deserted place, this is no desert, for we are told of the lush green grass (thus also indicating a time in the spring when the previous fall's grain supplies would be low at best)...

We are told that some five thousand men ate at this messianic banquet in the wilderness, which was indeed an enormous crowd, and all the more so if women and children were also present, as is likely (cf. Matt. 14:21). In fact, this would have well exceeded the population of the city of Capernaum (about two thousand people at that time). Perhaps we should think, as Lane suggests, that Isa. 25:6–9, which refers to the messianic one feasting with his people in the wilderness, is echoed here.[80]

24. Daniel J. Harrington:

No commentary (*Meet St. Mark Today*, 2011)

25. Vincent J. Taylor:

Many commentators suggest that the reference to the green grass points to the springtime, and thus to the Passover season; cf. Gould, 118; Swete, 133; Lagrange, 169; Plummer, 173; Allen, IOO; Turner, 19; Bartlet, 200. The inference, while probable, is not certain since green grass might be found in sheltered places and near streams as late as July. Cf. Schmidt, 191. Dalman, SSW, 174 f., describe the grass, not as a grass-plot, but as the exuberant wild growth of herbs which, in the spring and throughout most of the rainy season, cover the uncultivated ground in the district about the lake and even in the mountains.[81]

---

79. Beavis, *Mark*, 106.
80. Witherington III, *The Gospel of Mark*, 219–20.
81. Taylor, *The Gospel According to St. Mark*, 323.

26. Morna D. Hooker:

> The reference to the green grass has often been used in attempts to calculate the length of Jesus' ministry since grass is green in Palestine only in the spring: since Mark's arrangement of material is not necessarily chronological, however, this cannot be done. Possibly the phrase is meant to remind us that in the messianic age, the desert will be fertile (Isa. 35.1). It is appropriate that Jesus should feed the people in a fertile spot.[82]

27. R. Kent Hughes

> [No commentary] (*Mark: Jesus, Servant and Savior Volume 1* 1989)

28. Eckhard J. Schnabel:

> And the reference to the 'green grass' (v. 39) indicates that the time was spring, before grass turned brown in the summer heat, and thus a time when the village people would have just about consumed the harvest of the previous year.[83]

Finally, another option for readers is to employ a phrase and word search in Google Books:

1. Green grass
2. Mark 6:39
3. Psalm 23

Numerous writers, including many well-known commentators, concur that Mark 6 deliberately echoes Psalm 23. For example, BibleRef has an entry titled, "What does Mark 6:39 mean?" which declares:

> The note about the green grass continues the sheep and shepherd motif (Mark 6:34). Jesus had intended to take the Twelve away to rest, but He can't abandon the crowd. As our shepherd, Jesus gives us nourishment, safety, and peace (Psalm 23). He sacrifices Himself for His sheep and defends us against enemies (John 10:11–12).
>
> It is no coincidence that the greatest earthly king Israel ever had started as a shepherd boy (1 Samuel 16:11). David's years in the fields taught him responsibility and leadership. He learned how to calm his charges (1 Samuel 16:14–23) and how to protect

---

82. Hooker, *The Gospel According to Saint Mark*, 166.
83. Schnabel, *Mark*, 151–52.

them (1 Samuel 17:34–36). Most importantly, as a boy responsible for a good part of his family's livelihood that was regularly threatened by lions and bears, he learned to rely on God (1 Samuel 17:37).[84]

Multiple journal articles, dissertations, lectures, sermons, and podcasts reinforce the consensus that Mark 6 references Psalm 23. One notable example is a dissertation by Jonathan Bi Fan Cai, who completed his 2011 PhD thesis, "Jesus the Shepherd: A Narrative-Critical Study of Mark 6:30–44" at the Catholic University of America. He addresses Mark's mention of the green grass in the following passage:

> On the green pasture, the sheep now have their own compassionate shepherd. The situation of "sheep without a shepherd" has been rectified. As discussed earlier in v. 31, the phrase ἐπὶ τῷ χλωρῷ χόρτῳ ("on the green grass") alludes to Ps 23:1–2 (LXX 22:1–2) where Yhwh provides an eternal rest for the psalmist. The vivid description of the green grass then may allude to the eschatological change of the wilderness into the land of rest for the people of God in the eschaton. Stein argues that such an allusion is unlikely because "the actual verbal correspondence between 'green pastures' (*Tómov xlóns*) and 'green grass' (χλωρῷ χόρτῳ) is not great." But his argument misses the point because in an allusion "the degree of verbal correspondence between a given passage and the source to which it is said to allude is somewhat less than that of a quotation and may, in fact, be virtually absent." Thus the green grass here is not merely coincidental; it works perfectly with the shepherd-sheep imagery in v. 34. It makes very clear the picture of a good shepherd who tends passionately for his sheep. Mark continues to develop on this OT allusion in v. 41 to show Jesus as the shepherd providing a meal for his flock (Ps 23:5a [22:5a]). By working in the green grass to be part of the wilderness motif, Mark intricately weaves in the theme of Psalm 23 as the secondary line to support his claim that Jesus is a shepherd appointed by God (cf. Isa 40:11).[85]

Readers are invited to employ a search engine on the internet or WorldCat to discover how voluminous the literature on the subject is.[86]

To summarize: Professor Dale Allison's suggestion that the reference to green grass in Mark 6:39 may be intended to evoke Psalm 23 is very

---

84. Bibleref.com, "Mark 6:39."
85. Cai, "Jesus the Shepherd," 49–50. He modifies Stein, *Mark*, 315.
86. Cai, "Jesus the Shepherd"; Kim, "Exegesis: Mark 6:30–44."

much a mainstream view in scholarly circles. In addition, McGrew's assertion that the grass would have *only* been green in spring (when the Passover took place) is highly questionable: several commentators pointed out that it could also have been green in early summer.

Mark Goodacre and the Feeding of the Five Thousand: A Fatal Difficulty for McGrew's Hypothesis of Undesigned Coincidences

Similarities between two gospel narratives of the same event suggest they have the same source and origin. However, differences between narratives suggest that one (or both) narratives were partially composed of an independent source. One striking example of a contradiction/difference between the gospel narratives is Luke's account of Jesus Feeding the Five Thousand. This narrative contrasts with Mark and challenges the historical reliability of the two texts: Mark 6:30–35 and Luke 9:10–12 (see table 7). As readers also see, this example refutes McGrew's claim that different gospel accounts of the same episode dovetail nicely with one another and provide each other with mutual support. This claim is central to the hypothesis of Undesigned Coincidences, which she champions.

Table 7. Parallel Texts: Mark 6 and Luke 9 (ESV)

Mark 6	Luke 9
[30] The apostles returned to Jesus and told him all that they had done and taught. [31] And he said to them, *"Come away by yourselves to a desolate place and rest a while."* For many were coming and going, and they had no leisure even to eat.	[10] When the apostles returned, they reported to Jesus what they had done. Then he took them with him and *they withdrew by themselves to a town called Bethsaida*,
[31] And he said to them, "Come away by yourselves to a desolate place and rest a while." For many were coming and going, and they had no leisure even to eat.	
[32] And they went away in the boat *to a desolate place by themselves.*	Then he took them with him and *they withdrew by themselves to a town called Bethsaida,*

Mark 6	Luke 9
[33] Now many saw them going and recognized them, and they ran there on foot from all the towns and got there ahead of them.	[11] but the crowds learned about it and followed him. He welcomed them and spoke to them about the kingdom of God, and healed those who needed healing.
[34] When he went ashore he saw a great crowd, and he had compassion on them, because they were like sheep without a shepherd. And he began to teach them many things.	He welcomed them and spoke to them about the kingdom of God, and healed those who needed healing.
[35] And when it grew late, his disciples came to him and said, "This is a desolate place, and the hour is now late.	[12] Now the day began to wear away, and the twelve came and said to him, "Send the crowd away to go into the surrounding villages and countryside to find lodging and get provisions, for we are here in a desolate place."
	[13] But he said to them, "You give them something to eat." They said, "We have no more than five loaves and two fish—unless we are to go and buy food for all these people."

Nineteen years before *Hidden in Plain View* was released, Mark Goodacre, the current Frances Hill Fox Professor of Religious Studies at Duke University, published an article in *New Testament Studies* that engaged with the miracle of the Feeding of the Five Thousand. Goodacre specializes in the New Testament and Christian Origins. He earned his MA, MPhil, and DPhil at the University of Oxford. Goodacre is considered one of the leading experts on the intertextuality of the Gospels. In a six-part podcast, McGrew engages Goodacre's hypothesis of "editorial fatigue." Her podcast page says

> This series shows the enormous implausibility of Goodacre's editorial fatigue theories.
>
> Lay readers should be encouraged that so-called experts in Gospels studies do not have some special "line" on interpretive truth about the Gospels which allows them to discern that the evangelists are making factual changes in the stories. . .[87]

---

87. McGrew, "Editorial Fatigue." YouTube, May 26, 2024. video, https://www.youtube.com/watch?v=TXPCzlzXNBI. Interested readers may wish to listen to her six-part analysis.

McGrew holds nothing back. She considers Goodacre a "so-called expert." Readers must be the final judge of her evaluation.

He proposed that Luke and Matthew, the Gospel authors copying Mark, experienced "editorial fatigue." His paper supports Markan priority and provides numerous examples illustrating the differences between the gospel narratives. Crucially, he supplies a definition of the term "editorial fatigue":

> Editorial fatigue is a phenomenon that will inevitably occur when a writer is heavily dependent on another's work. In telling the same story as his predecessor, a writer makes changes in the early stages which he is unable to sustain throughout. Like continuity errors in film and television, examples of fatigue will be unconscious mistakes, small errors of detail which naturally arise in the course of constructing a narrative. They are interesting because they can betray an author's hand, most particularly in revealing to us the identity of his sources.[88]

Later, he provides several examples of "editorial fatigue." Highly relevant to this text is his evaluation of Luke's feeding the five thousand:

> The best example of the phenomenon, though, is Luke's version of the Feeding of the Five Thousand (Matt 14.13–21//Mark 6.30–44//Luke 9.10–17). In spite of, or perhaps because of, the familiarity of the story, a feature in Luke's account is sometimes [p. 51] missed. (21) Mark says that the disciples go away with Jesus into a desert place (εἰς ἔρημον τόπον, Mark 6.31). Luke, however, resets the scene in 'a city (πόλις) called Bethsaida'. (22) This then causes all sorts of problems when Luke goes on to agree with Mark:
>
> Mark 6.35b–36: 'And when the hour was already becoming late, his disciples having approached him were saying, "This is a desert place (ἔρημος ἐστιν ὁ τόπος) and already the hour is late; send them away so that they may go into the surrounding country and villages to buy something for themselves to eat."'
>
> Luke 9.12: 'And the day began to draw in and the twelve having approached him said, "Send away the crowd, so that they may go into the surrounding villages and countryside to lodge and find provisions because we are here in a desert place (ὧδε ἐν ἐρήμῳ τόπῳ ἐσμέν)."'
>
> The adjective used by both Mark and Luke is ἔρημος, lonely, desolate, abandoned. Clearly it is nonsense to say 'we are here in a desolate place' when in the Lucan setting they are not. After

---

88. Goodacre, "Fatigue in the Synoptics," 46.

all, if the crowd were in a city, they would not need to go to the surrounding villages and countryside to find food and lodging. (23) Further, since in Bethsaida food and lodging ought to be close to hand, Luke's comment that the day was drawing to a close lacks any relevance and, consequently, the feeding lacks the immediate motive that it has in Mark. In short, by relocating the Feeding of the Five Thousand, without being able to sustain the new setting with its fresh implications throughout, Luke has spoilt the story. (24)

Footnotes:

21. It is seen by Goulder, *Luke*, 433, though he treats this as an example of 'muddle', on which see my *Goulder and the Gospels* (JSNTSup, 133; Sheffield: JSOT Press, 1996), Chapter 11.

22. Some witnesses read κώμην, and others τόπον ἔρημον, but this simply shows that some scribes also felt our difficulty. The readings are discussed by Streeter, *The Four Gospels: A Study of Origins* (London: Macmillan, 1924), 569 and Creed, *The Gospel According to St Luke* (London: Macmillan, 1930), 128.

23. On the lodging element, which is unique to Luke, see Cadbury, *The Making of Luke-Acts* (London: SPCK, 1958), 250, and 'Luke's Interest in Lodging', *JBL* 45 (1926), 305-22. It is actually another possible example of careless editing on Luke's part: having added a reference to lodging, he is unable to develop this idea in the remainder of the pericope which naturally focuses on the feeding element (cf. the reference to 'prayers' as well as 'fasting' in Luke 5.33, an element that has dropped out in Luke 5.34//Mark 2.19; cf. Goulder, *Luke*, 109).

24. Explanations for the incongruity are lacking in the commentaries. The mystery is why Luke would want to relocate to Bethsaida. Nolland, *Word Biblical Commentary* Vol. 35A, *Luke 1-9.20* (Dallas: Word, 1989), 440, says: 'No really satisfactory explanation has yet been offered.' Marshall, *The Gospel of Luke, A Commentary on the Greek Text* (Exeter: Paternoster, 1978), 360, attempts one: 'The indications are that they are further round the E side of the lake than Bethsaida, possibly in Gentile territory (the Decapolis) where Jews might not be sure of a welcome.'[89]

In brief, "In Luke, this event, the feeding of five thousand, occurs at the town of Bethsaida—hardly an *isolated* and *remote place*." Here, Mark and Luke have an apparent contradiction over a significant element of the story: *where did the miracle occur?* If Mark and Luke were based on the

89. Goodacre, "Fatigue in the Synoptics," 50-51.

recollections of two eyewitnesses, we would expect the details they provide to dovetail nicely with one another, as McGrew proposes. Instead, we find two large jigsaw pieces that do *not* fit together: does the miracle occur in an isolated and remote place (as in Mark) or in the city of Bethsaida (as in Luke)? This kind of contradiction (difference?) is precisely the *opposite* of what the hypothesis of Undesigned Coincidences predicts.

What are the Most Likely Explanations for the Undesigned Coincidences in the Gospel Accounts of the Feeding of the Five Thousand?

The Gospel Authors Had Access to Previous Authors

If the Gospel authors had access to earlier authors, then what the later authors wrote was not a coincidence, as it is explainable in terms of literary dependence. Similarly, if the authors had access to identical oral traditions, it was a deliberate choice to include, exclude, edit, or redact the received information. An analysis of Matthew and Luke confirms that they both had access to Mark, and many scholars believe that John did, too. Therefore, the most logical explanation is that Matthew, Luke, and John decided to omit the word "green" from Mark's narrative for reasons unknown.

The Green Grass: Alternative Explanations

McGrew argues that the coincidence of Mark saying the grass was "green" is undesigned. The question that requires asking is how she knows. Where is her evidence? McGrew's opinion must be respected. However, other possibilities exist:

1. Mark added that the grass was green because he thought it would sound ornamental.[90]
2. Mark was making a theological allusion.
3. Mark was recalling Psalm 23.
4. Mark was recalling the Exodus from Egypt.
5. Mark was envisaging the messianic banquet.
6. Mark had multiple ideas in mind when he wrote the word "green."
7. Mark's remark that the grass was green was merely a coincidence.

---

90. Brown, *A Handbook to Old Testament Exegesis*, 181.

8. Mark wrote "green" to indicate the deserted place was not a *sandy* desert.
9. The green grass setting confirms that this is a deserted place. It is "a place that was not cultivated but was sufficient for flocks of sheep to be fed."[91]
10. Mark was unaware of Jerusalem's geography and climate. He wrote "green" simply because grass is usually green.
11. Mark had motives of his own that may forever elude us. In any case, it is circular reasoning to say that John's later retelling of the story reaffirms Mark's earlier tradition.
12. Satan deceived Mark into writing "green."

What Can We Know for a Fact About Mark's Account of the Green Grass?

The *Oxford Dictionary*, a gold standard reference, defines a "fact" as follows:

1. A thing that is known or proved to be true
2. Information used as evidence or as part of a report or news article.
3. The truth about events as opposed to interpretation.

According to the *Oxford Dictionary*, the green grass recorded in Mark 6:39 cannot be treated as a fact. (1) The claim narrated by Mark is *not* a thing known or proved to be true. (2) The information from Mark is unverifiable. Scholars generally acknowledged that Mark's Gospel was composed about forty years after the crucifixion and outside the land of Palestine. (3) Since the truth about the events recorded in chapter 6 of Mark's Gospel is unknown, it cannot be subject to absolute interpretation. Furthermore, it bears repeating:

1. It is not a fact that Mark *had* an independent source.
2. It is not a fact that Mark *is* an independent source.
3. It is not a fact that Mark's reportage is historical or reliable. Perhaps he was writing to develop the story further or make a theological point.
4. It is not a fact that Mark or his sources were well-informed. Presumably, he reported hearsay evidence and oral stories that had evolved over the previous thirty years.
5. It is not a fact that the Gospel authors did not makeup things.

91. Kostyuk, "The Function of Military Language," 163.

6. It is not a fact that Mark had highly accurate reports from people close to the facts.
7. It is not a fact that Mark was habitually honest.
8. It is not a fact that a Christian named Mark wrote Mark's Gospel.
9. It is not a fact that John is an independent source.
10. It is not even a fact that John's reportage is historical or reliable. Perhaps he was writing to develop the story further or make a theological point.
11. It is not a fact that John or his sources were well-informed. Presumably, he was reporting hearsay evidence and evolving oral stories about events approximately sixty years earlier.
12. It is not a fact that John had highly accurate reports from people close to the facts.
13. It is not a fact that John is habitually honest.
14. It is not even a fact that a disciple named John wrote John's Gospel.

Readers are encouraged to contemplate the following thoughts:
1. Just because an author writes something down does not mean he or she knows it to be true.
2. Writers, past and present, often make up things.
3. One gospel author should not be used to explain what another author means. Do proponents of the hypothesis of Undesigned Coincidences believe that John, writing almost twenty to thirty years after Mark, understood what Mark meant to say? (Did John ever meet Mark?)

One of the more challenging aspects of Bible study is comprehending what the author of the text means. What do they mean? Who says so? In Woody Allen's movie "Annie Hall," there is a famous scene in which Woody Allen's character is in a queue with his date, Annie, waiting to see a movie. Standing behind them, someone is expounding on Marshall McLuhan, a famous author. Allen thinks the man is an idiot and has no idea what he is talking about. Then, he leaves the line to speak directly to the camera. Immediately following, the man criticized by Allen comes and speaks to the camera in his defense. Allen resolves the dispute by pulling McLuhan from behind a counter to tell the man that his interpretation is wrong.

> Woody Allen: You don't know anything about Marshall McLuhan's work—

Man: Really? Really? I happen to teach a class at Columbia called TV, Media and Culture, so I think that my insights into Mr. McLuhan, well, have a great deal of validity.

Woody Allen: Oh, do you?

Man: Yeah.

Woody Allen: Oh, that's funny, because I happen to have Mr. McLuhan right here. Come over here for a second?

Man: Oh—

Woody Allen: Tell him.

Marshall McLuhan: I heard, I heard what you were saying. You, you know nothing of my work. How you ever got to teach a course in anything is totally amazing.

Woody Allen: Boy, if life were only like this.[92]

Allen's final words, "Boy, if life were only like this" carry a profound significance in our discourse.

How do readers know with certitude that Mark is reporting the truth? Could Mark have written in verse 39 that the grass was green, based on erroneous information? Determining the truth is highly interpretive and subjective on both sides of the religious aisle. Advocates of the hypothesis of Undesigned Coincidences cite the word "green" in Mark 6:39 for a distinctly theological purpose: to support their claim that the Bible is reliable (truthful) in its reportage. Therefore, the Bible is using the Bible to prove that it is truthful. This strategy is known as circular reasoning.

Why are Certain Words and Verses in Mark Omitted from Matthew and Luke's Accounts?

An undesigned coincidence occurs when one account of one event omits a piece or pieces of information, which is filled in, usually incidentally, by a different narrative, which helps to answer inquiries raised by the first. Cumulatively, undesigned coincidences lend support to the reliability of the Gospels:

1. If the overlap between two Gospel testimonies is correctly explained by deliberate design, such as collusion, one account's copying the other, or both accounts' copying a common source containing the overlapping information, then the cumulative case for undesigned coincidences is significantly weakened, as even proponents admit.[93]

92. "If Life Were Only Like This", *Annie Hall*, directed by Woody Allen (1977; Los Angeles, California: United Artists, 1981), DVD.

93. McGrew, "Undesigned Coincidences and Coherence for an Hypothesis," 801–28.

2. However, if the Gospels are independent accounts of Jesus' life, readers can safely assume they will not be direct copies of one another.

3. The McGrews argue that the Gospels are not identical but interlocking accounts of Jesus. By "interlocking," they mean that there are differences between the accounts. However, these differences are complementary and do not present discrepancies or contradictions.

4. The interlocking variations between the gospels illuminate, explain, and corroborate the different accounts. The most unusual attribute of these interlocking differences is that they appear entirely unintended.

5. The many small ways the Gospels interlock with and complement one another are too subtle and—on the surface—unimportant to have been planned by the four authors.

6. The corroboration of details in the Gospels is cumulative.

7. This "evidence" supports a cumulative argument for the Gospels' reliability. When the reader adds up all these undesigned coincidences, they create a picture of eyewitnesses giving accurate testimony.

However, the preceding argument overlooks something equally significant: omissions. Constructing a cumulative argument *against* undesigned coincidences from omissions in the gospel narratives is possible. Discussions about feeding the five thousand frequently appear in articles, lectures, and podcasts about undesigned coincidences. Detractors and skeptics express doubts about this narrative when comparing Mark to the later three remaining Gospels. Mark's report includes "facts" not mentioned in Matthew, Luke, or John:

1. And he said to them, "Come away by yourselves to a desolate place and rest a while." For many were coming and going, and they had no leisure even to eat (Mark 6:31, ESV).

2. Send them away to go into the surrounding countryside and villages and buy themselves something to eat (Mark 6:36, ESV).

3. So they sat down in groups, by hundreds and by fifties. (Mark 6:40, ESV).[94]

4. And those who ate the loaves were five thousand men (Mark 6:44, ESV).[95]

---

94. Aus, *Feeding the Five Thousand*, explains, "Yet the crowd of necessity had to be divided up into groups, for example by hundred and fifties, to facilitate the distribution of the bread and fish. The 5000 men could not have been fed by their standing all in one line. A symbolic progression of terms is not intended." (79n343)

95. Readers must note that *some, but not all*, of the alleged facts in Mark, are in

The Gospels are consistent and inconsistent with feeding the five thousand narratives. Noteworthily, and pointed out by Bible commentators, the Gospels share several features. Nonetheless, skeptics and detractors of the Gospels' reliability point out that differences exist between them. Additionally, in many ways, the gospel narratives here and elsewhere do not (e.g., the resurrection narratives). Moreover, several differences are more significant than the publicized similarities or undesigned coincidences.

Mark is "inconsistent" with the three later Gospels in numerous ways. However, believers can arbitrarily group features that interest them and forget those without interest. In short, the alleged similarities or undesigned coincidences between the Gospels are false or subjective.

Why, presuming the Gospel authors were familiar with Mark or his oral sources, would these writers cumulatively omit material from Mark? Why, if these authors were under the guidance of the "Holy Ghost," did they cumulatively omit passages and words from Mark? Or was it just an undesigned coincidence that Matthew, Luke, and John omitted these verses? These questions from silence remain unanswered by proponents of the hypothesis of Undesigned Coincidences. Any attempted answer is neither verifiable nor falsifiable.

Biblical Criticism Revisited

McGrew asks her readers to take the hypothesis of Undesigned Coincidences "for a test drive while setting aside the apparatus of critical scholarship." Her thinking seemingly resembles that of an 1893 encyclical authored by Pope Leo XIII: *Providentissimus Deus* ("On the Study of Holy Scripture.") His twenty-five-part letter engages with and repudiates the errors of Rationalists and "higher critics." Relevant excerpts are listed below (numbers in brackets refer to paragraphs within the encyclical):

1. Now, we have to meet the Rationalists, true children and inheritors of the older heretics, who, trusting in their turn to their own way of thinking, have rejected even the scraps and remnants of Christian belief which had been handed down to them. (10)

2. Hence it follows that all interpretation is foolish and false which either makes the sacred writers disagree one with another, or is opposed to the doctrine of the Church. (14)

3. The Church, "by reason of her wonderful propagation, her distinguished sanctity and inexhaustible fecundity in good, her Catholic unity, and her

---

Matthew or Luke, albeit in slightly different forms. However, omissions exist there, too.

unshaken stability, *is herself a great and perpetual motive of credibility, and an unassailable testimony to her own Divine mission."* (17)

4. But since the divine and infallible magisterium of the Church rests also on the authority of Holy Scripture, *the first thing to be done is to vindicate the trustworthiness of the sacred records* at least as human documents, from which can be clearly proved, as from primitive and authentic testimony, the Divinity and the mission of Christ our Lord, the institution of a hierarchical Church and the primacy of Peter and his successors. (17)

5. *There has arisen, to the great detriment of religion, an inept method, dignified by the name of the "higher criticism,"* which pretends to judge of the origin, integrity and authority of each Book from internal indications alone. (17)

6. To look upon it in any other light will be to open the door to many evil consequences. It will make the enemies of religion much more bold and confident in attacking and mangling the Sacred Books; and this vaunted "higher criticism" will resolve itself into the reflection of the bias and the prejudice of the critics. (17)

7. [H]istorical investigation should be made with the utmost care. (17)

8. In the second place, *we have to contend against those who, making an evil use of physical science, minutely scrutinize the Sacred Book* in order to detect the writers in a mistake, and to take occasion to vilify its contents. (18)[96]

Readers should examine the entire encyclical.

Earlier in this chapter, the Maximal Data approach was discussed. As readers have seen, McGrew is a leading advocate of this approach, arguing for the truthfulness of the New Testament. Several vital points of hers align with Pope Leo XIII's encyclical.

1. The Gospels are eyewitness reports of Jesus' life, death, and resurrection (e.g., John's Gospel) or (in the case of the Synoptic Gospels written by Matthew, Mark, and Luke) as biographical reports, written only twenty-five to thirty years after Jesus' death.

2. The Gospels are based on interviews with eyewitnesses who knew Jesus.

3. The Gospel authors are presenting reportage of actual historical events.

---

96. Leo XIII, "Encyclical *Providentissimus Deus.*", para. 10, 14, 17, 18.

4. "An undesigned coincidence provides reason to believe that both (all) of the statements that contribute to it are truthful."[97]
5. The "Undesigned Coincidences" validate the Maximal Data approach by providing evidence that the Gospels were composed of independent and reliable sources that fit together like pieces of a puzzle.
6. Pope Leo XIII attacked what he called the "higher criticism," arguing that it was harmful to religion. Similarly, McGrew invites her readers to take this hypothesis of Undesigned Coincidences "for a test drive while setting aside the apparatus of critical scholarship."[98]

Most noteworthy, this Christian apologetic assertion (1) is grounded in assumptions, guesses, and speculations and (2) employs an argument from silence. Perhaps, most significantly and disturbingly, the hypothesis of Undesigned Coincidences does not allow the texts (e.g., the Gospels) to speak for themselves. Does Mark 6 parallel Psalm 23, 2 Kings 4: 38–44, or the Exodus motif? Moreover, could Mark have deliberately composed chapter 6 of his Gospel, employing parts of the Hebrew Bible as a blueprint/template, rather than accidentally generating an undesigned coincidence? The parallels are striking. Christian apologists, Bible commentators, theologians, and the Church seemingly imply that they, as guardians of the truth, are the only ones capable of explaining what the original authors of the text meant to say. However, this statement may be too harsh. Readers must be the final judges.

Conclusion

Proponents of the hypothesis of Undesigned Coincidences argue that mentioning "green grass" in Mark 6:39 is an important detail that needs an explanation. Why does Mark write "green grass"? Lydia McGrew asks her readers to take the hypothesis of Undesigned Coincidences "for a test drive while setting aside the apparatus of critical scholarship."[99] In other words, readers should avoid consulting any of the following sources:

1. Approximately 400 biblical commentaries on the Gospel of Mark[100]
2. Numerous theses or dissertations (see table 8 below)

---

97. McGrew, *Hidden in Plain View*, 13.
98. McGrew, *Hidden in Plain View*, 15.
99. McGrew, *Hidden in Plain View*, 17.
100. Alter, *A Thematic Access-Oriented Bibliography*, 275–93.

3. Books devoted to Mark 6:40–46 and related matters (Psalm 23; 2 Kgs. 4: 38–44, the Exodus). WorldCat identifies several relevant classifications:

    a. Bible. Mark Relation to the Old Testament
    b. Bible. Mark VI, 30–33 Criticism, Narrative
    c. Feeding of the five thousand (Miracle)
    d. Criticism. Interpretations, etc.
    e. Bible. Psalms, XXIII
    f. Bible. Psalms, XXIII Criticism, Interpretation,
    g. Shepherds in the Bible (see table 9 below)

4. Biblical studies of allusions, analogies, metaphors, or symbolism in the Bible
5. Peer-reviewed journal articles discussing the topic.

Readers can evaluate the merits of this approach for themselves. Moreover, readers must peruse table 8 and table 9.

Table 8: Theses and Dissertations about the Feeding of the Five Thousand

Randy Craig Alcorn, The Historical-Biblical Context of the Shepherd Theme. Thesis, Dissertation, 1979.
Jonathan Bi Fan Cai, Jesus the Shepherd: A Narrative-Critical Study of Mark 6:30–44. Thesis, Dissertation, 2011.
LeRoy A. Campbell, The Background and Significance of the Feeding of the Five Thousand. Thesis, Dissertation, 1930.
Robert M. Fowler, Loaves and Fishes: The Function of the Feeding Stories in the Gospel of Mark. Thesis, Dissertation, 1981. [Scholars Press, Chico, Calif., 1981]
Robert M. Fowler, The Feeding Stories in the Gospel of Mark. Thesis, Dissertation, 1978.
William Ellison Jones, The Feeding of the Multitude: A Theological Analysis of the History of its Interpretation. Thesis, Dissertation, Duke University, 1997
Younggwang Kim, Exegesis: Mark 6:30–44, Thesis, Dissertation, Liberty University, Lynchburg, Va., 2021.
Oleg Kostyuk, The Function of Military Language in the Feeding of the Five Thousand Narrative (Mark 6:30–44): A Narrative-Cognitive Study, Thesis Dissertation, Andrews University, 2020

Janice A. Kraus, The Blessing of the Loaves & Fishes: Popular Apprehensions of the Eucharist in the Fourth-Century Christianity: Hints from Imagery. Thesis, Dissertation, 1995.
Jae Pil Lee, The Feeding of the Five Thousand in the Gospel of Mark (6:30–44): The Significance of the Wilderness Location. Thesis, Dissertation, 2006.
Ian D. Mackay, John's Relationship with Mark: An Analysis of John 6 in the Light of Mark 6–8. Thesis, Dissertation, 2004; Mohr Siebeck, Tübingen, 2004.
Elijah Mahlangu, The Miracle of the Multiplication of the Loaves of Bread in John 6:1–15: A Survey and Assessment of Recent Research. Thesis, Dissertation, 1991 University of South Africa, Pretoria, 1991.
Anthony Joseph Marshall, The Incident of the Loaves: A Historical-Critical Exegesis of Mark 6:30–44 and 8:1–10, Thesis, Dissertation, 2013.
Ulysses S. Randall, The Philosophical Possibility and the Historicity of the Feeding of the Five Thousand. Thesis, Dissertation, Andover Newton Theological School, 1930.
Matthew Wade Umbarger, Leviathan the Fleeing Serpent and Five Loaves of Bread: The Feeding of the Five Thousand, the Messianic Banquet, and Their Biblical and Ugaritic Background. Thesis, Dissertation, 2006, Ben-Gurion University of the Negev, [Beer-Sheva], 2006
Jack W. Vancil, The Symbolism of the Shepherd in Biblical, Intertestamental, and New Testament Material, Thesis, Dissertation, 1975.
Jeffrey D. Veitch, Ruling Banquets: Herod's Birthday and the Feeding of the Five Thousand in Mark and Matthew, Graduate Theological Union, 2011.

Table 9: Books about the Feeding of the Five Thousand

Roger David Aus. *Feeding the Five Thousand: Studies in the Judaic Background of Mark 6:30–44 par. And John 6:1–15.* University Press of America, Lanham, MD. 2010
Kenneth E. Bailey. *The Good Shepherd: A Thousand-Year Journey from Psalm 23 to the New Testament.* InterVarsity, Downers Grove, 2014
Jonathan Gan. *The Metaphor of Shepherd in the Hebrew Bible: A Historical-Literary Reading.* University Press of America, Lanham, MD., 2007
Jogy Cheruvathoor George, *Metaphor of Shepherd in the Gospel of Mark.* Peter Lang, Frankfurt am Main, 2015.
Joseph A. Grassi. *Loaves and Fishes: The Gospel Feeding Narratives.* Liturgical Press, Collegeville, MN, 1991.

Edmund Little. *Echoes of the Old Testament in the Wine of Cana in Galilee (John 2:1–11) and the Multiplication of the Loaves and Fish (John 6:1–15): Towards an Appreciation.* J. Gabalda, Paris, 1998.
Ian D. Mackay. *John's Relationship with Mark: An Analysis of John 6 in Light of Mark 6–8.* Mohr Siebeck, Tübingen, 2004.
Walter A. Maier, Lutheran Church—Missouri Synod. *Form and Redaction Critical Analysis of the Gospel Accounts of the Feeding of the Five Thousand.* Commission on Theology and Church Relations, the Lutheran Church—Missouri Synod, St. Louis, 1973.
Geert van Oyen. *The Interpretation of the Feeding Miracles in the Gospel of Mark.* Wetenschappelijk Comité voor Godsdienstwetenschappen, Koninklijke Vlaamse Academie van België voor Wetenschappen en Kunsten, Brussel, 1999.
Eddy Dharmanand Savarimuthu. *Feeding Narratives in Mark.* GRIN Publishing, [Place of publication not identified], 2015.
James Silvester. *The Feeding of the Five-Thousand: An Exposition.* W. Barker, Portsmouth, 1922.

3

The Philip Controversy and Summary of Problems with the Hypothesis of Undesigned Coincidences

3.1 WHY DOES JOHN MENTION PHILIP IN HIS ACCOUNT?[1]

> 1 After this Jesus went away to the other side of the Sea of Galilee, which is the Sea of Tiberias. 2 And a large crowd was following him, because they saw the signs that he was doing on the sick. 3 Jesus went up on the mountain, and there he sat down with his disciples. 4 Now the Passover, the feast of the Jews, was at hand. 5 Lifting up his eyes, then, and seeing that a large crowd was coming toward him, *Jesus said to Philip, "Where are we to buy bread, so that these people may eat?"* 6 He said this to test him, for he himself knew what he would do. *7 Philip answered him, "Two hundred denarii worth of bread would not be enough for each of them to get a little."* 8 One of his disciples, Andrew, Simon Peter's brother, said to him, 9 "There is a boy here who has five barley loaves and two fish, but what are they for so many?" 10 Jesus said, "Have the people sit down." Now there was much grass in the place. So the men sat down, about five thousand in number (John 6:1–10, ESV).

---

1. McGrew, *Hidden in Plain View*, 107–13; Blunt, *Undesigned Coincidences*, 283.

A SECOND FREQUENTLY REFERENCED example of an alleged undesigned coincidence in the narratives of the feeding of the five thousand occurs in the Gospel of John. Jesus asks Philip where they can buy bread for five thousand people. This question strikes McGrew as strange. In her book, *Hidden in Plain View*, she rhetorically inquires, "Why Philip? . . . There is, in fact, no particular reason apparent in John for Jesus' selection of Philip for this question."[2] Almost one hundred and seventy years earlier, Blunt asked almost an identical question: "Why should this question have been directed to Philip in particular?"[3] Any answer given can only be a guess, hunch, or speculation from silence, as there is no way of verifying it. Blunt, the McGrews, and others offer various explanations. To begin with, however, they offer several caveats:

1. If we had the Gospel of St. John but not the other Gospels, we should see no special reason why Jesus's question should have been addressed to *Philip* in particular, and we would probably ascribe Jesus's choice of Philip to accident.[4]

2. If we had the other Gospels, but not that of St. John, the puzzle over Jesus's question to Philip would never have arisen, for these Gospels make no mention of the question having been addressed expressly to *Philip*.[5]

3. Philip was not one of the most prominent disciples.[6]

4. Philip was not one of the inner three (Peter, James, and John).[7]

5. Philip was not the treasurer of the group. That was Judas Iscariot.[8]

6. McGrew acknowledges that "It is possible that Philip was selected at random," although she rejects that opinion.[9]

Blunt and McGrew argue that an example of an undesigned coincidence is when Jesus uniquely asks Philip a question in John 6:5, supported by the information provided about Philip in Luke 9:10. In passing, Luke casually in passing mentions that "Philip was of Bethsaida." Therefore, this passage is considered undesigned and unplanned. This presumed fact is the

---

2. McGrew, *Hidden in Plain View*, 108.
3. Blunt, *Undesigned Coincidences*, 283.
4. Blunt, *Undesigned Coincidences*, 283.
5. Blunt, *Undesigned Coincidences*, 283.
6. McGrew, *Hidden in Plain View*, 108.
7. McGrew, *Hidden in Plain View*, 108.
8. McGrew, *Hidden in Plain View*, 108.
9. McGrew, *Hidden in Plain View*, 108.

"interlocking" key and undesigned coincidence that fits like a glove or a missing part in a puzzle.

1. This miracle of feeding the five thousand took place in a deserted area near the town/village of Bethsaida.
2. Philip was from Bethsaida.
3. It was appropriate for Jesus to direct his question to Philip.
4. Philip knew the neighborhood and most likely knew where bread could be purchased.
5. Therefore, it was logical for Jesus to ask Philip the question.

Roger Aus provides another answer.

> Jesus asks Philip in 6:5–6, "'Where are we to buy bread for these people to eat?'" 6) He said this to test him, for he himself knew what he was going to do." This reversal of the disciples' asking Jesus the same question in Mark 6:37b par. is due to the Fourth Evangelist. John also emphasizes Jesus' sovereign authority and foreknowledge elsewhere (cf. 2:25; 6:64; and 13:11).[10]

Moreover, a multitude of Christian apologists, Bible commentators, and theologians present a wide array of opinions and provisos, each offering a unique perspective on the question Jesus poses to Philip:

1. Jesus does not ask Philip or the other disciples where they can buy bread because they already know there is not enough bread in the nearby towns to feed 5,000 people.
2. Jesus' question to Philip holds a profound significance. It is not a mere inquiry about bread but a test of Philip's faith and understanding. [John 6:6 is clear: "He said this to test him, for he himself knew what he would do." In the Gospel of John, Jesus is the Son of God and knows everything.]
3. Jesus does not ask Philip or the other disciples where they can buy bread because Jesus knows he can perform a miracle and produce sufficient bread to feed 5,000 people.
4. Jesus does not ask Philip or the other disciples where they can buy bread because he wants to perform a miracle for his purposes.
5. Jesus does not ask Philip or the other disciples where they can buy bread because he genuinely wants them to buy bread.

---

10. Aus, *Feeding the Five Thousand*, 127.

6. Jesus employs the question to prepare and instruct his disciples (6:5–9, 12–13, 16–21; cf. 4:27–28).[11]

7. Jesus' question to Philip is intended as a learning opportunity to deepen his understanding and faith.

Background on the Apostle Philip

The name of the apostle Philip occurs sixteen times in the Christian Scriptures before Jesus' ascension. Significantly, McGrew writes, "Aside from the lists of the disciples and the passage in question, Philip comes up on only a few occasions, *all of them in John*." (Italics added for emphasis.)[12] Philip's name appears four times in the list of the twelve disciples (Mark 3:18; Matt. 10:3; Luke 6:14; Acts 1:13) and four more times in John's Gospel when Philip becomes a disciple (John 1:43, 45, 46, 48).

Only the Gospel of John tells the readers how and why Philip and Nathanael decided to follow Jesus. This account, therefore, lacks multiple attestation. John reports that Jesus went into Galilee the day after Simon Peter and Andrew had decided to become Jesus' disciples. John writes, "The next day Jesus decided to go to Galilee. He found Philip and said to him, 'Follow me'" (1:43, ESV).

John 1:45–49 describes how Nathanael became a disciple. The text reads:

> Philip found Nathanael and said to him, "We have found him of whom Moses in the Law and also the prophets wrote, Jesus of Nazareth, the son of Joseph." Nathanael said to him, "Can anything good come out of Nazareth?" Philip said to him, "Come and see." Jesus saw Nathanael coming toward him and said of him, "Behold, an Israelite indeed, in whom there is no deceit!" Nathanael said to him, "How do you know me?" Jesus answered him, "Before Philip called you, when you were under the fig tree, I saw you." Nathanael answered him, "Rabbi, you are the Son of God! You are the King of Israel!" (ESV)

John's report elaborates on why Philip followed Jesus and became his disciple. The reason was that Philip professed his belief that Jesus was the one written about in the law of Moses and the prophets. If this means Jesus was the Messiah, then the question needs to be asked: was Philip cognizant of the biblical requisites to be the Messiah? Another question that is required

---

11. Köstenberger, *Encountering John*, 99.
12. McGrew, *Hidden in Plain View*, 108.

is: Was Philip a scholar of the Torah? Was Philip more knowledgeable than any Pharisee of his day who knew the Torah yet was unaware that Jesus was the one written about in Moses' law and the prophets?

Readers must ask themselves if this alleged reality is plausible. Sakari Häkkinen, writing in *HTS Teologiese Studies*, sheds light on this relevant question.

> Literacy was even more limited in Judea and Galilee than in the rest of the Roman Empire. Writing was confined mainly to scribal circles and high priestly administrations. Oral communication dominated at all levels of the society, completely so in the villages...
>
> Even if the Galilean villagers would have had possession of some scrolls, which they most probably did not, they would not have understood it read to them, because they spoke a dialect of Aramaic that deviated from the Hebrew of the sacred texts. They would have known the existence of the sacred scriptures, because it was deposited in the Temple and supposedly to be read or rather recited on ceremonial occasions. Some fragmentary knowledge of the scripture may also have been mediated to villagers through Pharisees and other scribal representatives of the temple-state. Having some knowledge of the scriptures and even the ability to recite them did not, however, mean literacy in the sense of ability to read.[13]

Significantly, did Philip know that Jesus was (according to Matthew and Luke) conceived through a virgin, thereby eliminating his paternal lineage to David? It is noteworthy that John does *not* provide information about Philip's age, marital status, education, knowledge of the Torah, religious beliefs, or prior knowledge of Jesus. Presumably, Philip had some knowledge of the Bible since he referred to the laws of Moses and the prophets. He and his brother were probably about twenty years of age or younger. John also informs his readers (1:44) that "Philip, like Andrew and Peter, was from the town of Bethsaida."

On top of that, Philip's name occurs seven additional times, but only in John's Gospel. John 6:5 states that Jesus asked Philip where he could buy bread and that he then answered Jesus' question in verse seven. Six chapters later, John 12:21–22 reports that some Greeks came to Philip and made a request, asking permission to see Jesus. In the next verse, his name appears twice: Philip told Andrew, and then he and Andrew passed the request on to

---

13. Häkkinen, "Poverty in the First-Century Galilee," 8. cf. Horsley, *Jesus in Context*, 29, 89–92.

Jesus. Finally, John 14:8–9 records a question Philip asked Jesus at the Last Supper and Jesus' response.

Background on Bethsaida

In Jesus' time, the three towns/villages of Bethsaida, Chorazin/Korazim, and Capernaum were the most prominent and influential along the northern shore of the Sea of Galilee (See Map). Several passages in the Gospels single out these locales. According to Matthew, mighty works occurred in these three cities. Jesus performed at least three miracles at Bethsaida: he healed a blind man (Mark 8:22–26), walked on water (Mark 6:45–52), and fed at least five thousand people (Mark 6, Matthew 14, Luke 9, and John 6). John 12:37 reports, "Even after Jesus had performed so many signs in their presence, they still would not believe in him" (John 12:37, ESV). For their stubborn unbelief, the people of Bethsaida, Chorazin, and Capernaum earned a curse from him:

> 13 Woe to you, Chorazin! Woe to you, Bethsaida! For if the mighty works done in you had been done in Tyre and Sidon, they would have repented long ago, sitting in sackcloth and ashes. 14 But it will be more bearable in the judgment for Tyre and Sidon than for you. 15 And you, Capernaum, will you be exalted to heaven? You shall be brought down to Hades (Luke 10, ESV).

Their location is approximately three to five miles from each other. Capernaum, the most prominent of the three villages, is only about three miles west of the probable locations of Bethsaida. In 2006, Frank Zindler wrote a stimulating twenty-seven-page article about Capernaum in *The Journal of Higher Criticism*.[14] In the article, he argued that Capernaum was a literary artifact rather than a real place. Therefore, the events that are said to have occurred there are *not* historical. Among the arguments put forward by Zindler are the following:

1. Capernaum is unknown in the Hebrew Bible.

2. The Capernaum in Josephus is not the equivalent of the Capernaum of the Gospels.

3. The archaeological evidence is difficult to evaluate.

4. The silence of Origen (c. 185–254 CE) is significant because he lived only about forty-five miles from the presumed location of Capernaum.

5. Studies on Capernaum in the literature are biased.

14. Zindler, "Capernaum—A Literary Invention," 1–27.

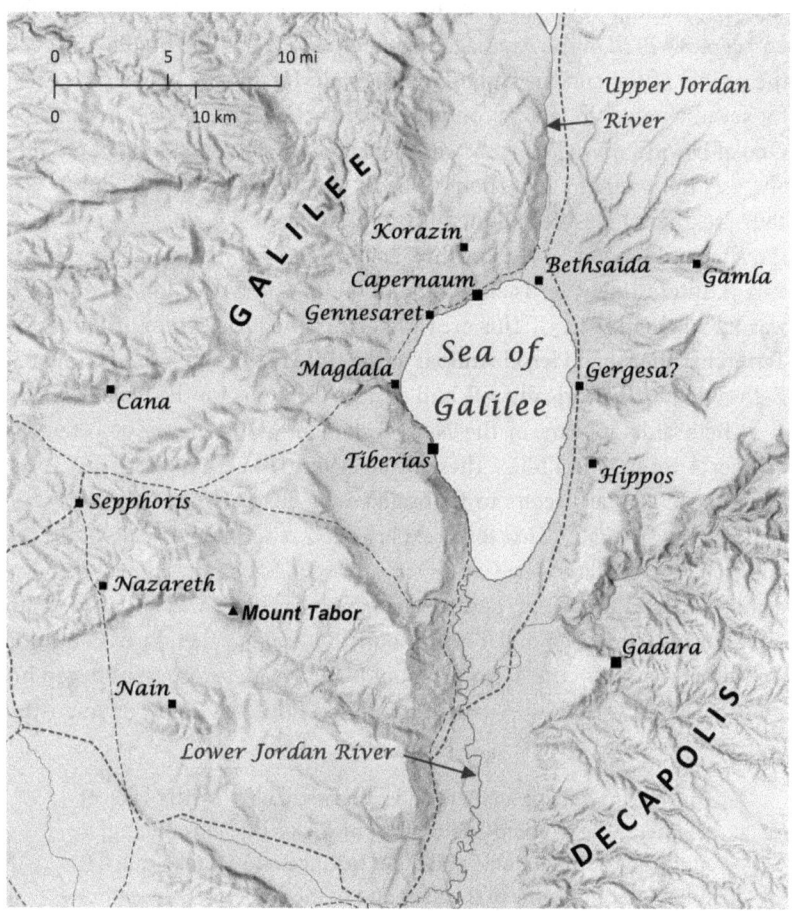

Map: Jesus Ministry in Galilee Maps used with permission
from the Bible Mapper Atlas (biblemapper.com/blog).

Chorazin sits on a hillside two miles north of the presumed location of Capernaum. Bethsaida is near the northern tip of the Lake/Sea of Galilee, on the east side of the upper Jordan River. However, its exact site still needs to be verified. Rami Arav and other archaeologists believe that et-Tell is the site of the New Testament Bethsaida. It (et-Tell) is a 20-acre mound that rises 147 feet above the Bethsaida Plain.[15] Mendel Nun argues for el-Araj. Regardless, the New Testament (Mark 6:45; John 1:44) and Josephus (*Life* 298–406) situate Bethsaida on the lakeshore (i.e., the Sea of Galilee).

15. Arav, "Bethsaida," 64.

Excavations revealed that the settlement at Bethsaida existed in the 10th century BCE in the Aramaean kingdom of Geshur. Bethsaida had been the capital of the ancient kingdom of Geshur. Its royal family, which ruled for several generations, was connected by marriage to the Davidic dynasty. One of David's wives, Ma'acah, was the daughter of Talmai, king of Geshur. She was the mother of Absalom (2 Sam. 3:3), who fled to the land of Geshur seeking refuge after killing his brother (2 Sam. 13: 28–33). Previously, the ancient kingdom of Geshur had been friendly to the Israelites (Joshua 13:13). Interestingly, Jesus also withdrew to this area after John the Baptist was killed (Matt. 14:13). This area was under the jurisdiction of Philip the Tetrarch rather than Herod Antipas at the time. So Geshur and the town of Bethsaida were historically safe and refugee locations for the Israelites.

Bethsaida appears in the New Testament as the home of Peter, his brother Andrew, and Philip. These three fishermen became Jesus' disciples. The Gospel of Mark refers to Bethsaida as a village (*komē* in Mark 8:23), not as a city (*polis*).[16] This town experienced rebuilding under Philip the Tetrarch, one of Herod the Great's sons. In 4 BCE, he inherited it upon the death of Herod the Great. Seventeen years later, in 14 CE, with the death of Augustus, Philip enlarged and rebuilt Bethsaida. Therefore, Bethsaida was rebuilt by Philip the Tetrarch about fifteen years before Jesus began his ministry. Afterward, Philip named it Julias in honor of Emperor Augustus' daughter. Josephus writes:

> And to the village of Bethsaida [located] next to the lake of Gennesar, he granted the dignity of a city by [introducing] a multitude of inhabitants and other fortifications, and he called it Julias after the name of the daughter of the emperor. (*Antiquities* 18.28)

Roger Aus comments, "She died in 29 CE at the age of eighty-seven and was later deified by her grandson, the emperor Claudius, in 42 CE."[17] According to Josephus, Philip "died at Julias; and when he was carried to that monument which he had already erected himself beforehand, he was buried with great pomp" (*Antiquities* 18, 4, 4; Whiston, 382).

Was Jesus' Question to Philip a Literary Device?

Bethsaida means 'house of the fishers,' 'house of hunt,' and 'place of fishers.' Its etymology is from (1) the noun *beth*, house, and (2) the verb *sud*, to fish or hunt. Fish, of course, are significant in this story. Therefore, it is worth

---

16. Arav, "Bethsaida," 67.
17. Aus, *Feeding the Five Thousand*, 120.

considering the name of Bethsaida and its (fishy) origins. This fact suggests that the story may be partly a literary creation. Additionally, Mark 1:17 narrates that Jesus called his disciples to become "fishers of men."

Scholars point out that Jesus' choice of location is of other significance. Bethsaida ("house of the fishers") is located just north of the Sea of Galilee, to the east of the place where the Jordan River enters. Since the Jordan River is the eastern boundary of Galilee, Bethsaida is *not* in Galilee but in Iturea. Rami Arav elaborates,

> Bethsaida was under the jurisdiction of Philip Herod the brother of Herod Antipas. According to the testimony of Josephus, Philip Herod was different from his brother and much more beloved by his subjects. In case of adversity Jesus could find refuge at Bethsaida and it seems that he made quite good use of this possibility.[18]

Thus, Jesus placed himself outside the jurisdiction of Herod Antipas, and within that of the mild Philip the tetrarch from whom no violence was to be feared.[19]

Therefore, although Herod could not reach Jesus in this new "fishy place," Jesus' followers could. Matthew (14:13–14), in particular, explains how Jesus' disciples and many thousands of others flocked to be around Jesus as word spread of his teachings. Coincidentally, "Bethsaida had been rebuilt by Philip the Tetrarch about a quarter century before Jesus had begun his ministry."[20] Unknown and subject to speculation is whether several Gospel authors "conjoined" historical realities and deliberately implemented literary devices in their stories (a proposal that is neither verifiable nor falsifiable):

1. Bethsaida means "house of the fishers," and Jesus declares his disciples are to become "fishers of men" (Mark 1:17; literary pun).

2. The disciples were sent on a mission to hunt for food (literary pun).

3. One of Jesus' miracles was the miraculous multiplying of the loaves and fish (a literary pun, based on 2 Kgs. 4: 42–44, which narrates a similar miracle by Elisha).

4. The name Philip, which coincides with that of Philip the Tetrarch, the founder of Bethsaida, and Philip, the father of Alexander the Great, was a potential literary pun (This text rejects that interpretation.).

18. Arav, "Bethsaida and the Ministry of Jesus around the Sea of Galilee."
19. Asimov, *Asimov's Guide to the Bible*, 853–54.
20. Asimov, *Asimov's Guide to the Bible*, 854.

5. Philip the Tetrarch died and was buried there (a rejected literary pun).

6. Bethsaida was the location of the miraculous feeding because it was outside Herod Antipas's jurisdiction (historical fact).

7. Bethsaida is significant biblically and historically as a safe refuge for the Israelites, adding another layer of context to its importance.

New Testament scholar Robert M. Price, in one of his Bible Geek podcasts, was asked about Philip's question, "noting that the question is a setup used in ancient dialogues by their authors." Babinski, summarizing Price, comments, "So Jesus could have meant the question rhetorically, just the author's means of telegraphing in literary fashion the miracle punch to follow. Per some commentators, it's a typical Johannine set up and illustrates 'how the fourth Gospel author wrote.'"[21]

Speculations: Why Mention Philip?[22]

McGrew rhetorically inquires, "Why Philip? . . . There is, in fact, no particular reason apparent in John for Jesus' selection of Philip for this question."[23] Similarly, Blunt wrote, "Why should this question have been directed to Philip in particular?"[24] Writers can offer speculations, just as the McGrews and Blunt did.

1. Outside the lists of the disciples' names in the Synoptic Gospels and Acts, John is the only gospel writer mentioning the apostle Philip in the New Testament. (Philip the apostle is not to be confused with Philip the evangelist, mentioned a few times in Acts.) Philip's name is mentioned eleven times in the New King James Version of John's Gospel and just three times in the other Gospels. Therefore, the questions asked by McGrew and Blunt are incomplete, misleading, and disingenuous. Additionally, they need to inquire why (1) John incorporates Philip's name eleven times into his gospel and (2) why the Synoptic authors omit his name. Richard Carrier, a detractor, proposes that "The Gospel of John picks the Disciple Philip into a bunch of stories (in John 1; John 6; John 12; and John 14), using him to perform story

---

21. Babinski and Reppert, "Tim McGrew replies to Ed Babinski's Critique of his Discussion of Undesigned Coincidences" timestamp 7:34 p.m. See also Price's March 16th, 2012 episode of the Bible Geek podcast at https://itunes.apple.com/us/podcast/the-bible-geek-show/id360861303

22. McGrew, *Hidden in Plain View*, 107–13; Blunt, *Undesigned Coincidences*, 292–93.

23. McGrew, *Hidden in Plain View*, 108.

24. Blunt, *Undesigned Coincidences*, 292.

functions where previous authors didn't."[25] However, his proposal is neither verifiable nor falsifiable.

2. John is confirming John. John 1:44 states, "Philip, like Andrew and Peter, was from the town of Bethsaida. Therefore, perhaps, the author of John *deliberately planned* (a designed plan) to say that "factoid" because it would make his gospel narrative sound more realistic. Philip, being from Bethsaida, would know where to find food. Additionally, it is irrelevant that Luke 9:10 mentions Jesus and the disciples going to Bethsaida. Furthermore, proponents note that Luke did *not* report feeding the five thousand occurring in Bethsaida.

3. Carrier criticizes McGrew's explanation of why John presumably forgot to mention in John 6 that the scene was near Bethsaida. However, earlier, all the Synoptic Gospels locate the scene near Bethsaida. Since the composition of Mark is usually dated to c. 65–70, Matthew to c. 80, and Luke to c. 85, presumably, readers of John's Gospel would already be familiar with that fact. Noteworthy, the composition of John was about 95 to 110.[26] The subject of academic debate is whether John had access to the Synoptic Gospels, oral traditions forming the Synoptic Gospels, or other sources of information.[27] It is unknown whether his information was from independent sources. Therefore, perhaps John did not think the information was necessary for the storyline.

4. John's author could have been familiar with Luke's placing of the feeding story in Bethsaida and reused that as Philip's hometown. Once again, that "factoid" would make John's Gospel narrative sound more realistic. Philip, being from Bethsaida, would have known where to find food.

5. In his work, *The Gospel According to John*, D.A. Carson speculates, "It is possible that John maintains his interest in Philip because of continued contact with him in later life."[28]

---

25. Carrier, "There are No Undesigned Coincidences."

26. Carrier, "There are No Undesigned Coincidences."

27. Several scholars and commentators argue that John was *not* composed independently of the Synoptic Gospels. See Barker, *John's Use of Matthew*; Barrett, *The Gospel According to St. John*; Bauckham, *The Gospels for all Christians*; Lindars, "John and the Synoptic Gospels," 287–94; Moloney, *The Gospel of John*; North, *What John Knew and What John Wrote*; Smith, *John Among the Gospels*; von Wahlde, *The Gospel and Letters of St. John*.

28. Carson, *The Gospel According to John*, 158.

6. John selects Philip because of his close geographical connection to the brothers Andrew and Peter. The odds of selecting Philip are one in three.

7. An indirect point is that John could have asked Andrew or Peter the identical question for the same rationale. They were all from Bethsaida and knew where food could be procured.

8. Perhaps the author of John's Gospel was closely connected with Philip and his family, or one of his sources had a close relationship with them.

9. D.A. Carson, citing tradition, offers the possibility that in later years, the author of John was geographically close to Philip. "Eusebius (H. E. III. xxxi. 3) cites Polycrates to the effect that Philip, one of the Twelve, was buried in Hierapolis, a city in Asia Minor, the province where the apostle John apparently ministered for the last twenty-five years of his life. But this evidence is of uncertain value; Polycrates may have confused Philip the apostle with Philip the Evangelist (cf. Acts 6:5; 8:5ff.)."[29]

10. John 5:2–47 reports that healing at the Pool on the Sabbath occurs in Bethsaida and follow-up conversations. John 6:1 says, "After this Jesus went away to the other side of the Sea of Galilee, which is the Sea of Tiberias." Therefore, the scene shifts to northern Galilee by boating across the water. Carrier offers speculation (unverifiable) that John's edit was out of order. "The original text *may well have placed* this scene near Bethsaida." (Italics in original)[30]

The McGrews, J.J. Blunt, and others have presented various speculations, but the validity of these arguments cannot be verified or falsified. One interesting question posed by Jesus in John's Gospel is notably absent from the Gospels of Mark, Matthew, and Luke. McGrew raises why this question only appears in John, but the other evangelists may have a ready explanation for its absence in their gospels.

1. Jesus asked no question concerning 'where to buy bread' because the disciples had already spoken up before Jesus could pose the question.

2. The disciples insisted that Jesus "[s]end the crowd away so they can go to the surrounding villages and countryside and find food and lodging because we are in a remote place here." Therefore, the disciples must know where food is available.

---

29. Carson, *The Gospel According to John*, 158.
30. Carrier, "There are No Undesigned Coincidences."

3. Presumably, Jesus did not need to ask Philip where to buy food because if the disciples from Galilee knew there was food and lodging in the surrounding villages, many of the five thousand, being from the area, must also have known where food could be procured.

Last, it bears repeating that John 6:6 explains the reason for Jesus' question. It was good storytelling and rhetorical: Jesus was testing Philip. "And this he said to prove him: for he himself knew what he would do" (ESV).

John Confirms John

Previously, it was suggested that John confirmed what he had written himself. John 1:44 states, "Philip, like Andrew and Peter, was from the town of Bethsaida." Therefore, John 6:5 is self-confirmed by John 1:44. Several times, John incorporates this literary device.

1. John confirms his references to a character named Nicodemus (who appears only in John).
    a. Nicodemus visits Jesus one evening to discuss his teachings: John 3:1–21
    b. Nicodemus reminds his colleagues in the Sanhedrin that the law requires that a person be heard before being judged: John 7:50–51
    c. Nicodemus assists in preparing and burying Jesus' dead body: John 19:39–42
2. John confirms his narrative of the soldier piercing Jesus on the side.
    a. A soldier pierces Jesus' side with a spear: John 19:34
    b. Thomas demands to put his hand in Jesus' side: John 19:25
    c. Jesus offers Thomas the opportunity to place his hand in Jesus' side: John 19:27
3. John confirms his narrative that Jesus is the Lamb of God/Paschal Lamb: John 1:29, 36–37.
    a. John the Baptist says, "Behold the Lamb of God, who takes away the sin of the world!" John 1:29
    b. John the Baptist says, "Behold the Lamb of God!" John 1:36
    c. John is the only Gospel in which Jesus dies at the same hour, just after noon, to demonstrate that Jesus is the Lamb of God unequivocally.

d. Jesus dies at the same place (Jerusalem) as the Passover lambs.
   e. Jesus dies at the hands of the same people, the Jewish leaders, especially the priests, as the Passover lambs.
   f. The month of Nissan falls under the sign of the Lamb. Coincidentally, during the first century, the spring equinox, the time of Passover, was in the zodiac sign of Aries the Lamb. It was the age of the Lamb.
   g. John 19:37 is the only Gospel in which a Roman soldier pierced Jesus' side with a spear rather than break his legs on the cross so as not to violate the prohibition in Exodus 12:46 about breaking the bones of the paschal lamb.
4. John confirms his claim that Jesus is a deity.
   a. "In the beginning was the Word, and the Word was with God, and the Word was God. He was in the beginning with God. All things were made through him, and without him was not any thing made that was made" (John 1:1–3, ESV).
   b. Jesus tells the Samaritan woman at the well, "I who speak to you am he" (John 4:26, ESV).
   c. Jesus says to the crowd, "Truly, truly, I say to you, before Abraham was, I am" (John 8:58, ESV).
   d. Later, in another discourse, Jesus says, "I and the Father are one" (John 10:30, ESV).
   e. Jesus says to Philip, "Have I been with you so long, and you still do not know me, Philip? Whoever has seen me has seen the Father" (John 14:9, ESV).
   f. Thomas answers Jesus, "My Lord and my God!" (John 20:28, ESV)[31]
5. John confirms his assertion that Jesus performs signs. The Greek word *semeion* means signs. In the Gospel of John, "sign" is also used to mean "miracle." Unlike the Gospels of Mark, Matthew, and Luke, John does not record many miracles of Jesus. Academics usually identify seven listed in John, six *explicitly referred to as "signs"* in the text. The seven signs are:

1. changing water into wine at the wedding at Cana (John 2:1–11);

---

[31]. Antitrinitarians refute these cited verses that allegedly support the opinion that Jesus is God.

2. healing the royal official's son (John 4:46–54);
3. healing the paralyzed man at the pool of Bethesda in Jerusalem (John 5:1–15);
4. feeding the multitude (five thousand) (John 6:5–14);
5. walking on water (John 6:16–21);
6. healing the man born blind (John 9:1–7); and
7. raising Lazarus from the dead (John 11:1–45).

Andreas J. Köstenberger points out that signs are vital because they are central to John's Christology. Especially noteworthy are verses John 20:30–31:

> Now Jesus did many other signs in the presence of the disciples, which are not written in this book; but these are written so that you may believe that Jesus is the Christ, the Son of God, and that by believing you may have life in his name (John 20:30–31, ESV).

Regarding the signs in John, Köstenberger elaborates:

> 33 There are seventeen occurrences of the term *semeion* in John's gospel: 2:11, 18, 23; 3:2; 4:48, 54; 6:2, 14, 26, 30; 7:31; 9:16; 10:41; 11:48; 12:18, 37; and 20:30. John 2:11 refers to Jesus' changing water into wine; 2:18 to the Temple clearing; 2:23 and 3:2 make general reference to "the signs" Jesus is doing; in 4:48, Jesus chastises people for their insistence on "signs and wonders" in order to believe; 4:54 refers to Jesus' healing of the nobleman's son; 6:2 talks about signs Jesus is doing upon the sick; 6:14 relates to Jesus' feeding of the multitudes; 6:30 records the Jews' request for yet another sign; 7:31 asks, in the context of discussion over Jesus' healing of the lame man (cf. 5:1—15), whether the Christ will do more signs than Jesus; 9:16 makes reference to Jesus' opening the eyes of a blind man: 10:41 says that John the Baptist did not do any signs; 11:47 and 12:18 refer to Jesus' raising of Lazarus; 12:37 concludes that even though Jesus did all these signs, the Jews still did not believe in him; and 20:30 notes that Jesus did many other signs, but that the evangelist selected certain signs to lead his readers to faith in Jesus. Some commentators, while acknowledging the six signs listed below, may also include additional signs.[32]

The academic literature on "signs" is extensive.

---

32. Köstenberger, *Theology of John's Gospel and Letters*, 324.n33.

Why Philip's Being from Bethsaida Doesn't Explain Why Jesus Asked Him Where to Buy Food: A Refutation of the Alleged Undesigned Coincidence in John 6:5

Is the argument that Jesus' question to Philip counts as an undesigned coincidence sustainable? Does it make sense? Are there viable and rational alternative explanations for the question Jesus poses to Philip in John 6? Do counterarguments exist that challenge and refute this apologetic? What follows is a list of counterarguments culled from the literature. Many of these talking points are from the previous section, which engaged and interacted with the "green grass" argument.

1. There is no methodology for determining how anyone can decide what is a coincidence.
2. There are no criteria for determining what is and is not designed.
3. There are no criteria for determining what counts as a casual, offhand reference.
4. Writers are free to invent details, unlike narrators of eyewitness accounts:
    a. The "undesigned coincidences" associated with feeding the 5,000 show that the gospel writers worked from the same source or sources, which tells the readers nothing about whether the story is true. As blogger Ed Babinski says, "I have read different versions of the Robin Hood story. There is some overlap. Is this evidence that the Robin Hood story is true? No. Not at all."[33]
    b. John's author could have been familiar with Luke's placing of the feeding story in Bethsaida and reused that as Philip's hometown.
    c. Jesus addresses Philip: "How are we to buy bread so that these people may eat?" This passage echoes the question asked by Moses to the Lord: "Where am I to get meat to give all these people?" (John 6:5; cf. Num 11:13). Several explanations are possible: (1) both the feeding and Jesus' question are historical and accurate reportage, (2) the feeding is historical and accurate reportage, but the question was a literary embellishment designed to echo Numbers 11:13, and (3) the feeding and question are nonhistorical. None of these options can be verified or falsified.
5. The story has developed from vague to specific over time.

---

33. Babinski and Reppert, "Tim McGrew replies to Ed Babinski's Critique," timestamp January 15, 2011 12:54 p.m.

a. Mark and Matthew, the earliest tellers of the story, do not mention where the miraculous feedings took place. They are incredibly vague on where it took place. It was a "solitary," "isolated," and "remote" location. Jesus reaches it by boat instead of via named roads. In the earliest telling of the story by Mark, Bethsaida is mentioned. However, it is not the site of the miracle. Instead, it is the place they sail to after leaving the site of the miracle. Only in the later Gospel of Luke is a location for the miracle supplied: Bethsaida.[34]

b. Luke and John were presumably working from the same source materials. This assumption tells the reader very little about whether the source materials describe actual events—specifically, whether Jesus asked Philip the question about where to buy bread. This statement in John can neither be verified nor falsified.

6. Alleged undesigned coincidences must be weighed against "undesigned discrepancies." (See table 6.)

a. The apologist also makes too much of the question addressed to Philip, "Where shall we buy bread for these people to eat?" This question overlooks that in the earliest version of the story, the apostles tell Jesus where the people can get food "in the surrounding towns and villages" (which are unnamed, as noted above). Therefore, in the earliest versions, there was no question concerning "where to buy bread," as in John's version of the story, because the disciples had already spoken up first and insisted that Jesus: "Send the crowd away so they can go to the surrounding villages and countryside and find food and lodging because we are in a remote place here."[35]

b. In John's Gospel, Jesus asks his apostles where to buy fish. In the other gospels, it is not Jesus asking the question but the apostles asking the question of Jesus: a complete reversal. The reader must examine the text diligently and thoroughly.

c. In the Gospel of Matthew, Peter and Andrew were fishermen living in Capernaum (Matthew 4:13). On the other hand, the Gospel of John says Peter and Andrew were, like Philip, from

---

34. Babinski and Reppert, "Tim McGrew replies to Ed Babinski's Critique," timestamp February 26, 2013 7:34 p.m.

35. Babinski and Reppert, "Tim McGrew replies to Ed Babinski's Critique," February 26, 2013, timestamp 7:34 and April 12, 2013, timestamp 7:58 p.m.

Bethsaida (John 1:44): "Philip was from Bethsaida, of the city of Andrew and Peter." This example is a weak instance of a possible discrepancy. The disciples could have been born in Bethsaida and later moved to Capernaum.

    d. Randall Rauser comments: "In other words, in any eclectic collection of texts, one will inevitably find various points of surprising agreement. And by counting the coincidental hits and dismissing the misses, one gets a skewed sampling of the data."[36]

7. Babinski: McGrew and another apologist have been focusing on the "feeding of the multitude" story, claims the undesigned coincidences are piled on top of one another. However, other scholars point out that the undesigned coincidences argument is based more on human ingenuity and attempts to boost the significance of some coincidences while ignoring all the discrepancies and alternate explanations.[37]

8. McGrew: "It could be utterly coincidental, a one-out-of-twelve chance that he [Jesus] picked some disciple at random [Philip]."[38]

9. McGrew: "Why did he ask Philip? And you know I mean it could just be random. Maybe Jesus just grabs a random disciple to give a hard time to, but that's not very satisfying."[39]

10. Amy and Daron: In the example mentioned, Phillip, being from Bethsaida, does not solve the hierarchical problem because Peter is also from Bethsaida. The question remains: Why did Jesus turn to Philip (a minor character) to ask the question instead of asking Peter (a significant character)?[40]

11. Babinski: John 1:44 says, "Philip was from Bethsaida, of the city of Andrew and Peter." So, how many disciples were familiar with those fishing towns on both sides of the river? Probably lots.[41]

12. Mark is the first Gospel identifying Philip (Mark 3:14–19). If Philip's name were a literary invention, there would be no way of verifying or

---

    36. Rauser, "A New Defense of the Historical Reliability of the Bible."

    37. Babinski and Reppert, "Tim McGrew replies to Ed Babinski's Critique," February 26, 2013, timestamp 7:34 p.m. and April 12, 2013, timestamp 7:58 p.m.

    38. McGrew, "Undesigned Coincidences in the Gospel of John."

    39. Chardayoyne and McGrew, "Episode 62: Undesigned Coincidences."

    40. Amy and Daron, "Undesigned Coincidences". See timestamp 7:35 a.m.

    41. Babinski and Reppert, "Tim McGrew replies to Ed Babinski's Critique," February 26, 2013, timestamp 7:34 p.m.

falsifying the reason why Mark invented that name. There are several hypotheses, including the following:

a. Mark was writing for his Greek or Roman readership. Philip was a prominent and well-known Greek name. It was non-Jewish. Wikipedia identifies numerous personages with that name:

Kings of Macedon

Philip I of Macedon

Philip II of Macedon, father of Alexander the Great

Philip III of Macedon, half-brother of Alexander the Great

Philip IV of Macedon

Philip V of Macedon

New Testament

Philip the Apostle

Philip the Evangelist

Others

Philiippus of Croton (c. 6th century BC), Olympic victor and legendary hero

Philip of Opus, one of Plato's students

Philip of Acarnarania, a physician

Philip (son of Antipater), general of Alexander the Great

Philip (son of Machatas), builder of Alexandria on the Indus

Philip (first husband of Berenice I of Egypt, son of Amyntas, and first husband of Berenice I

Philip, brother of Lysimachus and youngest son of Agathocles of Pella

Philip, one of the sons of Lysimachus from his wife Arsinoe II

Philip (satrap), Greek satrap of Sogdiana and governor of Parthia

Philip I Philadelphus, ruler of the Hellenistic Seleucid kingdom

Phillip II Philoromaeus, the last ruler of the Hellenistic Seleucid kingdom

Lucius Marcius Philippus (disambiguation), multiple Roman statesmen

Philippides of Paiania, Greek son of Philomelos, archon of nobility, basileus 293/2 BC.

Herod Philip I, son of Herod the Great and husband of Herodias

Herod Philip II, "the Tetrarch," son of Herod the Great and ruler of Ituraea and Trachonitis

b. Assuming Mark's Philip was a literary invention, Matthew, Luke, and John (who based their accounts of the feeding of the 5,000 on Mark's) would have been trapped and forced to use that name. The reason John selected Philip as the apostle to whom Jesus addresses his question about buying food is open to speculation: neither verifiable nor falsifiable.

If the advocates of the hypothesis of Undesigned Coincidences want to say there is missing information here, then why would biblical commentators and readers not question all the missing information about Jesus, which is not contained in the Gospels but merely tangentially referenced?

4

Summary of Problems with the Hypothesis of Undesigned Coincidences

EYEWITNESS TESTIMONY AND MAXIMAL DATA

A QUOTE FROM NEW Testament scholar Bart Ehrman, who did extensive research on the subject of memory while writing his book *Jesus Before the Gospels*, is strikingly relevant here:

> It is flat-out amazing to me how many New Testament scholars talk about the importance of eyewitness testimony to the life of Jesus without having read a single piece of scholarship on what experts know about eyewitness testimony. Some (well-known) scholars in recent years have written entire books on the topic, basing their views on an exceedingly paltry amount of research into the matter. Quite astounding, really. But they appear to have gone into their work confident that they know about how eyewitness testimony works, and didn't read the masses of scholarship that shows they simply aren't right about it.[1]

McGrew and proponents of the "Maximal Data" approach argue that the Gospels are *not* documents written forty to sixty years after Jesus' death. Instead, they are either eyewitness reports of Jesus' life, death, and resurrection (e.g., John's Gospel) or (in the case of the Synoptic Gospels written by Matthew, Mark, and Luke) biographical reports, written only twenty-five

---

1. Ehrman, "Eyewitness Testimony: The Importance of Actual Eyewitnesses."

to thirty years after Jesus' death. *Moreover, the Gospels focus on interviews with eyewitnesses who personally knew Jesus. Therefore, the Gospel authors are presenting reportage of actual historical events.* In Hidden in Plain View, McGrew writes, "An undesigned coincidence provides reason to believe that both (all) of the statements that contribute to it are truthful."[2] Consequently, the presence of "undesigned coincidences" in the gospel narratives validates the Maximal Data approach by providing evidence that the Gospels are composed of independent and reliable sources, which fit together like pieces of a puzzle.

McGrew does not provide information from experts about eyewitness testimony, memory, or the reliability of oral traditions. Moreover, the bibliography of *Hidden in Plain View* lacks researchers in related fields. McGrew's familiarity with the works of Elizabeth Loftus, Daniel Schacter, or other experts in these fields is unknown. Presumably, skeptics and detractors may argue that if she is familiar with the research, then for the benefit of her readers, she should address the issues it raises regarding the unreliability of human memory.

The hypotheses of Undesigned Coincidences and Maximal Data related to the life of Jesus have been subject to debate and skepticism. Some experts in relevant fields argue that there is insufficient evidence to support these hypotheses. These critics have pointed out that there are no first-hand accounts of Jesus or his disciples.[3] This lack of eyewitness accounts raises concerns about the validity of the stories presented in the Christian Bible, which were composed in *koine* (Hellenistic) Greek by anonymous authors using unknown sources. The stories were written between twenty-five and sixty-five years *after Jesus' death* and center on unconfirmed local accounts. While proponents of the hypothesis of Undesigned Coincidences hold a different view, the lack of concrete evidence remains a contention among scholars and skeptics.

Explaining Differences between the Gospel Narratives

The question that demands attention is how McGrew knows that the Gospels' authors were *not* employing compositional devices. However, this raises further questions about the alleged appearance of undesigned coincidences in the Gospels. One such question is how readers can determine where facts begin and end. Another question is distinguishing between factual information and embellishments or legendary details. Moreover, how much of the

---

2. McGrew, *Hidden in Plain View*, 13.

3. However, they fail to acknowledge 1 Corinthians 9:1 and 15:8 when Paul claims to have seen Jesus.

SUMMARY OF PROBLEMS 151

information presented in the Gospels is historically accurate? Additionally, it is essential to determine what can be considered a contradiction, difference, or omission in the Gospels. These are all crucial questions that require engaging when examining the validity and accuracy of the Gospels and the hypothesis of Undesigned Coincidences.

Presume that the Gospel authors Matthew, Luke, and John (1) existed, (2) were first-hand eyewitnesses, (3) had lengthy, detailed discussions with all of the women, all of the disciples, all other relevant people, and also (4) knew that the information recorded in Mark was complete and accurate. Nonetheless, for personal reasons, they wrote their *enhanced*, redacted narratives years after the completion of Mark's Gospel. Question: Would these new narratives merely be considered "differences," or would they be contradictions? If they are *not* contradictions, then what should they be called? If the Gospels' authors incorporated undesigned coincidences into their narratives, would these new narrative passages (i.e., undesigned coincidences) merely be considered "differences," or would they be contradictions?

In the eyes of skeptics and detractors, Christian apologists, Bible commentators, and theologians supporting the hypothesis of Undesigned Coincidences engage in complex and convoluted reasoning to reconcile differences in the text. Instead of letting the text speak for itself, they may come across as saying, "Let me explain to you what the Gospel authors meant to say." By doing so, they may give the impression that they are the sole arbiters of truth and are the only ones capable of accurately understanding the original author's meaning.

The agenda of the McGrews is apparent and, in part, openly acknowledged. They are unabashed, committed, conservative Christian apologists defending (1) the authority of Scripture, (2) the final truth of Scripture, (3) the unity of Scripture, and (4) the historicity and reliability of the New Testament.[4] Reverend Bosco Peters, in a book review of *Hidden in Plain View*, writes:

> Lydia McGrew's book (again betraying the context of the circles she moves in) shifts between biblical inerrancy and eyewitness' differing accounts. If inerrancy is held, then eyewitness' differences must be only apparent. They can be harmonized. But, if there is a real (unharmonizable) eyewitness difference, then inerrancy must be given away. In this case, you simply cannot have your cake and eat it.[5]

4. In her podcasts, McGrew says she does not advocate biblical inerrancy.
5. Peters, "Undesigned Coincidences." Rev. Peters has a BTh (Hons) Melbourne College of Divinity, BSc (Canterbury), Dip Tchg (Christchurch) and was Former lecturer and examiner in Church, Ministry and Sacraments for LTh at College House

Stanley Porter and Bryan Dyer clarify that harmonization is one approach to explaining at least some of the differences encountered when studying the Gospels.[6] They quote Craig L. Blomberg's definition of harmonization: "The attempt to reconcile seeming contradictions in the Gospels by arguing that the Gospel writers are describing separate events or different aspects of a single event."[7] Frequently, McGrew fails to engage with biblical criticism, discuss the significance of research on eyewitness testimony, memory, and the reliability of oral traditions, or provide her listeners with vital information that challenges the hypothesis of Undesigned Coincidences. Among the things she neglects to do are the following:

1. Defining the crucial terms coincidence, fact, eisegesis, exegesis, and casual(ness),

2. Examining and sharing research about coincidence,

3. Reviewing the literature examining the relationship between Mark 6 and Psalm 23, the Exodus motif, 2 Kings 4: 38–44, the controversy about Bethsaida, and discussing in depth the topics of literary devices, symbolism, and motifs.

Crucially, the McGrews admit that reading the works of Paley and Blunt caused them to reexamine the long-overlooked hypothesis. After reading their works, they read the New Testament and found other undesigned coincidences. Later, they wrote books, journal articles, and papers and presented lectures and podcasts online supporting the hypothesis of Undesigned Coincidences. In other words, they started with a conclusion (undesigned coincidences exist) and then found a way to make their evidence (i.e., primarily, the New Testament) support it.

Licona's text includes an essential chapter, "Important Considerations on Historical Inquiry Pertaining to the Truth in Ancient Texts." A critical section of focus is "Horizons." He begins the chapter saying

> Horizon may be defined as one's "preunderstanding."37 It is how historians view things as a result of their knowledge, experience, beliefs, education, cultural conditioning, preferences, presuppositions and worldview. Horizons are like sunglasses through which a historian looks. Everything she sees is colored by that horizon.[8]

Institute of Theology, Christchurch.

6. Porter and Dyer, "The Synoptic Problem," 4.
7. Blomberg, "The Legitimacy and Limits of Harmonization," 144.
8. Licona, *Resurrection of Jesus*, 38.

In footnote 37, he elaborates, "Meyer (1979), 97. Preunderstanding is the hearer's total relationship (intellectual, emotional, moral) to the thing expressed."

After about twelve pages, Licona engages with a relevant topic: "On the Possibility of Transcending Horizon." He proposes six tools that, when combined, can be effective guides that bring us closer to objectivity" (i.e., toward transcending horizons).[9]

1. Method can serve as a means toward achieving greater objectivity. Method encompasses many parts, including the manner in which data are viewed, weighed and contextualized; criteria for testing the adequacy of hypotheses; and the fair consideration of competing hypotheses.
2. The historian's horizon and method should be public. It is certain that at least portions of the historian's horizon can be public or open to scrutiny... Moreover, historians should be clear about the methods they employ for achieving results.
3. Peer pressure may also be helpful in minimizing the impact of horizon on the historian's work.
4. Submitting ideas to unsympathetic experts may assist in minimizing the negative impact of horizon.
5. Account for the relevant historical bedrock. Some facts are so strongly evidenced that they are virtually indisputable. These facts are referred to as "historical bedrock" since any legitimate hypothesis should be built on it. If a hypothesis fails to explain all of the historical bedrock, it is time to drag that hypothesis back to the drawing board or to relegate it to the trash bin.
6. Detachment from bias is nonnegotiable.[10]

About "undesigned coincidences," the relevance of Licona's balanced words should be evident to the perceptive reader. Those who will understand will understand.

A related opinion is found in the work by Matthew McCormick, a distinguished professor in the Philosophy department at California State University—Sacramento. Among the courses that he teaches are Critical Thinking, Inductive Logic, Knowledge and Understanding, and Rationality. A detractor, his book *Atheism and the Case Against Christ* offers a valuable

---

9. Licona, *Resurrection of Jesus*, 38; cf. Meyer, *The Aims of Jesus*, 97.

10. Licona, *Resurrection of Jesus*, 52-62. Readers must diligently examine these pages.

resource for those on *both* sides of the religious aisle. He presents a comprehensive (lengthy) list of questions that can significantly enhance one's critical thinking and decision-making skills. When applied diligently, these questions can solidify any discourse about undesigned coincidences. They are as follows:

- Are there data?
- What exactly are the data?
- Have I conducted an exhaustive search?
- If there were significant counterevidence, would my search have found it?
- What else could explain the data?
- What would disprove the hypothesis?
- Has my enthusiasm for any particular hypothesis affected the evidence I have searched for or emphasized?
- Have I adequately considered other alternatives?
- Has search satisfaction led me to stop looking prematurely?
- Have I thought about it long enough?
- Has my enthusiasm for a hypothesis led me to relax evidential standards for it or increase them for competing hypotheses?
- Am I prepared to change my mind in light of new or different evidence?
- Hypothetically, what information would change my mind?
- If there are personal, psychological, or social factors that tilts my evaluation of the evidence, would I be aware of it? What are they?
- If there are factors that are filtering my access to information, would I be aware of them? What are they?
- Have I given more or less important pieces of information their appropriate weight?
- Has the order of my consideration of the evidence affected my evaluation when it shouldn't have?
- Has the recency or remoteness of some evidence in time affected my evaluation when it shouldn't have?
- Is my memory supplying me with a representative picture of the relevant experiences?

- Am I applying principles of justification here that are consistent with the ones I use normally?
- Do I sustain a high level of open-mindedness during the search and evaluation phase?
- Are the estimates of likelihoods or probabilities that I am employing accurate or realistic?
- Would the conclusion drawn withstand a reasonable level of skepticism?[11]

Unlike McGrew's hypothesis of Undesigned Coincidences and Maximal Data approach, the scientific method is a multi-step inquiry methodology. Using the scientific method limits the influence of bias and preconceived notions and enhances the results' quality. The scientific method comes in various versions. Some versions have more steps, while others may have only a few. These steps include the following:

1. Observation/Question
2. Research topic area
3. Hypothesis
4. Test with experiment
5. Analyze data
6. Report conclusions

Remembering the specific components required when employing the scientific method is essential.

1. Employ careful and attentive observation.
2. Form relevant and testable questions based on the observations.
3. A crucial element of the scientific method is the application of rigorous skepticism. This incorporation is essential as cognitive assumptions can distort how one interprets the observation, and skepticism plays a vital role in avoiding such biases, ensuring the objectivity of the research.
4. In hypothesis testing, it is crucial to consider the null hypothesis or the no-difference hypothesis. This is a type of hypothesis that assumes changing a variable will not affect the outcome. It is tested against the alternative hypothesis and reflects the possibility of no observed change in the experiment. (For instance, in biblical studies, a null hypothesis could be that mentioning green grass in Mark 6:39 is inconsequential.)

11. McCormick, *Atheism and the Case Against Christ*, 221–23.

Understanding the null hypothesis is fundamental to understanding the scientific method.

5. A good hypothesis should be *falsifiable*, meaning it can be proven false.
6. The scientific method attempts to disapprove a conclusion and offer alternatives honestly.
7. Any good science experiment must always serve its one primary function: to prove or disprove a hypothesis.
8. *Scientists generally report their results in academic or scientific journals, where other scientists have checked and verified each report in a peer review process.* In theology, text and journal publishers can verify the publication by blind review process with experts in the field.

Advocates and detractors of the hypothesis of Undesigned Coincidences can follow a multi-step process to examine it thoroughly. Readers should carefully evaluate whether the proponents or detractors utilize the scientific method to test this hypothesis. This approach will ensure an intellectually honest analysis of the topic and its potential implications.

5

Conclusion

The Cumulative Argument against the Hypothesis of Undesigned Coincidences

THIS TEXT REVIEWS AND discusses the green grass and the question Jesus asked Philip at length but does not rehash them here. Instead, it presents extensive reasoning and assessments that challenge the hypothesis of Undesigned Coincidences.

1. There is *no* existing methodology for how anyone can identify and decide what is a coincidence.
2. There are *no* criteria to determine what is and is not designed (i.e., *not planned, unpremeditated,* or *unintentional*).
3. Research substantiates the fact that coincidences happen.
4. There are *no* criteria for determining what counts as a casual reference.
5. If Matthew had access to Mark, Luke had access to Mark (and perhaps Matthew), and John had access to the Synoptic Gospels or their sources, then obviously, these authors were *not* writing independently.
6. If Matthew had access to Mark, Luke had access to Mark (and perhaps Matthew), and John had access to the Synoptic Gospels or their sources, these authors *cannot* corroborate each other.
7. If the Gospel authors copied from prior authors or used them as sources, they *would* appear to fit together like pieces of a puzzle.
8. "Redaction criticism reminds us that the evangelists wrote with more than (though not less than) historical interest. They were preachers and teachers concerned with applying the truths of Jesus' life and

teaching to specific communities in their day. This theological purpose of the evangelists has sometimes been missed, with a consequent loss of appreciation for the significance and application of the alleged history that the evangelists narrate."[1] This reality is not to deny that the gospel accounts may sometimes contain kernels of historicity.

9. Writers are free to invent details, whereas, in eyewitness accounts, witnesses report what they experienced.
10. The gospel stories have developed from vague to specific over time.
11. Alleged undesigned coincidences must be weighed *against undesigned discrepancies*.
12. If the advocates of undesigned coincidences concur that information is missing, why should investigators and researchers not question all the missing information about Jesus, which is not contained in the Gospels but is tangentially referenced?
13. The use of literary imitation can explain some coincidences.
14. Some undesigned coincidences disappear when the *assumed knowledge of an audience* is brought into view.
15. The evangelists were as careless and forgetful as other authors in antiquity. An undesigned coincidence between two Gospels may result from two sloppy authors accidentally omitting minor details, with one evangelist recording a detail neglected by his counterpart.
16. Even if the Gospels contained multiple undesigned coincidences, it would *not* support the conclusion that *eyewitnesses* were the direct source or that their reportage was accurate.
17. Investigators, researchers, and readers have to deal with four authors working with different source materials, with their redactional interests and compositional techniques, writing in a foreign language, and writing to different audiences, sometimes decades apart. Unsurprisingly, the complex "writing a Gospel" process would be expected to give rise to apparently 'undesigned' coincidences.
18. It is impossible to verify (or falsify) that the Gospel authors accurately reported the facts, did not make things up, and wrote in good faith.
19. The similarities between the various gospel accounts of an event may derive from popular stories, while the differences may arise from the evangelists' creativity (or carelessness) or their sources.

---

1. Carson and Moo, *Introduction the New Testament*, 112.

20. Undesigned coincidences can be found in entirely fictional stories like *Star Trek* and *Star Wars*.
21. Undesigned coincidences are essentially harmonization under a different name.
22. Undesigned coincidences are traditional apologetics dressed in a new garb.
23. Anyone can harmonize anything.
24. Advocates of the hypothesis of Undesigned Coincidences assume that the material in the Christian Bible is historically reliable.
25. It is impossible to verify whether the Gospel authors were close to or somewhat removed from the events they allegedly reported.
26. It is unknown if all the gospel accounts were eyewitness reports or if they included material passed down secondhand through written or oral tradition. Luke writes in his prologue that his information is secondhand.
27. The cumulative collection of undesigned coincidences *fails* to demonstrate that the writers were well-informed or habitually truthful. Besides, even habitually truthful people can be wrong, accept inaccurate information, and pass it along.
28. The inconvenient truth is that the hypothesis of Undesigned Coincidences, the Maximal Fact hypothesis, and their accompanying "cottage industry" rest on sandy foundations. Their hypothesis is like a house built on sand (see Matt 7:26).

The cumulative case methodology supports or refutes a position by showing that it is a more reasonable view, considering all the available evidence, than some alternative hypothesis. This method involves using various arguments, *none of which are definitive*. However, each argument strengthens the evidence for the position advocated. Instead of proving the conclusion with absolute certainty, the goal is to establish a conclusion that is more likely to be accurate than false. It is important to note that while each argument or piece of evidence may be imperfect and have limitations, considering them as a whole leads to a more definite conclusion.

The argument *for* the hypothesis of Undesigned Coincidences rests on the assumption that the New Testament narratives are reliable. However, it is essential to note that the Gospel authors remain anonymous, and their accounts were composed several decades after the events they reported. Moreover, the Gospels were composed in various locations and decades apart, in sophisticated Greek rather than the native Hebrew or Aramaic, and not by uneducated fishermen disciples, as some may believe. Furthermore, the Gospels contain divergent or contradictory narratives with omissions, often composed for theological reasons. Scholars have demonstrated that later Gospel authors and others may have copied, edited, or redacted earlier works of unknown origin. This reality means that the Gospels were *not* independently composed, so they *cannot* corroborate each other.

It is worth restating that readers need to answer the following questions. Assume that the four Gospel authors are reporting on the feeding of the five thousand or resurrection episodes. The people involved in these episodes spoke Aramaic, as did the witnesses. However, the Gospel authors wrote their reports in sophisticated Greek, nearly word for word, about thirty to seventy years after translating the Aramaic conversations. *Do you think it is likely that the Gospel authors could accurately report almost word for word on the Aramaic conversation translated into Greek decades later?* Also, do you believe that the authors' compositions were independent works?

Most notably, there is *no* methodology to determine what counts as a coincidence. There are *no* criteria to determine what is not designed (i.e., unplanned, unpremeditated) or unintentional. Moreover, there are *no* criteria to determine what is merely a casual reference in the Gospel texts. Therefore, accurately evaluating undesigned coincidences is impossible. In her book *Hidden in Plain View*, McGrew warns readers early on that identifying undesigned coincidences is fraught with uncertainty.

> I will be using the phrase "undesigned coincidences" throughout the book, and I should say at the outset that *there are gray areas when it comes to the question of whether something counts as an undesigned coincidence argument* (Italics for emphasis)[2]

The arguments presented here request that readers consider all the counterarguments mentioned earlier and overwhelmingly challenge the hypothesis of Undesigned Coincidences. However, it is essential to recognize that the Gospels may still contain some elements of historical truth. Two critical questions that need further scholarly investigation are the reliability of the Gospels and the best way to separate fact from fiction.

It is the readers' responsibility to interpret Lydia's text, podcasts, and interviews charitably or not. However, the real question is whether the authors of the Gospel texts intended to write precisely with full attention and awareness. They may have chosen to omit some related information, which another author happened to mention. Readers must ask why the authors added or excluded material from their respective Gospel, even though it is

---

2. McGrew, *Hidden in Plain View*, 13.

an unanswerable question. Matthew copies Mark, and Luke copies Matthew and Mark. It is not clear whether John had access to the Synoptic Gospels. If the three latest authors had access to prior Gospels, they presumably composed their works with full attention and awareness. If this stance is correct, it is unlikely that there are any undesigned coincidences in the Gospels.

The central message of this text is that the alleged undesigned coincidences among various documents are *not* substantial enough to prove the historical reliability of the Gospels and other New Testament books. The idea of undesigned coincidences is criticized as overly simplistic and naive when used as a Christian apologetic. This text holds significance as it engages and systematically challenges this hypothesis. It presents readers *with a compelling cumulative argument* against the hypothesis of Undesigned Coincidences and its assertion of the historical accuracy of the Gospels.[3] The overall impact of this cumulative argument solidifies the *unsustainability* of the hypothesis of Undesigned Coincidences. Ultimately, it is up to the readers to judge the success or failure of this argument.

---

3. As Thomas Huxley aptly put it in 1870, "The great tragedy of Science [or we could add "theology"]—the slaying of a beautiful hypothesis by an ugly fact." Huxley, "Opening Address," 402. Or, Thomas à Kempis, a German-Dutch canon (1380–471), wrote the phrase "Man proposes, but God disposes," a translation of the Latin phrase "Homo proponit, sed Deus disponit" from Book I, chapter 19, number 2, of *De Imitatione Christi*, 39.

Bibliography

Allison, Dale. "Psalm 23 (22) in Early Christianity: A Suggestion." *Irish Biblical Studies* 5 (1983) 132–37. https://doi.org/https://biblicalstudies.org.uk/pdf/irish-biblical-studies/05-3_132.pdf.

Alonso, Facundo. "Planning on a Prior Intention." *Journal of Ethics and Social Philosophy* 18 (March 2020) 813–50. https://doi.org/10.26556/jesp.v18i3.850.

Alter, Michael J. "An Author Based Analysis of Resurrection Texts." *Socio-Historical Examination of Religion and Ministry* 4 (2023) 1–119.

———. *The Resurrection and Its Apologetics: Jesus' Death and Burial*. Vol. 1. Eugene, OR: Resource Publications, 2024.

———. *A Thematic Access-Oriented Bibliography of Jesus's Resurrection*. Eugene, OR: Resource Publications, 2020.

Alter, Michael J., and Darren M. Slade. "Dataset Analysis of English Texts Written on the Topic of Jesus' Resurrection: A Statistical Critique of Minimal Facts Apologetics." *Socio-Historical Examination of Religion and Ministry* 3 (2021) 367–92. https://doi.org/10.33929/sherm.2021.vol3.no2.09.

Amy and Daron. "Undesigned Coincidences, August 4, 2011." https://str.typepad.com/weblog/.

Anscombe, Gertraude E. *Intention*. 2nd ed. Oxford: Blackwell, 1963.

Arav, Rami. "Bethsaida." In *The Routledge Encyclopedia of the Historical Jesus*, 64–67. New York: Routledge, 2006.

———. "Bethsaida and the Ministry of Jesus Around the Sea of Galilee." https://bibleinterp.arizona.edu/articles/2000/ara248019.

Archer, Gleason L., and Gregory Chirichigno. *Old Testament Quotations in the New Testament*. Chicago: Moody, 1983.

Asimov, Isaac. *Asimov's Guide to the Bible: Two Volumes in One: The Old and New Testaments*. New York: Wings, 1981.

Aus, Roger David. *Feeding the Five Thousand: Studies in the Judaic Background of Mark 6:30–44 par. and John 6:1–15*. Lanham: University Press of America, 2010.

Babinski, Ed, and Victor Reppert. "Tim McGrew Replies to Ed Babinski's Critique of His Discussion of Undesigned Coincidences." http://dangerousidea.blogspot.com/2011/01/tim-mcgrew-replies-to-ed-babinskis.html?showComment=1361932493909#c4700614804211144770.

Baird, William. "New Testament Criticism." In *ABD*, 1:730–36. New York: Doubleday, 1992.

Barclay, William. *Barclay's Guide to the New Testament*. Westminster John Knox, 2008.

Barker, James W. *John's Use of Matthew*. Minneapolis: Fortress, 2015.

BIBLIOGRAPHY

Barrett, Charles Kingsley. *The Gospel According to St John: An Introduction with Commentary and Notes on the Greek Text.* 2nd ed. Philadelphia: Westminster John Knox, 1978.

Bauckham, Richard. *The Gospels for All Christians: Rethinking the Gospel Audiences.* Grand Rapids: Eerdmans, 1998.

———. *Jesus and the Eyewitnesses: The Gospels as Eyewitness Testimony.* Grand Rapids: Eerdmans, 2006.

Beavis, Mary Ann. *Mark.* Grand Rapids, MI: Baker Academic. 2011.

Beitman, Bernard D., and Magda Osman. "Can You Accurately Estimate Coincidence Probabilities?" https://www.psychologytoday.com/us/blog/connectingcoincidence/201904/can-you-accurately-estimate-coincidence-probabilities.

Berra, Yogi. "Quotesweekly.Com." https://www.quotesweekly.com/43-coincidence-quotes/.

"Best Commentaries on Mark: Best Commentaries." https://bestcommentaries.com/mark/.

BibleRef.com. "Mark 6:39." https://www.bibleref.com/Mark/6/Mark-6-39.html.

Black, C. Clifton. *Mark.* Nashville, TN: Abingdon. 2010. https://www.amazon.com/dp/0687058414/?tag=bestinclass-20

Blomberg, Craig. "The Legitimacy and Limits of Harmonization." In *Hermeneutics, Authority, and Canon,* 135–74. Grand Rapids: Zondervan, 1986.

———. *Matthew: An Exegetical and Theological Exposition of Holy Scripture.* Nashville, TN: B & H, 1992.

Blunt, John J. *Undesigned Coincidences in the Writings both of the Old and New Testament: An Argument of Their Veracity: With an Appendix Containing Undesigned Coincidences Between the Gospels and Acts and Josephus.* New York: John Carter, 1847.

Bock, Darrell, L. *Mark.* New York, NY: Cambridge University Press. 2015.

Boren, Braxton. "Whitefield's Voice." In *George Whitefield: Life, Context, and Legacy,* 167–89. Oxford: Oxford University Press, 2016.

Boring, M. Eugene. *Mark: A Commentary.* Louisville: Westminster John Knox, 2006.

Brierley, Justin, Bart Ehrman, and Timothy McGrew. "Bart Ehrman vs Tim McGrew—Round 2." YouTube, March 17, 2016. Video, https://www.youtube.com/watch?v=Gm-nx8yNK30.

Broach, Elise. *Shakespeare's Secret.* New York: Henry Holt, 2005.

Brown, William P. *Handbook to Old Testament Exegesis.* Louisville: Westminster John Knox, 2017.

Bull, Emma. *Bone Dance: A Fantasy for Technophiles.* 2nd ed. New York: Orb, 2005.

Burger, Edward B., and Michael P. Starbird. *Coincidences, Chaos, and All that Math Jazz: Making Light of Weighty Ideas.* New York: W.W. Norton, 2005.

Cai, Jonathan Bi Fan. "Jesus the Shepherd: A Narrative-Critical Study of Mark 6:30–44," 2011.

Cambridge English Dictionary. "Coincidence." https://dictionary.cambridge.org/us/dictionary/english/coincidence.

CARM. "Eisegesis." https://carm.org/dictionary/eisegesis/.

Carrier, Richard. "There Are No Undesigned Coincidences: The Bible's Authors Are Simply Changing Up Their Sources • Richard Carrier." https://www.richardcarrier.info/archives/16428.

Carroll, Lewis. *Through the Looking Glass: And What Alice Found There*. Philadelphia: Henry Altermus Company, 1897.
Carson, D. A. *The Gospel According to John*. Leicester: Inter-Varsity, 1991.
———. *Matthew 13–28*. Grand Rapids: Zondervan, 2010.
Carson, D. A., and Douglas J. Moo. *An Introduction to the New Testament*. 2nd ed. Grand Rapids: Zondervan, 2005.
Cavett, Dick. "Dick Cavett Quote." https://www.azquotes.com/quote/702441.
Chabris, Christopher, and Daniel Simons. *The Invisible Gorilla: And Other Ways Our Intuition Deceives US*. London: HarperCollins, 2010.
Chardavoyne, Michael, and Lydia McGrew. "Episode 62: Undesigned Coincidences." https://veracityhill.com/episodes/episode-62-undesigned-coincidences.
Chesterton, Gilbert Keith. "The Human Will and the Decline of Empire." https://www.oxfordreference.com/display/10.1093/acref/9780191826719.001.0001/q-oro-ed4-0002890;jsessionid=44BFA7C373519890568DE73A524781FA.
Clines, David. "Historical Criticism: Are Its Days Numbered?" *Teologinen aikakausskirja* 6 (2009) 542–58. https://www.academia.edu/2256745/Historical_Criticism_Are_its_Days_Numbered.
Collins, Adela Yarbo. *Mark: A Commentary*. Minneapolis, MN: Fortress. 2007.
Coupland, Douglas. "*Girlfriend in a Coma*." https://www.brainyquote.com/quotes/douglas_coupland_411428.
Cranfield, C.E.B. *The Gospel According to St. Mark*. Cambridge, U.K.: Cambridge University Press. 1959/1977.
Davies, W. D., and Dale C. Allison. *A Critical and Exegetical Commentary on the Gospel According to Saint Matthew*. Vol. 2. London: T & T Clark, 1997.
Derrett, J. Duncan. "Daniel and Salvation-History." *The Downside Review* 100 (1982) 62–68. https://doi.org/10.1177/001258068210033805.
Diaconis, Persi, and Frederick Mosteller. "Methods for Studying Coincidences." *Journal of the American Statistical Association* 84 (1989) 853–61. https://doi.org/10.1080/01621459.1989.10478847.
Dictionary of Biblical Imagery, (Downers Grove, IL: InterVarsity, 1998), s.v. "Grass.,"
Donahue, *The Gospel of Mark*. Collegeville, MN: Liturgical. 2005
Edwards, James R. *The Gospel of Mark*. Grand Rapids, MI: Eerdmans. 2002.
Ehrman, Bart. "Biblical Scholars Don't Typically Call Themselves Biblical Historians." https://ehrmanblog.org/can-biblical-scholars-be-historians/.
———. "Eyewitness Testimony: The Importance of Actual Expertise." https://ehrmanblog.org/eyewitness-testimony-the-importance-of-actual-expertise/.
———. "How Can We Possibly Know a Scribe's Intentions? My Most Important Theoretical Reflection." https://ehrmanblog.org/how-can-we-possibly-know-a-scribes-intentions-my-most-important-theoretical-reflection/.
Ens, Paul, and Dale Allison. "Apologists Turn on Christian Resurrection Scholar (Feat. Dr Dale Allison)." YouTube, February 27, 2023. Video, 3;15 https://www.youtube.com/watch?v=oSpQ83bR5yk.
Falk, Ruma, and Don Macgregor. "The Surprisingness of Coincidences." *Advances in Psychology* 14 (1983) 489–502. https://doi.org/10.1016/s0166-4115(08)62252-59.
France, R.T. *The Gospel of Mark*. Grand Rapids: Eerdmans, 2002.
———. *The Gospel of Matthew*. Grand Rapids: Eerdmans, 2007.
Fraser, Paul. "The Use of Scripture in Saint John's Gospel." https://catholic-resources.org/John/OT-citations.html

Foster, Meadhbh I., and Mark T. Keane. "Why Some Surprises Are More Surprising than Others: Surprise as a Metacognitive Sense of Explanatory Difficulty." *Cognitive Psychology* 81 (2015) 74–116. https://doi.org/10.1016/j.cogpsych.2015.08.004.

Fryer, N. S. "Matthew 14:14–21. The Feeding of the Five Thousand. A Grammatico-Historical Exegesis." *In die Skriflig/In Luce Verbi* 21(1987) 27–42. https://doi.org/10.4102/ids.v21i84.1318.

Garland, David E. *Mark*. Grand Rapids, MI: Zondervan. 1996.

———. *A Theology of Mark's Gospel: Good News about Jesus the Messiah, the Son of God*. Grand Rapids, MI: Zondervan. 2015.

Gloer, Hulitt. "Old Testament Quotations in the New Testament." In *Harper's Bible Dictionary*, 1047. Nashville: Holman Bible Publishers, 1991.

Godfrey, Neil. "The Point of the Dionysiac Myth in Acts of the Apostles, #1." https://vridar.org/2013/08/28/the-point-of-the-dionysiac-myth-in-acts-1/.

Goodacre, Mark. "Fatigue in the Synoptics." *New Testament Studies* 44 (1998) 45–58. https://doi.org/10.1017/s0028688500016349.

Gould, Stephen Jay. *The Flamingo's Smile; Reflections in Natural History*. New York: W.W. Norton, 1985.

Grassi, Joseph A. *Loaves and Fishes: The Gospel Feeding Narratives*. Wilmington, DE: Michael Glazier, 1992.

Green, John, and David Levithan. *Will Grayson, Will Grayson*. New York: Dutton, 2010.

Griffiths, Thomas L., and Joshua B. Tenenbaum. "From Mere Coincidences to Meaningful Discoveries." *Cognition* 103 (2007) 180–226. https://doi.org/10.1016/j.cognition.2006.03.004.

Guelich, Robert A. *Mark 1–8:26*. Dallas, TX: Word. 1989

Gundry, Robert H. *Mark: A Commentary on His Apology for the Cross*. Grand Rapids: Eerdmans, 2000.

Häkkinen, Sakari. "Poverty in the First-Century Galilee." HTS Teologiese Studies / Theological Studies 72 (2016): 1–9. https://doi.org/10.4102/hts.v72i4.3398.

Harrington, Daniel J. "Biblical Criticism." https://www.oxfordbibliographies.com/display/document/obo-9780195393361/obo-9780195393361-066.xml

Healy, Mary. *The Gospel of Mark*. Grand Rapids, MI: Baker Academic. 2008.

Henderson, Suzanne Watts. *Christology and Discipleship in the Gospel of Mark*. Cambridge: Cambridge University Press, 2006.

Henry, Jane. "Coincidence Experience Survey." *Journal of the Society for Psychical Research* 59 (1993) 97. @article{Henry1993CoincidenceES, title={Coincidence Experience Survey}, author={Joseph Henry}, journal={Journal of the society for psychical research}, year={1993}, volume={59},pages={97–108},url={https://api.semanticscholar.org/CorpusID:148543614}}

Henten, J.W. van. "Daniel 3 and 6 in Early Christian Literature." In *The Book of Daniel: Composition and Reception*, 149–69. Leiden: Brill, 2001.

Holladay, Carl R. "Biblical Criticism." In *Harper's Bible Dictionary*, 129–33. San Francisco: Harper & Row, 1985.

Hooker, Morna D. *The Gospel According to Saint Mark*. Peabody, MA: Hendricks 1992.

Horatio, Thomas. "Some Thoughts on 'Undesigned Coincidences' in the Gospels." https://thomas-horatio.medium.com/some-thoughts-on-undesigned-coincidences-in-the-gospels-fb3652021868.

Horsley, Richard A. *Jesus in Context: Power, People & Performance*. Minneapolis: Fortress, 2008.

Hühn, Eugene. *Die alttestamentlichen Citate und Reminiscenzen im Neuen Testamente.* https://ia804704.us.archive.org/28/items/DieAlttestamentlichenCitateUnd ReminischenzenImNeuenTestamente/huhn_die-alttestamentlichen-citate-und-reminiscenzen-im-neuen-testamente.pdf.

Huxley, Thomas H. "Address to the British Association for the Advancement of Science / Delivered by the President, Thomas H. Huxley, at Liverpool, September 14, 1870." https://www.nature.com/articles/002399a0.

Johansen, Mark K., and Magda Osman. "Coincidences: A Fundamental Consequence of Rational Cognitio." *New Ideas in Psychology* 39 (2015) 34–44. https://doi.org/10.1016/j.newideapsych.2015.07.001.

Johnson, Franklin. *Quotations of the New Testament from the Old.* Kessinger. 2008.

Jones, David A. "Old Testament Quotations and Allusions in the New Testament." https://www.logos.com/product/10225/old-testament-quotations-and-allusions-in-the-new-testament.

Jung, Carl G. *The Structure and Dynamics of the Psyche.* New York: Pantheon, 1960.

———. *Synchronicity: An Acausal Connecting Principle.* Translated by R.F.C. Hull. Princeton: Princeton University Press, 2011.

Keener, Craig S. *A Commentary on the Gospel of Matthew.* Grand Rapids: Eerdmans, 1999.

Keener, Craig S., and Lydia McGrew. "Foreword." In *Hidden in Plain View: Undesigned Coincidences in the Gospels and Acts,* 7–9. Chillicothe, OH: Deward, 2017.

Kempis, Thomas à. *De Imitatione Christi.* Jac. Bern. Jouret, 1840.

Kidd, Thomas. "The Science of Sound: Whitefield's Massive Crowds." https://www.thegospelcoalition.org/article/the-science-of-sound-whitefields-massive-crowds/.

Kim, Younggwang. "Exegesis: Mark 6:30–44." https://digitalcommons.liberty.edu/masters/800/.

King, Brian, and Martin Plimmer. *Beyond Coincidence.* New York: St. Martin's, 2006.

Koester, Helmut. *Introduction to the New Testament.* 2nd ed. NY: Walter de Gruyter, 2000.

Koestler, Arthur. *Janus: A Summing Up.* New York: Random House, 1978.

Köstenberger, Andreas J. *Encountering John: The Gospel in Historical, Literary, and Theological Perspective.* Grand Rapids: Baker Academic, 1999.

———. *Theology of John's Gospel and Letters.* Grand Rapids: Zondervan, 2009.

Kostyuk, Oleg. "The Function of Military Language in the Feeding of the Five Thousand Narrative (Mark 6:30–44): A Narrative-Cognitive Study." https://digitalcommons.andrews.edu/dissertations/1737/.

Lambert, Derek, and Dale Allison. "Challenge Dr. Dale C. Allison Jr With Your Questions | New Testament Scholar." YouTube, April 5, 2022. https://www.youtube.com/watch?v=ohvL5F0CgHA.

Lane, William L. *The Gospel of Mark.* Grand Rapids, MI: Eerdmans. 1974.

Leo XIII, Pope. "Providentissimus Deus (November 18, 1893): Leo XIII." https://www.vatican.va/content/leo-xiii/en/encyclicals/documents/hf_l-xiii_enc_18111893_providentissimus-deus.html.

Licona, Michael R. "Lydia McGrew Answered." https://www.risenjesus.com/lydia-mcgrew-answered.

———. *The Resurrection of Jesus: A New Historiographical Approach.* Downers Grove: IL: IVP, 2010.

———. "Was Mark Confused Pertaining to the Location of the Feeding of the 5,000?" https://www.risenjesus.com/mark-confused-pertaining-location-feeding-5000.

———. *Why are There Differences in the Gospels?: What We Can Learn from Ancient Biography*. New York: Oxford University Press, 2017.

Lindars, Barnabas. "John and the Synoptic Gospels: A Test Case." *New Testament Studies* 27 (1981) 287–94. https://doi.org/10.1017/s0028688500006688.

MacDonald, Dennis R. *Homeric Epics and the Gospel of Mark*. New Haven: Yale University Press, 2010.

Marcus, Joel. *Mark 1–8*. New York: Doubleday, 2000.

Mariottini, Claude. ">Republicans v. Democrats = Old Testament v. New Testament." https://claudemariottini.com/2006/08/07/republicans-v-democrats-old-testament-v-new-testament/.

Marks, David F., and Richard Kammann. *The Psychology of the Psychic*. Amherst, N.Y.: Prometheus, 2000.

Marotta, Krisan. "John's Use of the Old Testament." https://www.wednesdayintheword.com/john-oldtestament/.

McClatchie, Jonathan. "Undesigned Coincidences in the Gospels: A Reply to John Nelson." https://jonathanmclatchie.com/undesigned-coincidences-in-the-gospels-a-reply-to-john-nelson/.

McCormick, Matthew S. *Atheism and the Case Against Christ*. Amherst, N.Y.: Prometheus, 2012.

McDowell, Sean. "Unique Evidence for the New Testament: Interview with Lydia McGrew." https://seanmcdowell.org/blog/unique-evidence-for-the-new-testament-interview-with-lydia-mcgrew-about-unintended-coincidences-1.

McGrew, Lydia. "About Me," https://www.lydiamcgrew.com/about.

———. "About Me," https://www.lydiamcgrew.com/about

———. "Editorial Fatigue, Probably Not 6." YouTube, May 26, 2024. Video, https://www.youtube.com/watch?v=TXPCzlzXNBI.

———. *The Eye of the Beholder: The Gospel of John as Historical Reportage*. Tampa, FL: DeWard, 2021.

———. "The Green Grass: Undesigned Coincidences vs. Symbolic Invention." https://open.spotify.com/episode/5e6Lz7zylPdzultC9gSz6h.

———. *Hidden in Plain View: Undesigned Coincidence in the Gospels and Acts*. Chillicothe, OH: DeWard, 2017.

———. "How the Bible's Obscure 'Coincidences' Demonstrate Its Reliability: An Interview with Lydia McGrew." https://www.biblegateway.com/blog/2017/10/how-the-bibles-obscure-coincidences-demonstrate-its-reliability-an-interview-with-lydia-mcgrew/.

———. "Is Jesus John's Mouthpiece? Reconsidering Johannine Idiom." *Conspectus : The Journal of the South African Theological Seminary* 32, no. 1 (October 2021) 42–57. https://doi.org/10.54725/conspectus.2021.2.2.

———. "On Credentials, Philosophy, and NT Studies." http://lydiaswebpage.blogspot.com/2018/05/on-credentials-philosophy-and-nt-studies.html.

———. "Undesigned Coincidences." https://lydiaswebpage.blogspot.com/2011/01/undesigned-coincidences.html.

———. "Undesigned Coincidences and Coherence for an Hypothesis." *Erkenntnis* 85 (2018) 801–28. https://doi.org/10.1007/s10670-18-0050-54.

———. "Undesigned Coincidences in the Gospel of John." *Modern Reformation*, (2019). https://www.modernreformation.org/resources/essays/undesigned-coincidences-in-the-gospel-of-john. Interviewed by Shane Rosenthal.

Meyer, Ben F. *The Aims of Jesus*. London: SCM, 1979.

Moles, John. "Jesus and Dionysus in The Acts of The Apostles and Early Christianity." *Hermathena*, 180 (2006) 64–104.

Moloney, Francis James. *The Gospel of John*. Edited by Daniel J. Harrington. Collegeville, MN: Liturgical, 1998.

———. *The Gospel of Mark*. Peabody: MA: Hendrickson, 2002.

Montefiore, C. G. *The Synoptic Gospels*. 2nd ed. Vol. 1. London: Macmillan, 1927.

Mullins, Michael. *The Gospel of Mark*. Dublin: Columba, 2005.

Nelson, John. "'Undesigned Coincidences' in the Gospels." https://www.behindthegospels.com/p/undesigned-coincidences-in-the-gospels.

Nicolai, Carsten. "Alva Noto Quote." https://www.azquotes.com/quote/833370.

Nicole, Roger. "New Testament Use of the Old Testament." In *Revelation and the Bible Contemporary Evangelical Thought*, 135–51. Grand Rapids: Baker, 1958.

North, Wendy E.S. *What John Knew and What John Wrote: A Study in John and the Synoptics*. Lanham, MD: Lexington, 2020.

obstinateguy (@obstinateguy). "Coincidence, if traced far enough back, becomes inevitable". Tumblr. April 16, 2024. https://www.tumblr.com/obstinateguy/828933571 31/coincidenceif-traced-far-enough-back-becomes

O'Neill, J. C. "Biblical Criticism." In *The Anchor Yale Bible Dictionary*, 725–30. New York: Doubleday, 1996.

Osborne, Grant R. *Matthew*. Grand Rapids: Zondervan, 2010.

Oxford English Dictionary, "Coincidence." https://www.oed.com/dictionary/coincidence_n?tl=true

Paley, William. *Horae Paulinae, or, the Truth of the Scripture History of St. Paul: Evinced by a Comparison of the Epistles which bear his name, with the acts of the apostles, and with one another*. London: Printed for F.C. and J. Rivington, 1822.

"Parallel Passages in New Testament Quoted from Old Testament: Part II—Study Resources." https://www.blueletterbible.org/study/misc/quotes02.cfm.

Parker, Neil Ronald. *The Marcan Portrayal of the "Jewish" Unbeliever: A Function of the Marcan References to Jewish Scripture: The Theological Basis of a Literary Construct*. New York: Peter Lang, 2008.

Paul, Ian, and Lydia McGrew. "What Do Interlocking 'Coincidences' Say About the Reliability of the NT?" https://www.psephizo.com/biblical-studies/what-do-the-interlocking-coincidences-say-about-the-reliability-of-the-nt/.

Perkins, Pheme. *Mark*. Nashville, TN: Abingdon, 1995.

Peters, Bosco. "Undesigned Coincidences." https://liturgy.co.nz/undesigned-coincidences.

Petersen, Jonathan. "How the Bible's Obscure 'Coincidences' Demonstrate Its Reliability: An Interview with Lydia McGrew." https://www.biblegateway.com/blog/2017/10/how-the-bibles-obscure-coincidences-demonstrate-its-reliability-an-interview-with-lydia-mcgrew/.

Plummer, Robert L. *40 Questions About Interpreting the Bible*. 2nd ed. Grand Rapids: Kregel Academic, 2010.

Pope, Msgr. Charles. "What Was the Climate and Weather of Israel Like at the Time of Jesus?" https://blog.adw.org/2014/07/what-was-the-climate-and-weather-of-israel-like-at-the-time-of-jesus/.

Porter, Stanley E., and Bryan R. Dyer. "The Synoptic Problem: An Introduction to Its Key Terms, Concepts, Figures, and Hypotheses." In *The Synoptic Problem: Four Views*, 1–26. Grand Rapids: Baker Academica, 2016.

Ranke-Heinemann, Uta. *Putting Away Childish Things: The Virgin Birth, the Empty Tomb, and Other Fairy Tales You Don't Need to Believe to Have a Living Faith*. San Francisco: HarperSanFrancisco, 1994.

Rauser, Randal. "A New Defense of the Historical Reliability of the Bible." https://www.christianpost.com/voices/defense-historical-reliability-of-the-bible.html.

Raven, Alan, Francois P. Viljoen, and Timothy van Aarde. "The Impact of the Hebrew Scriptures, and Especially the Torah, on James's Thought, Terminology and Teaching." *In die Skriflig / In Luce Verbi* 56 (December 2022). https://doi.org/10.4102/ids.v56i1.2801.

Sandoval, Chris. "Amazon Book Review of *Hidden in Plain View*: 'Undesigned coincidences do not always arise from independent eyewitnesses.'" https://www.amazon.com/gp/customer-reviews/R1OFEOV0NEQQ6R/ref=cm_cr_dp_d_rvw_ttl?ie=UTF8&ASIN=1936341905.

Savarimuthu, Eddy Dharmanand. "The Feeding Narratives in Mark: Studying the Significance by a Comparative Analysis." Master's Thesis, University of Innsbruck 2013.

Schnabel, Eckhart J. *Mark: An Introduction and Commentary*. Downers Grove, IL: Inter-Varsity. 2017.

Setiya, Kieran. "Intention." https://plato.stanford.edu/archives/win2022/entries/intention/.

Smith, Dwight Moody. *John Among the Gospels: The Relationship in Twentieth-Century Research*. Minneapolis: Fortress, 1992.

Stein, Robert H. *Mark*. Grand Rapids: Baker Academic, 2008.

———. *Studying the Synoptic Gospels: Origin and Interpretation*. 2nd ed. Grand Rapids: Baker Academic, 2001.

Strauss, Mark L. *Mark: Zondervan Exegetical Commentary on the New Testament*. Grand Rapids: Zondervan, 2014.

Taylor, Vincent J. *The Gospel According to St. Mark*. London, U.K.: Palgrave Macmillan. 1966.

Towner, W. Sibley. *Daniel*. Louisville: John Knox, 1984.

Toy, Crawford Howell. *Quotations in the New Testament*. New York: Charles Scribner's Sons, 1884.

Tripp, Jeffrey, and Derek Lambert. "The FAILURE of 'unDESIGNED Coincidences' | Christian Apologists Are Wrong." YouTube, September 22, 2023. Video, https://www.youtube.com/watch?v=3oFoM1wtNow.

Turton, Michael A. "*Historical Commentary on the Gospel of Mark*". http://www.michaelturton.com/Mark/GMark06.html.

Twelftree, Graham H. *Jesus the Miracle Worker: A Historical & Theological Study*. Downers Grove, IL: InterVarsity, 1999.

Tyson, Neil deGrasse. "When a Coincidence Seems Amazing, That's Because the Human Mind Isn't Wired to Naturally Comprehend Probability & Statistics." Twitter, July 29, 2014. https://twitter.com/neiltyson/status/494196567445098498.

Venn, John. *The Logic of Chance; An Essay on the Foundations and Province of the Theory of Probability, with Especial Reference to Its Application to Moral and Social Science*. London: Macmillan, 1866.
Wahlde, Urban C. von. *The Gospel and Letters of John*. Grand Rapids: Eerdmans, 2010.
Wallace, J. Warner. *Cold-Case Christianity: A Homicide Detective Investigates the Claims of the Gospels*. Colorado Springs, CO: David C Cook, 2013.
Watt, Caroline A. "Psychology and Coincidences." *European Journal of Parapsychology* 8 (1990–991) https://doi.org/http://www.koestler-parapsychology.psy.ed.ac.uk/Documents/EJPv8_Watt.pdf.
Wilkins, Michael J. *The NIV Application Commentary: Matthew*. Grand Rapids: Zondervan, 2004.
Witherington III, Ben. *The Gospel of Mark*. Grand Rapids, MI: Eerdmans. 2001.
Wright, N. T. *Mark for Everyone*. Louisville: Westminster John Knox, 2001.
———. *The Resurrection of the Son of God*. Minneapolis: Fortress, 2003.
Zindler, Frank. "Capernaum—A Literary Invention." *Journal of Higher Criticism* 12 (2006): 1–27.

Names Index

Allen, Woody 120–21
Alonso, Facundo 15n46
Alter, Michael J. xii–xiii, 7, 59, 125n100,
Amy 146
Andrew 63, 129, 132–33, 136, 139–41,
    145–46
Anscombe, Gertraude E. 15n46, 16
Arav, Rami 135, 136n16, 137
Archer, Gleason L. 22, 23n63, 29
Asimov, Isaac 137n19,
Aus, Roger David 66n3, 68n8, 73, 77,
    89, 11n94, 127, 131, 136
Austin, David xix, 87

Babinski, Ed 138, 144–46
Baird, William 19, 20n57
Barclay, William 47
Barker, James W. 46n74, 49n97, 139n27
Barrett, Charles Kingsley 49n27, 139n27
Bauckham, Richard 36n74, 39, 49n27,
    139n27,
Beavis, Mary Ann 67n7, 110, 11n79
Beitman, Bernard D. 9, 11
Berra, Yogi 11
BibleRef 112
Black, C. Clifton 67n7, 109
Blomberg, Craig L. 1n1, 75, 79n20, 152
Blunt, John J. xv, 2, 4, 13, 18, 55, 60, 80,
    90, 95, 129n1, 130, 138, 140, 152
Bock, Darrell 1n1, 67n7, 108
Boren, Braxton 79
Boring, M. Eugene 67n7, 86, 109–10
Bowman, Robert M. 1n1
Boyd, Greg 1n1
Brierley, Justin 35

Broach, Elise 10
Brown, William P. 118
Bull, Emma 10
Burger, Edward B. 9, 11

Cai, Jonathan Bi Fan 113, 126
CARM 33
Carrier, Richard 102–3, 138–40
Carroll, Lewis 65
Carson, D.A. 50, 75, 79n20, 139–40,
    158n1
Cato 44
Cavett, Dick 10
Chabris, Christopher F. 36
Chardavoyne, Michael 146n39
Chesterton, Gilbert Keith 11
Clines, David 19, 20n57
Collins, Adela Yarbo 105
Collins, C. John 1n1
Coupland, Douglas 9
Craig, William Lane 1n1
Cranfield, C.E.B. 169

David 26, 30, 133
Davies, W. D. 68n8
Derrett, J. Duncan 68n8
Diaconis, Persi 10, 12, 14
Dittmar, Wilhelm 22
Donahue, John R. 67n7, 107

Eddy, Paul Rhodes 1n1,
Edwards, James R. 104–5
Ehrman, Bart 7, 15n46, 16n47, 35, 149
Elisha 66–67, 86, 105, 137
Ens, Paul (Paulogia) 95n36, 96n37

174 NAMES INDEX

Euripides 58
Evans, C. Stephen 1n1
Evans, Craig A. 1n1

Falk, Ruma 12n37
Fales, Evan vii, xx
Foster, Meadhbh I. 13
France, R. T. 67n7, 75–76, 79, 104
Frankenstein, Victor 81
Franklin, Benjamin 80
Fryer, N. S. 74n11, 82, 83n22

Garland, David E. 1n1, 106
Gilson, Tom 1n1
Gloer, Hulitt 20–21, 30
Godfrey, Neil 59
Goodacre, Mark 114–16, 117n89
Gould, Stephen Jay 10
Goulder, Michael 117
Grassi, Joseph A. 67, 127
Green, John 9
Griffiths, Thomas L. 12, 14
Guelich, Robert A. 107–8
Gundry, Robert H. 58, 77n19, 97, 108

Habermas, Gary 1n1, 2
Harrington, Daniel J. 19, 111
Healy, Mary 67n7, 109
Henderson, Suzanne Watts 65–66
Henry, Jane 12
Henten, J.W. van 68n8
Holladay, Carl R. 19n55
Hooker, Morna D. 112
Horatio, Thomas 39, 40n81–82, 101
Hühn, Eugene 22, 30
Huxley, Thomas 161n3

James 130
Jesus ix, xv–xvi, xix, 2, 13, 17, 20, 26–29, 31, 34–35, 37, 39, 41, 50, 52, 56, 58–59, 61–64, 66–67, 69–75, 77–89, 91–94, 96–99, 101–3, 105–7, 110–14, 116, 122, 124, 129–46, 148–50, 157–58
John (Apostle) xvi, 13, 17, 30–32, 36, 39, 49, 51, 57–58, 60, 62, 73, 96, 99, 101–3, 118, 120, 123, 129–30, 132–33, 138–42, 145, 148, 151, 157, 161
John the Baptist 86, 136, 141, 143
Johansen, Mark K. 12, 13n38
Jones, David A. 29
Joseph II 100
Josephus, Flavius 135–37
Judas Iscariot 35, 130
Juel, Donald H. 109
Julias 136
Jung, Carl G. 10
Jung, Charles 11

Keener, Craig 1n1, 55, 56n111, 76, 79n20
Kempis, Thomas à 161n3
Kidd, Thomas 80n21
Kim, Younggwang 113n86, 126
King, Brian 43n85
Koester, Helmut 50
Koestler, Arthur 10n27
Köstenberger, Andreas J. 132n11, 143
Kostyuk, Oleg 119n91

Lambert, Derek 41n84, 94–95, 97n39
Lane, William L. 1n1, 104
Lazarus 143
Leo XIII, Pope 123–25
Licona, Michael R. 44–46, 88–89, 152n8, 153
Lindars, Barnabas 36n74, 49n97, 139n27
Loftus, Elizabeth 150

MacDonald, Dennis R. 59, 68, 102
Maier, Paul 1n1
Marcus, Joel 85, 107
Mariottini, Claude 33
Mark 6 ix, 13, 21, 29, 43, 62–73, 77, 79, 84, 87–90, 92–94, 96–99, 101–2, 104, 106–7, 109–15, 119, 121–22, 125–28, 131, 134–35, 152, 155
Marks, David F. 14
Marotta, Krisan 25, 29
Marshall, David 1n1
McCormick, Matthew S. 153, 155n11
McDowell, Sean 1n1, 17

NAMES INDEX

McGrew, Lydia xi, xiii, xv, 1–8, 13–18, 20n58, 21, 23–24, 29–31, 34–35, 37–46, 50–57, 59–61, 65, 90–97, 99–101, 103, 115–16, 118, 123–25, 129n1, 130, 132, 138, 140, 146, 149–50, 151n4, 152, 160
McGrew, Timothy xv, 1, 5, 18, 35, 90
McClatchie, Jonathan 101
Meyer, B.F. 153
Michelangelo 30
Moles, John 59
Moloney, Francis James 49n97, 109, 110n77, 139n27
Montefiore, C. G. 68n8
Montgomery, John Warwick 1n1
Moses 26, 30, 67, 69–72, 98, 105, 108, 110–11, 132–33, 144
Mosteller, Frederick 10, 12, 14
Mozart 100
Mullins, Michael 66n3
Murray, Abdu 1n1

Nathanael 132
Nelson, John 39, 40n81–82, 101
Nicolai, Carsten (Alva Noto) 10n26
Nicole, Roger 20–22, 30
North, Wendy E.S. 49n97, 139
Nun, Mendel 135

Osborne, Grant R. 76, 79n20
Oxford Languages 9

Paley, William xv, 2, 18, 55, 60, 152
Parker, Neil Ronald 24n65
Paul (Apostle) 3, 32, 52, 58, 91, 150n3
Paul, Ian 15, 56
Perkins, Pheme 110
Pervo, Richard 59
Peter (Apostle) 34–35, 63, 124, 129–30, 132–33, 136, 139–41, 145–46
Peters, Bosco 151
Petersen, Jonathan 3
Philip (Apostle) vii, xv–xvi, 62–63, 88, 129–34, 136–42, 144–48, 157
Plutarch 44–45
Plummer, Robert L. 18–19

Pope, Msgr. Charles 93
Porter, Stanley E. 152
Price, Robert M. 138

Ranke-Heinemann, Uta 58
Rauser, Randal 146
Raven, Alan 30n67
Rhoads, David 110

Sandoval, Chris 41, 110
Savarimuthu, Eddy Dharmanand 66, 67n5, 128
Schacter, Daniel 150
Schnabel, Eckhard J. 112
Schweizer, Eduard 98
Setiya, Kieran 15n46
Singh, Khan Noonien 53
Smith, Dwight Moody 36n74, 49n97, 139n27
Spock 53
Stein, Robert H. 47, 67n7, 106, 107n67, 113
Strauss, Mark L. 87n25, 108

Taylor, Vincent J. 107, 111
Torley, Vincent xix, 34, 39n79
Towner, W. Sibley 68n8
Toy, Crawford Howell 22, 29
Tripp, Jeffrey 41
Turek, Frank 1n1
Turton, Michael A. 66
Twelftree, Graham H. 102
Tyson, Neil deGrasse 10

Venn, John 11

Wahlde, Urban C. von 49n97
Wallace, J. Warner 1n1, 35, 36n73
Watt, Caroline A. 14, 15n44
Whitefield, George 79–80
Wilkins, Michael J. 76, 77n18, 79n20
Williams, Peter J. 40, 101
Witherington, Ben 111
Wright, N. T. 68n8, 102

Zindler, Frank 134

Subject Index

Allusion(s) 17, 20, 22–30, 53, 59, 65, 76, 90–91, 94–95, 98, 107–9, 113, 118, 126
Annie Hall 120, 121n92
Aramaic 48, 58, 133, 159–60

Bacchae 58–59
Bethsaida xv–xvi, 77–80, 84, 86–89, 114, 116–18, 130–31, 133–41, 144–46, 152
Biblical criticism xv, xvii, 18–20, 23–24, 60, 90–91, 123, 152

Capernaum 77–78, 86, 88, 111, 135, 145–46
Causal(ness) 9–12, 14–15, 34, 43, 65
Chorazin 78, 134–35
Coincidence xi–xiii, xvii, 4, 8–12, 14–15, 17, 42, 51, 56, 58, 60, 91, 93, 103, 118, 144, 152, 157, 160
Compositional Devices Hypothesis 44
Credentialism Controversy xv, 6–7
Critical scholarship 18, 52–53, 123, 125
Cumulative Argument 68, 90, 122, 157–61

Dictionary of Biblical Imagery 91

Editorial fatigue 115–16
Eisegesis 32–34, 91, 152
Exodus Motif ix, 65, 68–72, 125, 152
Ezekiel 34 104, 106, 109–10

Fact (defined) 119

Feeding of the five thousand ix, xv–xvi, 13, 15, 60–131, 139, 143–44, 148, 160
Fish 34, 64, 66, 68, 71, 73, 82–83, 85, 87, 111, 115, 122, 129, 136–37, 145
Frankenstein 81

Green grass xv–xvi, 15, 21, 43, 61–62, 64, 67–68, 87–88, 90, 92–114, 118–19, 125, 144, 155, 157

Harmonization 42, 59–60, 92, 152, 159
Hidden in Plain View xv, 1, 3–5, 41, 50, 57, 60–61, 115, 130, 150, 160

John 6 29, 43, 62–65, 72–73, 88, 93–94, 98, 101–2, 107–8, 127–48

Lamb of God 141
Literary dependence 35, 37, 118
Loaves of bread 82–87
Logistics 72–85

Maximal Data xvi, 2–3, 124–25, 149–50, 155
Meaningfulness 14
Methodology xvii, 18, 21, 32–33, 42, 51, 57, 60, 91, 96, 144, 155, 157, 159–60

1 Corinthians 15:3–4 32, 91

Passover 13, 15, 43, 62, 72, 90, 92–94, 99, 101–3, 107–8, 111, 114, 129, 142

SUBJECT INDEX

Philip Controversy vii, xvi, 129–48
Psalm 23 ix, 13, 15, 21, 65–68, 90, 94–100, 106, 112–13, 118, 125–26, 152

Quotation(s) 20–30, 58, 113,

Romeo and Juliet 53

Scientific method xvi, 155–56
Sea of Galilee 62, 77, 87, 89, 103, 129, 134–35, 137, 140
Sea of Tiberias 34, 62, 140
Shepherd(s) 13, 15, 63, 67, 69, 71, 86, 96–99, 103–4, 106–10, 112–13, 115, 126–27
Sitting 27, 66, 74, 78–79, 83, 97

Star Trek 42, 53, 159
Star Wars 42, 53, 159
Synoptic Problem 47–50

Theses 125–26
Transcending horizons xvi, 153
Through the Looking Glass 65
2 Kings 4:38–44 65–67

Undesigned (defined) 8–9
Undesigned Coincidence (defined) xv, 1–2, 16, 121, 130–31

Witness (Eye-Witness) xi, 35–37, 48, 50, 54, 80, 88, 103, 158, 160

X-ray machine 58

www.ingramcontent.com/pod-product-compliance
Lightning Source LLC
Chambersburg PA
CBHW072129160426
43197CB00012B/2045

Separation of the People, Separation of the Land